DANGEROUS PEOPLE, DANGEROUS PLACES

Norman Parker

DANGEROUS PEOPLE, DANGEROUS PLACES

JOHN BLAKE

Published by John Blake Publishing Ltd,
3 Bramber Court, 2 Bramber Road,
London W14 9PB, England

www.johnblakepublishing.co.uk

First published in hardback in 2007
This edition 2011

ISBN: 978 1 84358 312 7

British Library Cataloguing-in-Publication Data:

A catalogue record for this book is available from the British Library.

Design by www.envydesign.co.uk

Printed in Great Britain by CPI Bookmarque, Croydon CRO 4TD

1 3 5 7 9 10 8 6 4 2

Papers used by John Blake Publishing are natural, recyclable products made from
wood grown in sustainable forests. The manufacturing processes conform to the
environmental regulations of the country of origin.

CONTENTS

1. Norman the Writer   1
2. Lucero, Guerrilla Queen   7
3. The Curse of Driver Mills   33
4. On the Side of the Angels   43
5. For a Country Fit for Dogs to Live In   51
6. Rebel Without a Pause   65
7. The Cocaine Factory   81
8. The Number of the Beast   105
9. Be Careful What You Wish For   117
10. See and Blind, Hear and Deaf   137
11. The Day the Music Died   160
12. The Hit Man   167
13. Dave the Rave   171
14. Tigers   215
15. The Day of the Dead   229
16. My Spirit Beast   247
17. Parker of the Express   265
18. Jew Boy   287

CHAPTER ONE
NORMAN THE WRITER

In 1994, I was released from prison after 24 continuous years. Lest anyone should think that the appropriate reaction was to perform cartwheels down the street and party till dawn, I should add that I had spent the previous nine months partially free in a prison hostel and for three years prior to that I had been in Ford Open Prison. So it was not so much an individual act of being released as a succession of minor degrees of increasing freedom.

With each increasing degree came the greater realisation that, whatever novelty I found in my new surroundings and whichever problems I had in coming to terms with them, there was one inescapable reality that I would have to deal with sooner rather than later. I would have to find a way to earn a living.

My immediate prospects were not particularly good. I had passed a Bachelor of Arts Honours degree in prison, but had no actual work experience of anything. Coupled with the facts that I was now 50 years old and had a conviction for murder, it made for a CV that was anything but attractive to a prospective employer.

However, I had started to write in my last months at Ford. *Parkhurst Tales* was a collection of short stories, based on factual incidents that had happened in various jails. My incarceration notwithstanding, I had managed to accumulate a wide circle of friends and acquaintances over the years. Now I used them to 'network' my way to a book deal.

My work came to the attention of Frank Delaney, the writer and TV presenter. He was impressed, agreed to write a foreword and set out to get me a two-book deal with Random Century. At the same time, Mike Mansfield, the music impresario, had visited me at Ford with a view to pitching a TV series to the networks based on *Parkhurst Tales*.

It had been all too easy, really. But I was soon to come face to face with the reality of the false promises and let-downs of the media world. Frank Delaney suddenly got the job of presenting *The Book Programme* on Sky and was unable to continue his involvement. After a series of meetings, the TV project also came to nothing.

I still managed to get a book deal with a £3,000 advance though. *Parkhurst Tales* was duly released and promptly became a bestseller, selling more than 20,000 copies in hardback. I did the rounds of the many TV chat shows and found that it was a medium I handled quite well. I had realised by now that, to be a successful author, one who actually makes a living out of writing, one also had to be an ardent and resourceful self-publicist.

My second book, *The Goldfish Bowl*, was a full-length story set in Kingston Prison, Europe's only prison exclusively for lifers. The book launch was long on location, but short on timing. 'Grouchos' might have been something of a media cliché, but it still had plenty of potential for publicity. However, the Dunblane shooting massacre was all over the media. The main question the (mostly female) journalists asked was, 'Why should we write anything positive about somebody who'd also killed by shooting?'

For me, trying to establish myself as a serious writer, it was a major, if not unexpected, disappointment. I had discovered very early on that, for many people, I would always be 'Norman the Murderer' rather than 'Norman the Writer'. It wasn't something I agonised over or railed against the unfairness of the world about, but in my heart I knew that I would never escape the shadow of my convictions.

For that reason, I had always kept one foot in the – for want for a better term – underworld, a milieu where my criminal convictions were never held against me. To the contrary, in fact: I was widely known, trusted and respected – useful qualities for someone trying to make a living by crime.

But I was well aware of the high percentage of people fresh out of prison who had gone back in again. Further, my long-suffering and ever-loyal mother was doting on the fact that, at long last, she had me living with her again. I was ever mindful of the fact that I could easily break her heart.

Tragedy, though, was but a heartbeat away. Whether I was ill-starred or actively sought misfortune out by my choice of equally ill-starred and self-destructive companions, I couldn't discern. When it came, everybody was agreed that I hadn't had much luck in life.

I had met Janice through Ian, an old prison pal down on his luck. She was a petite, pretty 23-year-old, mixed-race girl with a serious drug problem that she funded through shoplifting. She used Ian's rundown flat as a base for her shoplifting forays.

It was a tempestuous relationship from the start. My character, fired in the furnace of the institution, was hard, unyielding, uncompromising and totally focused. It wasn't so much that I was selfish, rather just completely self-oriented from having to care only for myself for so long. At times, it must have seemed to Janice that I was inconsiderate.

For her part, she was also moulded by the institution, courtesy of the various sentences she had served. This was further compounded by her having to live by the chaotic and fratricidal rules of 'the street'. If her paranoia wasn't a clearly defined clinical condition, then its practical effects still served to make her distrustful of everyone. If it was a 'marriage' made in heaven, then the Great Creator must have been smiling while in the process of creation.

Before long we were deeply in love. That our characters and lifestyles were mutually destructive didn't seem to matter. And, even if it had, there was nothing we could do about it. Our love for each other was an addiction in itself. Both of us, in our own ways, were very strong. Together, when in unison, we were indestructible. Friends often commented on the fact that, at times, we seemed to 'shine' together.

Janice died in front of a train. Afterwards, the police told me that she had been the victim of a 'suicide-pact serial killer' (I discuss this in my book *Life After Life*). I was too devastated to consider the facts logically. Secretly, I blamed myself for not being there for her. It coloured every aspect of my existence.

It served to drive me even further into the arms of the 'underworld'. By a cruel irony, shortly afterwards I came into a lot of money. But, without Janice to spend it with, it meant nothing to me. Her death had irrevocably darkened my world.

My one remaining positive passion was to gain recognition as a serious writer. Painful though it was, I embarked on writing my fourth book (number three, *Parkhurst Tales 2* had been published a short time earlier). *Life After Life* was to be an account of all that had happened to me since my last months at Ford. If I had thought that it would exorcise the ghosts, I was to be disappointed.

Fearful that my latest literary effort might be ignored when finished, I set out to raise my public profile. Shortly after *Parkhurst Tales* was published, I found out that, as a published author, I was entitled to apply for a journalist's card. I had done so at the time with no journalistic intent whatsoever.

Even though free from jail, in truth I had been released only on 'life licence' and was forever under threat of being recalled to prison by the Home Office for any infraction of that licence. One of the restrictions I was under was that I couldn't travel abroad without Home Office permission. Received wisdom was that this was very difficult to get.

I reasoned that, if I was an accredited journalist, the Home Office would be reluctant to put me back in jail just for travelling abroad without permission. I knew that the European Court didn't even accept the legality of the 'life licence', so, even if the HO did 'recall' me, I would have a good legal case in Europe.

Now, just before the publication of my latest book, I thought I would use my journalist's card to get some articles published. But where should I start? Would the national press even consider someone with a criminal record like mine? And, even if they did, what would I write about?

As part of the round of launching my books, mostly in the media watering-holes of Soho, I had met and become friendly with some of the young men who worked and wrote for the lads' magazines. These had recently become something of a publishing phenomenon. Initially, I dismissed the medium, mostly because of the 'tits-and-bums' format. However, it was explained to me that the readership included many 'City boys', young men who worked for City banks and other financial institutions and had large disposable incomes. They were looking for a light-hearted and irreverent read to take their minds off the serious business of dealing in money. As a result, these magazines had become very fashionable.

The market leaders among the lads' mags were *Maxim*, *Loaded* and *Front*, with fluctuating circulation figures per month of around 500,000, 300,000 and 250,000, respectively. It was further explained to me that, on average, two people read every copy bought. So the prospect of reaching a readership of up to a million suddenly became very attractive to me.

One of the guys I had become friendly with was Bill Borrows, features editor at *Loaded*. A highly talented writer himself, he asked me to write for the magazine. He said that, if I could come up with a project, he would back it up by recommending me to the editor. I immediately began searching for a suitable subject.

I had always been interested in politics and was well informed about most of the ongoing conflicts in the world. I reasoned that I could hardly compete with most of the established journalists, who, through the power of their organisations, would have things largely sewn up. That ruled out many of the most easily accessible places. It left only the most dangerous and inaccessible ones.

Fortunately, my political viewpoint was decidedly left-wing, so I would have little difficulty in sympathising with many of the guerrilla movements. Whether this provided me with any sort of 'in' with them was another matter entirely. In jail, through the natural comradeship that springs up in shared oppressive situations, I had become friendly with several leading IRA men. One in particular, Gerry Kelly, was now a senior figure in Sinn Fein, the political wing of the IRA. I rang him and asked if he could recommend me to any guerrilla groups and provide an introduction.

Gerry baulked at the idea. He explained that, as a party, Sinn Fein just didn't do things like that. So I was back to square one.

Reading through some old newspaper articles that I had saved, I came upon one about Colombia. There had been a guerrilla war going on for almost 40 years. The article focused on the fact that the government had ceded a large area of land to the main guerrilla organisation, the Revolutionary Armed Forces of Colombia (FARC), where the latter had set up an unofficial 'capital' of their armed struggle. It was generally referred to as 'Farcland'. Government forces stayed out of the area. I had my idea for a story. I would go to Colombia and do a story on Farcland.

The next problem was for me to convince *Loaded* that I had some way of getting the story – that is, that I had some special access. The newspaper article had mentioned that FARC had a website and gave their address. I immediately emailed them, explaining that I was a journalist who generally sympathised with left-wing revolutions and asked permission to come to their 'capital' and do a story on them.

Their reply two days later was as disappointing as it was unhelpful. First, it was in Spanish, a language I didn't speak at all. With the translation came the second disappointment. They asked me to submit my request in Spanish.

However, I was confident that, once in Colombia, I could make contact with the guerrillas. Dangerous as the place was, I was savvy enough to know that modern-day guerrilla movements tried to avoid harming or killing journalists, because that only brought down a storm of criticism from journalists of every persuasion. Anyway, Parkhurst Prison had been a pretty dangerous place and I had survived that. So Colombia held no fears for me.

Non-committal though the reply from FARC had been, at least I could now say that I had been in contact with them. It was just a short step to saying that they were expecting me. With the encouragement of Bill Borrows, it was enough to sway *Loaded*. Perhaps they figured that, if I got myself killed, there would be a story for them in that!

A meeting was duly convened at *Loaded*'s offices, where they introduced me to my photographer for the trip. *Loaded* is 90 per cent a visual magazine, so that part of the story had concerned me. Now, with my own professional photographer, that was taken care of.

I had met several photographers during my Soho jaunts and, in general, I hadn't been impressed. I found them mostly to be narcissistic and obsessed by social status. Despite a thoroughly working-class accent, my photographer wasn't to disappoint.

Trent was a sharp-featured, anxious-looking guy in his early thirties. Stylish, well-pressed clothes fitted snugly to his slim figure and he hadn't a hair out of place. The word fastidious immediately sprang to mind. The first 20 minutes of the conversation were all about him and his work. Then he touched briefly on all the celebrities he knew, segueing neatly at the end into a story about him and his close friend, a famous DJ.

This was my first assignment. I wasn't about to grovel, but I would try to get on with everyone. In 'underworld' mode, I would have been readying myself to give this Trent a strong putdown. Instead, I focused on the promising things, namely his East End upbringing and his support for West Ham. I walked out of *Loaded*'s offices with an air ticket to Colombia, £1,200 in expenses and my first journalistic assignment.

CHAPTER TWO
LUCERO, GUERRILLA QUEEN

Now that I had my assignment, I set about doing some serious preparation. My first stop was the British Airways travel clinic in Regent Street. I was aware that I needed vaccinations against various diseases before I would be allowed to travel. What I didn't realise was just how many. Not only was Colombia one of the most dangerous countries from the point of view of political violence, but it seemed that the very environment was inimical to human life.

Next I considered what I should wear. No doubt professional journos in the field wore safari suits and other tropical kit. However, I didn't want to advertise my assignment to the Colombian government, because there might be restrictions on foreign journalists travelling to guerrilla-held territory. Jeans and T-shirts should be sufficient to allow me to blend in with the natives.

Finally, I read up on the current political situation to try to determine who the main players were. FARC were thoroughly Marxist-inspired. Their political agenda called for agrarian reform, protection of natural resources from multinational corporations and democratisation. With up to 20,000 men and women under arms, they were the biggest force in the field, apart from the Colombian Army. So successful had their military campaign been that the previous year the government had granted them a demilitarised zone the size of Switzerland in southern Colombia. This was where I was headed. FARC responded with an attack that reached the outskirts of the capital Bogotá.

The National Liberation Army, or ELN, were inspired by the Cuban revolution and had up to 5,000 men and women under arms. Although mostly fighting against the government, at different times and in different provinces they had been known to fight with FARC.

No South American revolution would be complete without its right-wing death squads, and this function was enthusiastically performed by the Autodefensas Unidas de Colombia, or AUC. An illegal paramilitary army, they numbered up to 5,000 men and were the sworn enemies of FARC and ELN. Although they were supposedly independent, informed sources said that they were merely an extension of the Colombian military and had close links with the drugs cartels. Guilty of many human-rights abuses, they were widely known as the 'head cutters' for their habit of decapitating victims after torturing them to death.

The Colombian Army largely comprised undertrained and unmotivated young men on national service. Regularly outfought and outgunned by FARC, they too had been accused of human-rights abuses by, among others, Washington's Human Rights Watch.

If every South American revolution is incomplete without its death squads, then it is similarly incomplete without the US. Sure enough, there was ongoing heavy US financial and military involvement. Under Plan Colombia, they were in the process of giving $1.6 billion in aid, 75 per cent of it in military assistance. They were currently training and equipping two elite Colombian anti-narcotics battalions.

All this added up to a very dangerous country indeed. The previous year, 5,000 people were killed in political violence, out of a total annual toll of 30,000 violent deaths. Journalists were not immune to this violence, either. Forty-six had been killed in the last ten years, and all sides frequently took journalists hostage. I assumed that I wouldn't be bumping into too many other foreign journalists in the field.

The air ticket provided by *Loaded* allowed me 12 days for the trip. However, it would take a day to get to Colombia and another day to get back. Once I was in Bogotá, it would take a further day to get down to FARC's jungle capital and another day to get back. Then there was the fact that Trent would be arriving from another assignment a day after I arrived. So, if everything went absolutely like clockwork, I would have a maximum of five, maybe six, days with the guerrillas, not a lot of time to do a detailed piece.

Other than the above, I had two other tight schedules to meet. I was still on life licence, which, among other things, entailed my reporting to

Henry, my probation officer, every two weeks. I could just fit the trip in and be back two days before my next appointment. Needless to say, I hadn't told Henry about the trip. He would have had to tell the Home Office, which, in effect, would mean my asking for permission to go. Henry had once given me permission to go on a short holiday to Spain not long after my release and had been given a terrible rollicking by the Home Office. They would have undoubtedly said no to Colombia.

An extra problem was that Henry lived in the tower block where I lived with my mother, only two floors above us. We often met in the lift. Just another of those little quirks of fate that seemed to plague my existence. So I would have to hope that Henry didn't miss all my normal comings and goings and ask about it at our next appointed meeting.

The other tight schedule was entirely more threatening of dire consequences. Marsha was a tall, stunningly beautiful, 28-year-old blonde with a figure to die for. Ferociously intelligent, she had two honours degrees and two masters' degrees and was currently studying for her doctorate, all in psychology. She was a strong personality and very demanding. She was also my girlfriend.

There were several ironies to the situation, not the least of them being that a prison governor had once remarked that he would have liked to put a whole team of psychologists in just to study me. Well, I didn't have a whole team, but I did have my very own personal full-time shrink now.

Marsha was also quite jealous. I had pointed out on several occasions that there weren't too many attractive women who were into short, balding 50-year-old ex-cons, but it had little or no effect. Now, on our last evening, I was reassuring her that everything would be all right. I would be safe, and back before she knew it.

Marsha looked at me with one of her studied cool looks, the ones that always unnerved me. I had stared down dangerous psychopaths in the jailhouse, but I always blinked with Marsha. 'And no looking at the women,' she said in a throaty growl.

It surprised me. I would be looking at the potential robbers, kidnappers, murderers and carriers of all the various Colombian diseases, but it hadn't occurred to me to look at the women. I was just about to say, 'Trust you to get your priorities right!' but thought better of it. 'Of course I won't, darling' was the best I could manage.

Marsha was also very strict about the observance of birthdays, especially her own. It just so happened that her birthday fell in about two weeks' time. I deliberately hadn't checked, but I knew it would be a close-run thing. 'And don't be late back for my birthday,' she purred.

The following day, a Friday and the day before my flight, was a frenzy of preparation. I must have checked, packed and unpacked my travelling bag six times. I was carrying Trent's camera and 40 rolls of film to give to him in Bogotá. For the umpteenth time, I wrapped the camera in tissue to protect it from in-flight damage.

Just as I was as sure as I could be that I had everything, my phone rang. An official-sounding voice informed me that they would like to speak to me concerning a matter at Kensington Police Station. The voice wouldn't be drawn on the nature of the matter, but I was told to ask for DC Keith Brown on arrival.

Now my mind really was racing. What could it be that they wanted to see me about? I racked my brains about anything I might have done, but couldn't come up with anything. I reassured myself that, if it was really serious, they wouldn't have bothered to phone: they'd just have come and arrested me. It wasn't a lot of consolation. Resignedly, I considered the possibility that it must be about the Colombia trip. I knew that everyone who travelled to Colombia, a drug-trafficking hotspot, was 'flagged' by having a note made of the fact. No doubt the combination of Colombia and my being on life licence had provoked them. At best, I could expect a stern warning; at worst, I might not walk out of the police station and instead be on my way back to a prison.

With considerable trepidation, I approached the front counter of Kensington Police Station and asked for DC Brown. There was no pressing of alarm bells or frantic phone calls. In fact, the desk officer hardly looked up at me. 'DC Brown works out of the office directly across the street,' he said, before returning to what he was doing.

'Across the street' was entirely more hospitable, in that there were large glass windows and a modern-looking reception area. On asking for DC Brown, I was politely asked to take a seat and promised that he would be with me very shortly.

Keith Brown was surprisingly young, hardly out of his twenties. He was also polite and very laidback. Apologising for keeping me waiting, he led me into a small office. I declined the offer of a cup of tea and settled back in a manner that I hoped would indicate that, while not being unduly worried, I would like to know what was going on.

'Your name's come up in connection with the Jill Dando murder,' said the detective constable.

My immediate reaction was one of relief. The murder of the television presenter was nothing to do with me. I very nearly said, 'Oh I thought it was something serious,' but realised that would sound flippant and insensitive.

Perhaps reading my expression, the DC added, 'We're not taking it too seriously. The computer's just thrown up your name.'

I mused on the fact that, whatever my journalistic pretensions, I would always be 'Norman the Murderer' to the police and their computers.

He then asked me where I was on 26 April the previous year, 1999, the date of Dando's death. I confessed that I hadn't a clue. I didn't keep a diary and, unless something significant had happened in my life on that day, I wouldn't ever be able to remember. The DC admitted that *he* couldn't remember where he had been on that day, either, a further indication that he wasn't taking this enquiry too seriously. And with that the interview was over.

The final surprise came as I was leaving. He asked me what my personal theory was about the Jill Dando murder. I remembered reading that she had been killed by a single pistol shot to the head. I opined that the killer was either an amateur or didn't really intend to kill. Many victims had survived one shot to the head. A professional would have administered the second shot to make sure.

By now, I was beginning to see just what a responsibility taking on this assignment had been. It was all very well my progressing one step at a time towards the goal of a successful piece, but there would be no prizes for *almost* getting there. If at any stage of the journey I fell, then there would be no story and I would have taken *Loaded*'s money and wasted it. In such circumstances I didn't expect them to sue me, but I was sure that would be the end of assignments for them. Further, no doubt word travelled quickly in the world of the lads' mags, and I wouldn't get any more work from any of them. Thus, my whole future as a journalist hung on the success or failure of this Colombia trip.

The flight was uneventful enough, although it was difficult to settle back and get comfortable with my arm still sore from all the injections. Nascent paranoia troubled me as I contemplated my coming encounter with Colombia's CIA-trained customs police. Would they question me about the camera and 40 rolls of film? Did ordinary people travel with 40 rolls of film? A small voice inside told me that it was all academic, anyway, since they would undoubtedly know exactly who I was.

In the event, I breezed through customs without so much as a word exchanged and, within minutes, was in a battered taxi making my way through the equally battered streets towards my hotel. Bogotá was a revelation, a large city in terminal stages of urban decay. Virtually every building looked tumbledown or seriously in need of repair. The roads were badly potholed so that, every now and again, drivers would have to slow and navigate around a particularly large chasm.

The hotel was a welcome surprise. While being a long way from five-star standards, at least it was clean and efficiently run. With an absolute minimum of fuss, I booked in and was soon in my room, the only troubling event being that the receptionist said she would have to keep my passport and return it to me later. Seriously tired now, I barricaded the door with a heavy table, positioned a heavy bedside lamp within easy reaching distance to clobber any intruder, and immediately drifted off into a dreamless sleep.

Even though out of jail over two years now, I sometimes woke up thinking I was still in a cell. The Bogotá hotel room spared me that, though. As consciousness dawned, I was immediately aware of the awful cacophony rising from the streets below as rush-hour drivers leaned on their horns. Then there was the heat. Bogotá is up in the mountains and is supposed to be cool. Virtually the whole of the rest of the country is down in the jungle. Acclimatisation was going to be a problem for me.

Trent wasn't due to arrive from Miami till the evening. Dangers or none, I wasn't going to skulk in my hotel room until then. Bogotá was there to be explored. As I mentally prepared myself for the foray into the unknown, I noticed the printed pamphlet on the bedside table. In passable English, it advised guests to leave all valuables in the hotel safe and warned that, in the event of their being approached by people claiming to be the police, they should not go with them but return to the hotel instead. Very reassuring! Coming on top of the official warnings by both the British and US governments for their nationals not even to travel to Colombia, it served to concentrate the mind wonderfully.

Trent had given me the number of a good friend of his, an English guy who had lived in Colombia for 20 years. Danny was in the music business and his club, London House, had been the first acid-house club in Colombia. He had married a Colombian woman and, after the club closed, had eked out a living importing CDs and deejaying. I remembered that Trent had told me that Danny was fluent in Colombian Spanish. I had already discovered that hardly anyone in Colombia spoke English.

Within 20 minutes, Danny was at my room. Or, rather, 20 minutes later, 'Hurricane Danny' hit my room. A big-built, rangy-looking guy in his early forties, he entered almost at a run. Everything was a hundred miles an hour with Dan, his body movements, his walking, his talking.

I considered myself a good judge of men and weighed him up quickly. There was a decidedly mad look in his eyes, but that was no disbarment, since many of my closest friends were quite mad. He had a bluff, easygoing personality and a ready wit. He soon had me laughing. The East End accent was reassuring, as was the quickly announced fact that he was a West Ham supporter. He confessed to having run with their hooligan arm, the Inter-City Firm, for a couple of years when he was younger. For me, this was even more of a recommendation. Not that I had any time for football hooliganism. There were plenty of things to fight over, and I just didn't consider football to be one of them. However, an immature outlook notwithstanding, the ICF were known for courage and loyalty to their mates. I was very big on loyalty.

Minutes into our conversation, I discovered the reason behind Dan's hundred-mile-an-hour approach. 'Want a quick line, Norm?' he asked, whipping out a small tin, flipping its lid and revealing its contents of white powder.

Back in London, where coke had found its way into every stratum of society, this was the prelude to many social encounters. But it wasn't for me. I wasn't arrogant enough to think that I could control it where so many others had failed. And I liked to be in control. Especially on this, my first journalistic assignment.

My 'No thanks, Dan' rebuffed him a bit and he looked closely to see if I had been offended. 'But you carry on, mate,' I added to show that there was no offence.

Dan needed little encouragement. In one fluid movement, he pinched some powder out of the tin, placed it on the back of his hand and snorted it up his nose.

Just for a second, as its effects hit him, he wasn't with me. Recovering quickly, he shook his head, refocused his eyes and broke into a crazy laugh. 'It's only about one pound fifty a gram out here, Norm. It keeps me going through the day.' He laughed again.

No doubt it did. I was laughing with him now. This Dan was quite a character and I would enjoy his company. However, with the serious business of the assignment always in the background, I pressed him on his knowledge of FARC's jungle capital. For a guy whose main interest was music, he was remarkably well informed about the politics. But, then, as he explained to me, the civil war was so much a part of every Colombian's life that they followed its twists and turns almost like some TV soap.

Dan confessed he'd never been deep into guerrilla-held territory himself, although he had been stopped several times by guerrilla roadblocks on routes leading to Bogotá when he'd been out doing DJ gigs. He said that they were easy enough to get on with, unless they thought you were working for the government. He also said that the people were very tired of the war and wanted peace, almost at any price.

Over the next couple of hours, Dan took me on a guided tour. His base, which he used almost as an office, was a record shop in an arcade just across the street. The owner was a close friend and the three assistants were all sometime party companions. Everywhere he went, everyone seemed to know and like him. As we sat drinking the strong Colombian coffee, Dan mentioned my assignment down in San Vicente, the guerrilla capital.

Universally, everyone we spoke to was shocked. They strongly advised against it, saying that I must be mad even to consider it. From a social perspective, it was all very interesting, but from a professional point of view it was quite depressing. It seemed that my assignment was going to be anything but straightforward.

That evening, we collected Trent from the airport. For Dan and Trent, it was a reunion of old friends and fellow West Ham supporters. The little tin and its contents took a right hammering. If nothing else, it helped them relax in the company of someone who, just a short while earlier, had been a complete stranger.

The following morning, it was down to business. To give credit where it was due, Trent knew when to party and when to work. At his suggestion, we made the rounds of all the agencies for further news of the situation. Reuters and a French news agency dismissed us out of hand as journalistic delinquents, pausing only to warn us of the seriousness of the situation. Clearly, *Loaded* didn't carry much weight with them. The lady at Médecins Sans Frontières tried to be more understanding. She warned us to stay close to the centre of San Vicente, as the roads surrounding it were contested and, should we be stopped by the 'wrong' group, we could expect to be murdered out of hand.

As we sat talking later that evening, Danny was clearly concerned for our safety. We'd had a busy and constructive day, as well as a lot of laughs. Already, a kind of camaraderie had sprung up between us, as often happens between Londoners in strange places. With it also came the rivalry. There was always friendly ribbing between East and West Londoners. At times, I had been hard pressed to keep up my end of it with both Trent and Dan from the East, but in general I gave as good as I got.

'Look, I've been thinking,' said Dan in a manner that suggested he was on the verge of something portentous. Trent and I stopped whatever it was that we had been doing and looked at Danny in expectation. 'You're my mate, Trent, and you, Norman, you're a fellow Londoner. I can't let you go down to San Vicente on your own. I'd never forgive myself if something happened. I'll come with you. You badly need someone who can speak the language. Trent's Costa Spanish will get you nowhere.' He stopped abruptly.

It was an emotional moment. Danny was a loyal guy. He, probably better than anyone, realised the dangers of our trip. Yet he was going to put himself in harm's way just to help us out. We both thanked him warmly and, with that, we all stumbled off to our beds.

Early next morning saw the three of us back at the rather inaptly named El Dorado Airport. This time, though, it was in the 'national' section. Through the large glass windows we could see the massive international jets and, dwarfed by them, the tiny twin-engined planes we were to travel in. As we booked three seats to San Vicente, we were immediately confronted by one of the many ironies of the Colombian situation. SATENA (Servicio Aéreo a Territorios Nacionales), the airline that would fly us to the guerrilla-held town, was run by the Colombian military. So much for our low profile!

The next shock came as we were about to board our little twin-engined 28-seater Fokker. We passed on the German jokes as we saw our luggage, and that of all the other 20 travellers, stacked on the runway around the plane. Each person had to identify his luggage (there were no female travellers) and carry it with him on to the plane. Danny told me that this was to ensure that no one managed to sneak a bomb on board. As I settled into my seat, I noticed that every one of the other passengers turned to look at us three foreigners.

The takeoff seemed to take ages. We didn't seem to be going fast enough. I remember thinking that I hoped we wouldn't run out of runway. Just as I was becoming seriously concerned, we bumped into the air and skimmed over the green canopy of a forest. The experience of cruising smoothly at 30,000 feet hadn't prepared me for the roller-coaster ride of flight in a small plane. As we dropped down from the heights of Bogotá, the warm updrafts from the jungle below buffeted us unrelentingly. Sometimes we dropped by as much as 50 feet, leaving our stomachs behind to catch up with the rest of us. At the same time, the pitch of the engine would change from a piercing screech to a halting, throbbing sound. Never once were we able to escape the knowledge that we were on a plane.

Below us, the Amazon rainforest stretched out in every direction, with no other distinguishing features whatsoever. There were no roads, no buildings, no electric pylons, no sign of any human presence at all. Occasionally, there would be a dark scar where a river intersected the jungle. I reflected that, should we come down, it would take hours, if not days, for help to reach us.

We made one stop, at a little jungle town whose name was as hard to pronounce as it was to find on the map, then it was on to San Vicente. This was the point of no return; there was no going back now.

San Vicente Airport was little more than a concrete strip in a jungle clearing. As we taxied after landing we saw a group of about eight guerrillas in military fatigues just beyond the perimeter fence. We had been warned that they would be expecting us, as they monitored the flight lists closely.

As we left the plane, the heat hit me. It was like being enveloped in an invisible hot mist. Within seconds, I was sweating from every pore on my body. My underwear was quickly saturated and I felt rivulets of cooler sweat running down my arms and legs. My love affair with the jungle was off to a very shaky start. I realised that this would be a very uncomfortable place to live, especially for someone used to mild European climates.

The terminal buildings were a collection of half-finished sheds. We stood in a group with several other travellers who we suddenly discovered were Colombian journalists. I had been so busy trying to keep my own identity a secret that it hadn't occurred to me to find out who else was travelling to San Vicente. 'There's no one here to talk to you, you know,' said the man from *El Tiempo*, the high-circulation Colombian daily. 'All the leaders are in Spain at a big peace meeting.'

It was not a particularly auspicious start. With fledgling feelings of impending doom, I climbed into a taxi and set out for nearby San Vicente. I consoled myself that it wasn't a particularly political piece I would be doing. So whether or not I managed to talk to any guerrilla leaders wasn't crucial. Just so long as I got some good background stuff on the guerrillas in general I'd be OK.

San Vicente was something more than a one-horse town. There were at least six of them standing in the high street. One urinated enthusiastically as we alighted from our taxi outside the hotel. It would have been nice to think that the Hotel Malibu had seen better days, but I feared it had always been a slum. At $8 a day, it was the best hotel in town. Unfortunately, that was no consolation whatsoever. The small dilapidated room with adjoining shower/toilet was rudimentary in the extreme. There were two ways of looking at it. It was either the worst hotel room I had ever been in, or the best cell. I decided to adopt the latter approach and set out to make the best of it.

With absolutely no incentive at all to sit in our rooms and sweat, the three of us soon congregated on a small veranda that overlooked the street. Unfortunately, it also overlooked the urinating horse, which suddenly decided to complete its ablutions by having a crap. As the stench of horseshit drifted up to the veranda, we decided that this was the cue for us to explore the town.

Carrying everything of value with us, we set off. The dusty streets, surrounded by broken-down two-storey buildings, looked like the Mexican towns in the old cowboy films. Higher up on the surrounding hills could be seen the tumbledown clutter of shanty towns. As we walked, swarthy, sinister, suspicious faces seemed to stare out at us from every doorway. It soon became apparent that we were the only gringos in town, and the first for a long while.

Danny and I had already fallen into an easy familiarity. His irreverent humour complemented mine in many ways. And we continued the rivalry that often springs up between Londoners from different areas of the city. It was especially keen between those from the East – that is the East End – and its environs and the rest. They definitely thought that they were sharper dressers, better money getters, could pull more women and were cleverer thieves. There was nothing malicious in it. In fact, it was all part of the rivalry to be funnier and cleverer with your mouth.

'Reminds me a bit of the East,' I said out of the corner of my mouth, as if I were afraid of being overheard. 'Definitely a touch of Brick Lane over there, so you two boys should be feeling quite at home.'

Their reply of 'bollocks!' was long and drawn out. 'You West London mob've got a few slums of your own, mate,' rejoined Dan.

'Yeah, but we ain't got all those outside toilets that you lot have still got.' My reply was met with another chorus of 'bollocks!' from the pair of them.

Suddenly, the narrow dusty streets opened out into a wide central square that was a riot of colourful graffiti and banners expressing revolutionary slogans. And there, right in front of us, was a one-storey slum, similarly bedecked with banners and slogans, which was obviously FARC's local office. A guerrilla in jungle fatigues, his weapon close by, lounged in a chair outside.

For melodrama, all that was missing was the strains of the theme from *High Noon* as the three of us advanced on the office. I reflected that this would be a crucial encounter. This would determine how much assistance, if any, we would get. In the event, Danny's fluent Colombian Spanish and ready wit proved invaluable. Soon he had the guerrilla laughing. He stood and shook hands and offered us a cup of coffee. Then he explained that there was no one here at the moment to talk to us and asked if we could come back in the morning.

Right next door to the office was the Yokomo Café. It was clean and the staff were friendly. We decided to make this our centre of operations.

Nine o'clock the following morning saw the three of us sitting outside the café eating breakfast. Jungle-fatigued guerrillas, with bandoleers of bullets around their chests and carrying automatic weapons, bustled in and out of the office. Strangely, FARC seemed to own few cars, for most came and went on trail bikes or in the yellow town taxis.

We soon saw that 9 a.m. was quite late by San Vicente standards. The town and, of course, the guerrillas had been up for hours and many had already gone off on their assignments for the day. We would have been there at least an hour earlier, but we had been held up by Trent. Jungle or no jungle, he clearly felt that there were certain standards to be upheld. His fastidiousness didn't come without a price, either. Danny and I had sat about for over an hour while Trent had washed, shaved, done his hair and generally attended to every detail of his toilet. Dan summed it up nicely. 'My old woman gets ready quicker than he does,' he muttered *sotto voce*.

But now we were ready to get down to business. There were real live heavily armed Marxist guerrillas to interview. However, on closer inspection, these guerrillas seemed considerably underwhelmed by our interest. It wasn't so much that they ignored us, just that everything else they had to do had a higher priority.

Then Lucero appeared. The Colombian journalists had told us of this beautiful guerrilla who held high political and military rank. She was married to a top FARC negotiator and had a seven-year-old daughter who was looked after by her family. Short, with eyes that seemed to flash and sparkle with amusement, Lucero was a veteran of many battles with the Colombian Army and had achieved almost legendary status. She listened while Danny explained what we wanted, but politely declined, saying she had important things to do. She suggested that we speak with Comandante Nora, who was out the back of the office.

Leaving Trent and me outside, Danny went in search of Comandante Nora. Within seconds, he was back, a pained look on his face. 'She's busy at the moment. We'll have to wait for a while,' said Dan. But there was something in his attitude that made me curious.

'What's she doing, then?' I asked querulously. The combination of the stifling jungle heat and the lack of cooperation was making me tetchy.

'Her fucking ironing,' replied Danny in similar vein.

There was something in his manner that indicated that he wasn't joking, but this I had to see. I walked inside and peered through a dusty window. Sure enough, there was Comandante Nora, AK-47 propped against a table, ironing her blouse.

While we were waiting, a portly, heavily moustachioed guerrilla called Comandante Mauricio came up and introduced himself. He had been sent to show us around the town. You didn't have to understand Colombian to discern that Mauricio was less than pleased with his assignment. But, as far as we were concerned, it was the most positive step so far. As Mauricio headed off on foot, we followed in his wake.

Over the next couple of hours we got an in-depth look at most of San Vicente's roadworks and municipal improvements. We trudged for miles along a network of hot dusty streets, none of which was paved or tarmacked. A few looked absolutely impossible to navigate in anything less than a tractor. Suddenly, we came across a road that was precipitously steep and deeply rutted. It may not have been the worst road in the world, but it was certainly in the top ten. Frustration must have made me blasé. Turning to Dan, I said, 'Definitely a touch of the Mile End Road there, mate.' The three of us laughed.

Mauricio may not have understood the language but no doubt sarcasm is internationally recognisable. His face like thunder, he advanced on me. With his finger, he beckoned for me to follow him. We had passed hundreds of tumbledown hovels in our progress through

San Vicente, but had looked into none of them. Suddenly, I was standing inside one.

The floor was of bare earth, with a couple of pieces of plastic matting scattered about. The roof was a patchwork of rusty and holed corrugated tin. The walls were made from an assortment of timber of different sizes, colours and types. The windows were just holes in the walls with torn material in the place of curtains.

There was one large room, with what must have been a bed in the middle. On this sat a tired-looking woman in her early thirties dressed in rags. At her breast a small infant was feeding. Around her feet sat several other small children. This was abject poverty in the extreme.

Mauricio spoke to Danny for him to translate, but his words were clearly for me. 'The government have never, ever done anything at all for these people. These are the ones they have given up on.'

It was meant as a rebuke and it had its desired effect. I was instantly both ashamed and embarrassed for making fun of such a situation. What had I been thinking of? I prided myself on having a social conscience. I wholeheartedly supported revolutionary movements such as FARC. I told myself it was the effect of the *Loaded* factor. Their readership wouldn't be the slightest bit interested in civic reconstruction in rural Colombia. *Loaded* was an irreverent, light-hearted read. Everything had to be a laugh or a putdown.

So how did I justify my writing for them? The answer to that was that, while the style of writing might appear to be light-hearted, the message was still there. Because the establishment controlled the media, socialist revolutions never got a fair press. This was an opportunity for me to get the message across to several hundred thousand people, who might normally baulk at the idea of reading a serious political piece about Colombia. Anyway, all ideology aside, I resolved to treat everything much more seriously from here onwards.

Then a little incident occurred that further defined what I was already discovering to be a difficult relationship with Trent. Danny and I had been strolling ahead, pointing things out to each other and talking, while Trent had been hanging back to photograph whatever took his interest. Suddenly he called me over. I thought it was to point out something. 'Look, Norman,' he said in a very level tone, 'this is your first assignment, so I'm really the senior man. When we're out like this you, should walk behind me.'

For a long second, I thought he was joking. Neither of us had completely relaxed with the other, so humour would have been difficult anyway. But as I stared into his face it dawned on me that he was serious.

Perhaps the rebuke from Mauricio had curbed my normally ebullient personality. Perhaps I was still striving to be as professional as possible. Maybe I was temporarily lost for words. As I turned and walked over to Danny, Trent struck out ahead.

Danny screwed up his face as I drew near and shook his head. 'He can be a bit of an arsehole at times,' he offered. If anything, it served to bring Danny and me closer. He was a decent guy who was embarrassed by such behaviour.

That evening, tired, uncomfortable in the suffocating evening heat and frustrated by our lack of real progress, we sat in what passed for the lounge of the Hotel Malibu. Occasionally we glanced at the one TV set, high on the wall. Suddenly, it had all our attention. There, all over the national evening news, was San Vicente Airport. And at the forefront of the screen, waiting to meet what looked like some sort of official delegation as they descended from the aircraft, was Lucero.

With Danny translating, we learned that this was FARC's official delegation returning from a peace conference in Spain. Travelling along with FARC's delegation were top ministers of the Colombian government. We had missed what was probably the biggest news event in the history of San Vicente, out looking at roadworks with Mauricio. With a growing feeling of impending doom, I retired to my room for the night.

The following morning I was up with the lark. If I was going to go down, I might as well go down fighting. If I upset a few guerrillas in the process, then so be it, but today I would get a few decent interviews no matter what. After I had rousted Danny from his room, we headed for the Yokomo Café.

Danny was like a child sneaking off from under a parent's control. 'What about Trent?' he asked, looking back over his shoulder. 'He's not going to like us going off without him.'

'Fuck Trent!' I replied. 'If he wants to lie in bed while there's work to be done, then that's his lookout. Anyway, I'm beginning to get the hump with his bad attitude.'

Danny didn't look convinced. He had a worried look on his face all through breakfast. I had brought my own camera with me, as had Danny. Neither of us was a photographer, but we had taken scores of photos of everything of interest. If Trent really threw a tantrum, I was looking at a situation of life without him.

I had just finished telling Dan that Lucero was top of the interview list when, as if on cue, she appeared. She collected a cup of coffee from inside FARC's office, then settled down to drink it in one of the chairs on the veranda outside, her AK-47 leaning against a nearby wall. I beckoned Dan to accompany me and we sat down in two chairs close by. In quick succession I showed her my National Union of Journalists card, a copy of my first book, *Parkhurst Tales*, complete with my photo on the back, and a copy of February's issue of *Loaded*.

I was slightly concerned about her reaction to the last of these. While being very professional and impressive in its layout, with well-written features and stories, there was no getting away from the fact that there were numerous photos of young scantily clad women in provocative poses. You didn't get much more liberated than a female guerrilla in FARC. Would Lucero be offended by what she might feel to be such less-than-serious treatment of women?

As she leafed through the pages, a broad smile spread across her face, revealing her perfect white teeth. She obviously couldn't understand the words, but the photos spoke for themselves. For several minutes, she was lost in the magazine. At last, she looked up, her eyes sparkling with humour. She pointed to the picture on the cover and asked Danny about it.

February's issue had the former Spandau Ballet member Martin Kemp on the cover and a story inside about his role as one of the Kray twins in the 1990 film *The Krays*. As Danny explained that he was a film star playing the role of a gangster, she suddenly pulled a.45 automatic from her waistband and held it to Kemp's likeness. 'This is what FARC does with gangsters,' she announced, still smiling broadly.

It was a great moment and just what I needed for the story. After asking her permission, we photographed her in several poses with the *Loaded* cover and the .45. It led nicely into the interview, too. On being asked how long she had been in FARC, Lucero replied, 'I was born a revolutionary.' From anyone else it would have sounded trite and would have smacked of melodrama, but, delivered with her beaming smile and sparkling eyes, it sounded just right from Lucero.

I mentioned the US involvement and asked if she was worried about the Americans and their superior technology. 'They are tall, with blue eyes. They will make good targets,' she retorted. When I asked about the reception for the delegation at the airport the previous day, she stopped for a moment and looked at me as if she were weighing me up. 'That was FARC's peace delegation returning from peace talks in Madrid. We were concerned that the Americans would try to assassinate them, so we insisted that several Colombian government ministers travel with them on the plane.'

So perhaps that explained why Mauricio was taking us out to see the roadworks. Not really knowing who we were, maybe they just wanted us out of the way.

I asked if being a guerrilla in FARC meant that a woman had to give up any hopes of a husband, children and family life. Lucero explained that many of the female guerrillas were married, with their children being looked after by relatives. That was her own situation. Her husband was one of the peace negotiators and their seven-year-old child was being looked after by her mother's family in her home town.

At this point, another uniformed guerrilla came out of the office and whispered something to Lucero. She quickly made her apologies and said that she had to leave, because she was wanted elsewhere. Without further ado, she mounted one of the several motorbikes parked outside the office and roared off in a cloud of dust, AK-47 strapped across her back.

In the absence of Lucero, Danny's thoughts now turned to Trent. 'I suppose I'd better go and see where Trent is,' he said, a concerned look on his face.

'He'll still be in the bathroom, mate,' I replied with the beginnings of a smile on mine.

Danny responded with a weak grin and, shaking his head, set off towards the hotel.

In no time at all, he was back. 'He's got the right fucking hump, Norm. I'd better warn you.' Now Dan was clearly worried.

'Fuck him, Dan. I'm beginning to get a bit fed up with this guy.' The annoyance was clear in my voice. 'Who does he think he is, anyway? I tell you something: I've been very tolerant up to now and tolerance is something I don't do very well. But I'm supposed to be in journalist mode. So I've put up with some of his bullshit. Back in England, on the street, I'd have steamed into him by now.'

'I know, Norm. I just don't want you to fuck up the assignment. To be honest, I've had my own fallouts with Trent in the past. He can be a bit of an arsehole at times. I know I've only known you a couple of days, but we seem to get on well and I'd like to think that we're mates. I'm not going to take sides, but I'm just trying to avoid any awkwardness.'

'I understand that, Dan. And, yeah, we do get on well together and I appreciate what you're trying to do. But pride is a bit of a fault with me and I'll only stand so much.'

As I finished, Trent suddenly appeared, beetling across the plaza, his arms swinging wildly and his face a study in anger. I sat back in my chair quite nonchalantly, not at all concerned. If it came to a punch-up, I was confident I could handle him. But I didn't know what the guerrillas would make of the two of us, supposedly professional journalists, battling away right outside their office.

While still 30 feet away, Trent beckoned me to come and meet him away from the front of FARC's office. I was out of my chair like a shot. Now it was my turn to swing my arms as I rushed towards him, serious violence firmly on my mind. 'Yeah, what do you want?' I asked aggressively as I closed on him, my face twisted into a scowl.

As Trent suddenly realised that I was right on the verge of steaming into him, his attitude abruptly changed. 'Hold up, hold up, mate. There's no need for this.' He stopped and held his hands out in front of him, as if to ward me off.

'Well what do you want? Coming rushing over here all aggressive, as if you're looking for a row. If it's a row you want, well, let's have it.' The anger just flowed out of me. It was a combination of the jungle heat, the failing assignment and Trent's attitude.

In the event, he turned out to be all bluff and bluster. 'No, Norm, it's just that I'm the senior man and you left me in the hotel.' There was a pleading tone to his voice now.

'Look, mate, don't give me all that shit. It might be my first foreign assignment, but I'm not a fucking idiot. If you want to lie in bed when there's things going on, well, that's up to you. Just don't expect me to sit outside your bedroom door waiting for you. And don't treat me with disrespect, OK, 'cause I don't take that from anyone.'

By now, Trent looked thoroughly crestfallen, his eyes focused on the floor, his shoes, anywhere but on mine. Suddenly, I felt sorry for him. I only wanted to put him in his place, not break his heart. 'Look, Trent,' I said in as conciliatory a tone as I could manage, 'if we're going to get this assignment done, we'll have to work together. As far as I'm concerned, we're all equals here, Danny, me, you, because we're all taking the same chance of getting killed or whatever. So let's just start again, eh?'

As I finished, I stuck out my hand. He shook it reluctantly, but I wasn't going to make an issue out of that. I wanted to get along with him only while we were on the assignment and in the jungle. I wasn't looking to be his pal back in the real world.

We both went to sit with Dan outside FARC's office. By now, there was only one guerrilla sitting inside and he said he was too busy to do an interview. So, left to our own devices, we decided to tour the town on our own.

Again, this was where Danny's fluent Colombian Spanish was crucial. We wandered from bar to bar, in and out of various cafés, and we stopped people in the street. Everyone seemed to know that we were English journalists. In every instance, Danny put them at their ease and very quickly had them laughing.

The story that we were uniformly told about San Vicente came as a surprise. People said that, before FARC came, there were four or five murders a week, which for such a small town was amazingly high. Now there was none and the place was virtually without crime. They pointed out the hospital and the school that FARC had built. The most amazing thing was that, despite being surrounded by coca fields, no one did coke. Nor did they smoke the Colombian grass. They were heavy drinkers, but there was a strong social stigma about taking drugs.

A sceptic might argue that the townspeople were so terrified of FARC that they only parroted the party line to us. But what was quite apparent was that there was absolutely no climate of fear. Unless they were all naturally consummate actors, they seemed like ordinary Colombians going about their social lives. In fact, many of the people we spoke to were in the advanced stages of inebriation, so their answers to our questions were all the more spontaneous. Further, all three of us were experienced in drug culture and the behaviour that goes with it. In all the bars and cafés we visited, we would have seen some sign of it, but there was none.

Now, while this might have been revelatory stuff for a piece in the *Guardian*, it was bad news for *Loaded* readers. Instead of their intrepid reporters filing a gripping article from Bandit City, capital of Bandit Country, it seemed that San Vicente was one of the safest, straightest places on earth.

By now, Saturday evening was upon us and all we had to show for our trip to Colombia was the interview and photo with Lucero and scores of photos of the local roadworks. Frustrated and depressed, I agreed to join Danny and Trent for a night out on the town. In the *Loaded* article, I might have written, 'But, when *Loaded* journalists' backs are against the wall, they know only one way to react: they go out on the piss.' But the truth was far more mundane. I had specifically asked Danny to hold back on the little tin while we were working. I didn't want Trent getting so off his face that he couldn't take a photo. Now that I had wasted their time dragging them down to San Vicente, I might as well let them go and enjoy themselves for a night. And, even though I didn't drink due to a stomach condition, I thought that, rather than sit in the hotel room, I might as well go out and get some fresh air.

As we wandered from bar to bar, Danny explained about the Colombian culture of drinking. There was a local highly potent drink brewed out of pure cane spirit, called *aguadiente*, which roughly translated as 'firewater'. Each area of the country was proud of the potency of its local *aguadiente* and there was great competition to brew the most potent drink. As was to be expected, San Vicente claimed that theirs was the strongest.

I had been listening carefully to all this, trying to discern which of my many allergies the *aguadiente* would affect. But, while the fermented brew would do little to improve my yeast infection, at least it wasn't made out of anything that would trigger an allergic reaction. Reluctantly at first, I joined them, but soon I was matching them drink for drink.

Carrying a couple of bottles of the stuff, we staggered down a particularly ill-lit street and came upon a funfair. It was rudimentary in the extreme compared with British funfairs, but in a Colombian jungle town it was a rare treat, made possible only by the fact that today was one of the local fiestas.

By now, the three of us were quite drunk. Not falling-down drunk or slurring-your-speech drunk, but sufficiently affected to stagger from time to time and generally talk nonsense. We staggered out of the funfair and into the darkened street again and towards what would be a pivotal moment in our whole trip.

Suddenly, around the corner of the narrow street came a sight that was both amazing and incongruous in the extreme. To the accompaniment of whistles and bells El Gusanito, or 'The Little Worm', thundered out of the darkness. El Gusanito was a kiddies' ride in the shape of a giant worm.

The head or engine that pulled the rest was a green plastic construction in the shape of a Disney worm's head, complete with large bulbous insect eyes and waving antennae. The construction completely obscured the farm tractor that it was mounted on. Behind it were eight two-wheeled cars, again covered with bright-green plastic, that made up the worm's body. The whole ride was festooned with multicoloured flashing lights and, every so often, a loud mournful siren would sound over the clamour of the whistles and bells.

Of all the things we might have expected to encounter in the darkened streets of San Vicente this was in the outer ranges of improbability. The three of us stood there, literally with our mouths open in surprise.

As it drew close, we saw that several of the cars were occupied by young children. Almost before I knew it, Danny and Trent had grabbed me by the arms and pulled me into one of the little cars with them. As we thundered off along the street, I suddenly discovered another aspect of the ride. As they rounded the many sharp corners of the narrow street, the children would lean out of the cars, wave their arms and scream at the startled passers-by. Other children and the occasional dog ran out of the darkened hovels we passed and howled after us.

This was somewhat less than dignified behaviour for supposedly serious, international journalists. Drunk or not, I couldn't help but feel slightly ridiculous. Danny and Trent were suffering no such qualms. Urging me to join them, they leaned out of the cars as we rounded the bends and screamed enthusiastically at the unsuspecting townsfolk.

By now I was caught up in the moment too. We rounded one particularly sharp bend and the three of us leaned out and screamed in unison at the three startled pedestrians standing on the corner. It was only as we flashed by that we noticed the jungle fatigues and automatic weapons. It was a three-man FARC patrol. In the event, they were more surprised than we were. I still have a clear picture of their startled faces as we disappeared into the darkness.

The central square acted as a terminus for the ride, and that was enough for me. Danny and Trent expressed their intention to visit the town's only brothel, somewhere up in the impenetrable blackness of the hills above San Vicente. It wasn't for me for a whole host of reasons, not the least of them being the almost palpable presence of the vengeful spirit of Marsha. I staggered off towards the hotel and oblivion.

The following morning, at breakfast outside the Yokomo Café, Danny and Trent regaled me with details of their visit to the brothel. In keeping with the rest of San Vicente, this seemed to be a bizarre establishment, too. According to their account, it was run by a bearded transsexual and had only two whores. Danny and Trent had monopolised these to such an extent that they had provoked a mini-riot, with outraged and impatient fellow customers banging on their room door and demanding access to the girls.

Sitting bleary-eyed and somewhat the worse for wear in the early-morning sun, I was aware of a growing feeling of embarrassment. What would FARC think of us? Every bit of credibility we might have had must surely have vanished. Would they even speak to us now?

The reality, though, was completely the opposite. Guerrilla after guerrilla came up to our table, laughing and slapping us across the backs. Mauricio was effusive and the normally taciturn Nora could be seen laughing behind her hands. Lucero larked about with Danny and he had them all laughing uproariously as he re-enacted events from the night before. It was intimated that they had been very suspicious of us previously and had thought that we might be spies. They had been watching closely everything we did.

In retrospect, our night out on the piss was probably the smartest move we could have made. No doubt the CIA and MI5 train their operatives to keep a low profile. So, for FARC, whatever we were, we definitely weren't spies. The only misgivings I had about that was that they might also conclude that we weren't serious journalists either.

However, over the next couple of days we got everything we could ever have hoped for. We were taken inside FARC's office, a place that had been strictly off limits to us before. There, under a large poster of Che Guevara that would surely have been a cliché in any other circumstances, we had FARC's ideology fully explained to us. The access-to-the-office bit was definitely a strategic mistake on FARC's part, because after that we were hardly ever out of the place.

We went on river patrol with Mauricio and three heavily armed guerrillas in a massive iron canoe. Afterwards, we went on township patrol. FARC definitely seemed to be popular. Everywhere we went people rushed out of their shacks to greet them effusively and discuss whatever problems they had, and, considering the degree of poverty, they certainly had plenty of those. It was all a visual feast for Trent, who was snapping away frantically in the background.

We were introduced to FARC's graffiti artist, a callow youth who would surely have been a social menace in any other society. It was he who was responsible for the literally hundreds of revolutionary slogans and icons plastered all over San Vicente. Purely as an acknowledgement to who we were working for, we got him to spray 'LOADED' in big yellow letters on a nearby wall.

Tuesday saw a major press conference at FARC's local HQ, just down the road at Los Pozos, and we were invited. The Colombian national press had arrived in force. TV crews in vans mounted with satellite dishes thronged the main square and nearby streets.

The star of the show was Raul Reyes, a small elderly bearded guy in jungle fatigues, who was number two in the guerrilla high command. He looked slightly bemused as he was first introduced to, then photographed with, the three English journalists from *Loaded*. The copy of the magazine had been deliberately left behind and I had instructed Danny to keep things as vague as possible, but still I saw Comandante Raul mouth the word 'Loaded' a couple of times with a quizzical look on his face.

It was my first real experience of a press conference, but, in the circumstances, I was a quick learner. I watched and listened as the representatives of the national press first introduced themselves and their media group, then asked their question. Comandante Reyes sat at a small table cluttered with microphones as dozens of heavily armed guerrillas scanned the surrounding countryside.

I just couldn't resist it. Clutching a piece from the *Independent* of a couple of months previously in which General José Serrano, the Colombian chief of police said, 'The SAS have given us great help in recent times,' I framed my question. Or, rather, the Colombian TV presenter who had agreed to help us did.

'Norman Parker, *Loaded*,' he said, live on Colombian national TV, as he acknowledged me standing next to him. 'Bearing in mind the human-rights allegations against the Colombian Army, what evidence does FARC have of the British SAS training the Colombian military?'

Comandante Reyes confessed that he didn't have such information to hand, but promised to seek it out as a priority. I wasn't disappointed in the slightest. The late Robin Cook, then the UK's Foreign Secretary, was forever wittering on about an 'ethical foreign policy'. Sheer and utter hypocrisy, of course. I just welcomed a chance, however small, to embarrass him for a moment.

I also took full advantage of the close proximity to so many leading Colombian journalists, as well as several from other South American countries. Speaking off the record, they were a rich source of information. On the subject of who profits from the drugs trade, the overwhelming consensus was that every party does, FARC, ELN, the paramilitaries, the cartels and the Colombian Army.

One informed me that a former president had resigned amid claims that his election campaign had been financed with drugs money.

All claimed that the US had its own agenda beyond that of drugs. 'The last thing the US wants is a Marxist Colombia,' said an Argentinean journalist. 'The Panama Canal has just been handed back and there is a nationalist, reformist government in Venezuela.'

'FARC are incredibly strong,' said another. 'They even have Stinger missiles. The Colombian military won't be able to cope and the US will have to send in troops. That will polarise the whole of South America and could well turn Colombia into another Vietnam.'

It was all heady stuff, but I didn't kid myself that *Loaded*'s City-boy readership would pause for a millisecond before doing their next line of charlie. However, wars are fought with information as well as bullets, and I had managed to fire a few shots.

Everywhere we went now, FARC patrols waved and swapped jokes with us. We were on first-name terms with many of the townspeople. However, time was running short. We had to be on the plane for Bogotá the following day. And, ignore it as I might try, the logistics dictated that I would be back on Marsha's birthday, but not until about nine in the evening.

Needless to say, I had neglected to mention that unfortunate fact in the daily phone calls I had made to her. To add insult to injury, her parents had flown in from their home abroad to be with us both on her birthday. Finally, I had to confess the awful truth.

There was a long moment's silence as I awaited the tirade that I knew must surely come. In the event, it was short and succinct. Of all the phone lines in the world to have a private conversation on, the line from the guerrilla capital at San Vicente was not the one. The CIA, MI5 and Colombian military intelligence closely monitored every call. So, together with all the other information they had gleaned about me over the past week, they now knew that I was a 'fucking wanker', just before Marsha put the phone down on me.

It was a sad parting between us and FARC. As a token of gratitude we had a cake made in a local shop. It was a creamy confection. Iced on it was:

To the FARC
Thanks for all your help
Danny, Trent & Norman, Loaded

We presented it to them in their office. It was an emotional moment. Lucero especially looked on the verge of being overcome. She recovered manfully though. Scooping a handful of cream from the top of the cake, she slapped it in Danny's face and a food fight ensued between the pair of them. An enduring memory is of the big blob of cream that ended up right on Che's nose.

The following morning, as we took off from the airport, FARC patrols waved goodbye from the perimeter. I reflected that not only had it been a successful first foreign assignment, it had also been a great adventure.

Back in London, *Loaded* were delighted with the results. I was thankful that we had so many photos to back our story up, because at times they looked decidedly sceptical. And I had to confess, if I hadn't experienced it myself, it would all be hard to believe.

The article was featured prominently in the August issue and I was relieved to see that they had edited my story only slightly from the original. My final line might have been pure '*Loaded*-ese', but in the circumstances it was rather apt. It went:

> *So the next time Sara Tara Whatever snorts a line of Charlie off the bonnet of her daddy's Roller, she might actually be doing something quite positive. Namely subsidizing civic reconstruction in some Colombian shanty town.*

CHAPTER THREE

THE CURSE OF DRIVER MILLS

Although the FARC story was my first real journalistic assignment, I had written an article for *Loaded* before. It was a crime story and, in view of my background, I was obviously trying to play from a position of strength. However, I didn't intend to concentrate solely on crime because I knew it to be something subject to the law of diminishing returns. For a start, the vast majority of criminals looked on the average journalist as nothing but a grass, a police informer. Many a criminal had had exposé articles written about him and had been arrested as a result. And for a story to have any worth one had to break new ground, reveal new facts. Once it became known that I was a crime journalist, fewer and fewer people would confide in me. So there would be no new facts to reveal and so no story of worth.

This particular crime story, though, would reveal previously unknown facts without compromising anyone. Further, in view of the fact that so many of the leading characters had walked in and out of my life over the past 30 years, it was quite a personal story, even though the crime at its centre was so well known as to be almost public property.

The Great Train Robbery is probably Britain's most famous – or infamous – crime. When a gang of men stopped the Glasgow-to-Euston mail train in the early hours of 8 August 1963 and robbed it of £2,500,000 in cash, it took its place in the history books as a unique case.

A brief examination of contemporary British crime reveals a phenomenon that was, to use a phrase of Thomas Hobbes, 'nasty, brutish and short'. It was inevitably characterised by a minimum of planning and a maximum of violence. The prolific and highly successful Bertie Smalls's bank-robbery gang even made a joke of it, calling themselves 'the Crash, Bang, Wallop Gang'.

'The Train' was different, though. Upwards of 15 men were involved in a highly detailed plan that was put together over several months. Trains were timed, signals examined, escape routes planned and transport for the loot and a hideout were bought.

The gang itself was something of a contradiction. Only a few of those caught (rumour has it that three got away) had experience of major violent crime. The rest were a mixture of lesser criminals, minor criminals and even a couple of 'straight-goers'.

The actual robbery went well enough. Inside information had told the gang that this particular load was worth taking. Communicating with walkie-talkies, the gang fixed a signal and stopped the train in a desolate part of Buckinghamshire in the early hours.

The 'high-value' coach was uncoupled from the rest of the train and shunted further up the track. The robbers then smashed their way in and intimidated the Post Office sorting staff working inside. Then they formed a human chain to pass the 120 mail bags filled with cash down the embankment. These were loaded into the backs of two Land Rovers and a lorry, which were then driven the 20 miles or so to Leatherslade Farm, the robbers' hideout. The robbery itself had taken just 35 minutes and they had stolen £2,631,684, approximately £20 million at today's values.

There was only one hitch. One of the robbers coshed the train driver, Jack Mills. Mills recovered, but he never worked again. The 25 guineas (£26.25) he received from British Rail and the £250 from the Post Office could hardly have been much consolation to him. Most of the robbers' loot was never recovered.

Mills died seven years later of bronchial pneumonia, chronic bronchitis and lymphatic leukaemia. At the inquest, Leonard Curley, the Home Office pathologist, emphasised that, in his opinion, there was nothing to connect the assault with his death. However, both his wife and son said that Mills was never the same man again, and many of the public certainly felt that the experience hastened his death.

This far is all pretty much common knowledge, as is the fact that most of the robbers were caught and sentenced to very long terms in jail. What isn't widely known, however, is the almost incredible catalogue of disaster and misfortune that has dogged many of them. It is almost as if they were cursed by the death of Driver Mills.

It was late August in 1963, and, although I was aware of the Great Train Robbery, my failing romance was totally at the centre of my concentration. It was a strange relationship by any standards: Susan, a fascist whose brothers were personal bodyguards to Sir Oswald Mosley; me, the son of Jewish parents. They had even prevailed upon me to look after guns they used for armed robberies. It had a predictable end.

Mad with jealousy over her latest infidelity, I confronted Susan in her parents' flat. Raging, she fetched the gun she used to keep under her pillow. Fortunately, her best friend Josephine was a witness to all this. The single shot came from the pistol I had been carrying.

Murder with a firearm was then a capital offence. The following morning, I sat in a cell at Marylebone Magistrates' Court, waiting to answer just such a charge. My parents were both law-abiding folk and knew nothing of courts and procedures. My legal representation had been arranged by a friend whose father had done several terms inside. As a result, through my door walked Brian Field, solicitor's clerk to John Denbigh Wheater. They would help me prepare my defence for my trial at the Old Bailey.

Or, at least, that had been the plan. You can imagine my consternation when, a few weeks later, both Wheater and Field were arrested and charged over the Great Train Robbery.

In the event, I was sentenced to six years for manslaughter and was sent to Wormwood Scrubs, where John Wheater became my library orderly and Brian Field my bridge partner. The latter experience was definitely part of the punishment. You learn an awful lot about a man when he is your bridge partner. Fortunately, it didn't last.

On the face of it, Brian Field was just a solicitor's clerk, but in reality he was a whole lot more than that. He had acted for Gordon Goody, also arrested for 'The Train', and other professional criminals in the past. In time, he had come to occupy that twilight world that sometimes exists between 'straight people' and the criminal fraternity. 'The Train' was his 'bit of work'. He had put up 'bits of work' in the past.

From a professional criminal's perspective, the trouble with Brian was that he thought it was all part of some jolly game. With his posh accent and his hail-fellow-well-met persona, he was what criminals call a 'silly bollocks'. Violent crime is a brutal dirty business and it was very apparent to everyone that, if things got nasty, Brian wouldn't have either the strength or the stomach to cope.

The 25-year sentence he received for his part in 'The Train' brought him right down to earth with a bump. Fortunately for him, before he could really come to terms with the enormity of the sentence, it was reduced on appeal to five years. The Appeal Court decided that he had only been party to buying the farm as a hideout and not to the planning of the actual robbery.

Brian served just over three years and the only hardship that befell him, apart from losing me as a bridge partner, that is, was that his wife divorced him. On release, he changed his name and started a new life.

By 1997, he had been free for ten years and was now a successful sales manager for an international publishing company. He had a pretty new wife, a Porsche and a nice flat in a select area, and was flush with money. It seemed that he had put his past behind him and successfully reinvented himself.

One weekend, he and his wife were driving home along the M4 in the Porsche after a short break in the country. Travelling in the opposite direction was a Mercedes carrying the daughter of Paul Raymond, her husband and their two children. The husband was driving. He had been drinking.

Suddenly, the Mercedes swerved and hit the central barrier. It hit at precisely the spot where the barrier had been bent downwards in an earlier collision.

The Mercedes took off like a water skier off a ramp. It hurtled through the air, turned upside down as it crossed the central reservation and, in a million-to-one accident, landed right on top of the oncoming Porsche. Brian Field, his wife and the four occupants of the Mercedes were killed.

I too was released from prison in 1967, but, unlike Brian Field, I changed neither my name nor my way of life. Once again, the ending was predictable. In 1970, I was sentenced to life imprisonment for killing another criminal.

In the 24 years I spent in the system, I met many thousands of notorious and violent criminals. I also met many of the 'train robbers' and, by comparison, they were nice guys. There was nothing vicious or nasty about any of them. And to those who would say, 'Ah, except that is, the violent and nasty crime they were convicted of', I would answer that, for their sins, they were sentenced to phenomenally long terms.

Charlie Wilson was a nice guy. Virtually nobody had a bad word to say about him, except perhaps the workers on the train he robbed. Charlie was a handsome-looking man, had a fine physique and possessed a personality full of wit and intelligence. I knew him through some of the darkest days of his 30-year sentence and never once saw him miserable or depressed.

Charlie was undoubtedly one of the most professional of the robbers, having previously been involved in the London Airport Robbery, when an audacious gang of ten men stole £62,000. If that doesn't sound much by today's values you must remember that you could buy a large London house for about £5,000 then.

He was among the first arrested for the Great Train Robbery and was sentenced to 30 years in 1964. Within a year, he had escaped from Birmingham's Winson Green Prison and fled to Canada. However, he was arrested there three years later and returned to England. He didn't walk free again until 1978.

After his release, Charlie made a lot of money as a gold smuggler. Together with others, he imported millions of pounds' worth of gold coins, melted them down and sold the gold as ingots, so avoiding paying VAT. In 1984, he was arrested for a £2.5 million VAT fraud, but the charges were dropped for lack of evidence.

The following year, he and another man were arrested for conspiracy to rob a security van while in possession of two shotguns. After he'd been four months on remand, the charges were dropped and two detective constables involved in the case were charged with conspiracy to rob and conspiracy to pervert the course of justice. A serious attempt had been made to frame Charlie.

In 1987, Charlie went to live in Spain. Perhaps he thought that it would be a case of 'out of sight, out of mind'. However a serious threat emerged from a completely different source. Early in 1990, he offended a powerful Holland-based drugs gang boss called Roy Adkins, after a friend of Charlie's mentioned Adkins's name in a court case. Some remarks Charlie had made about the case got back to Adkins.

Adkins was definitely not a man to cross. He had grown increasingly wealthy and powerful of late. With that status had come the paranoia, and he had ordered the deaths of several men. In April, Adkins sent two hit men to visit Charlie at his Spanish villa. Charlie was shot to death!

Roy James never had any need to become a criminal. He was a talented racing driver with the famous Brabham team and his future looked bright. Yet Roy liked to cock a snook at authority. Hence his role in the Great Train Robbery. He was sentenced to 30 years in 1964.

After his release in 1976, he tried to resurrect his racing career, but crashed the second time out. He then turned his hand to gold smuggling with Charlie Wilson and was subsequently cleared of a £2.5 million VAT fraud in 1984.

Shortly afterwards, Roy married Anthea, 30 years his junior and a bank manager's daughter, who worked in Roy's Hatton Garden jeweller's shop. By 1994, they were separated and arguing bitterly over their two children, whom Roy had custody of. The two main bones of contention were Anthea's drink problem and a dispute over the divorce settlement.

One weekend, Anthea had an access visit with her daughters. Later, she returned them to Roy's house, accompanied by her father. Soon a particularly acrimonious argument broke out. Roy snapped. He fetched a handgun from the house and shot Anthea's father three times in the shoulder. He then beat Anthea with the gun.

At his trial, he blamed the pressure of the Train Robbery and its aftermath for his mental condition, claiming that it had ruined his life. The trial judge accepted that he was suffering from a depressive mental illness and sentenced him to a comparatively merciful six years' imprisonment.

While in prison, he constantly complained that he felt ill. The prison authorities, as is their wont, accused him of malingering. Eventually, they allowed him to go to an outside hospital for tests. The hospital kept him in, saying that he had a serious heart condition that required immediate surgery. They operated the same day and saved his life.

Over the following months his health went from strength to strength and he was eventually released with no obvious ill effects. However, Roy felt a deep sense of gratitude to the medical profession. So, when given the opportunity to take part in a series of tests that would benefit future heart patients and needed ten human guinea pigs, Roy felt obliged to help. However, Roy died during the tests.

To those who knew him, Ronald 'Buster' Edwards's story is really sad. Of all the Robbers, Buster had the most likable personality. He was a shy and private man who, other than for a small group of friends, kept himself to himself. You had nothing to fear from Buster.

Generous and loyal to a fault, he would do anything to help a friend out. The irony is that so-called friends bled him of his share of the money while on the run. Buster didn't have a nasty bone in his body and abhorred violence, so he couldn't do a lot about it. Nearly penniless and with the pressure of life on the run becoming too much for him, he gave himself up in 1967 for a lesser sentence of 15 years. All he wanted was to be with his wife, June.

Although formerly enormously fat, Buster had a very determined nature. In prison he became a fitness fanatic, training for several hours every day. I trained regularly with him and, although ten years his junior and very fit myself, often struggled to keep up.

Buster was released in April 1975 and immediately began to struggle to survive. Being a Train Robber precluded him from most types of employment and he got little or no help from former friends. Within months, he was arrested and convicted of petty shoplifting, in Harrods of all places. This was widely interpreted as a cry for help. Unfortunately, no one was listening.

He then ran a flower stall outside Waterloo Station, where he became something of a local landmark. I used to see him nearly every day as I crossed the Waterloo Bridge to visit my girlfriend in North London. Often, I would stop and talk for a while.

I was fresh out of jail myself, and Buster warned me that it wasn't like the old days. Then, 'the chaps' used to rally round and help out a fellow 'face'. (You'll see a definition of 'chaps' in the glossary in Chapter 13.) He complained bitterly that no one had helped him. To add insult to injury, a film purporting to be of his life was made, starring Phil Collins. Nobody asked his permission or otherwise consulted him and he was given a derisory £5,000.

Although on the surface he seemed his usual, cheerful self, in private he became increasingly depressed. There was a lockup garage behind Waterloo Station where he used to keep his flower stall. One day, he got drunk, went into the lockup and hanged himself.

Tommy Wisbey was a trier, there can be no doubt about that. Despite almost criminal bad luck, he had pursued a thief's life for over three decades. For his part in the Great Train Robbery, he was sentenced to 30 years in 1964. The bad news then piled up very fast. Barely two years later, one of his daughters was killed in a car crash.

Then he lost all his money, which he had left in the safekeeping of 'friends'. In 1967, one of his few remaining friends tried to retrieve it for him. Jackie 'Scotch Jack' Buggie, a gangster, confronted a well-known London criminal in a nightclub. In front of several witnesses, Buggie was shot to death, then wrapped in a carpet and dumped at sea. Almost immediately, it was disturbed by a minesweeper and found by two off-duty policemen out fishing. However, no one was ever charged with the murder.

Wisbey was eventually released in 1974. In 1982, he was peripherally involved in another train robbery, but this time on a much smaller scale (so much for the deterrent effect of the 30-year sentence). Members of the gang would travel as passengers and let themselves into locked high-value coaches with specially made keys. Then they would throw the mailbags off the train, to be collected by others waiting at the trackside. Over £1 million worth of travellers' cheques went missing at the hands of the gang. Wisbey was convicted on a 'handling' charge and he was fined £500.

In 1989, after an extensive surveillance operation, he and another Train Robber, Jimmy Hussey, were arrested in connection with a drugs conspiracy. They were convicted of being in possession of 2.5 kilos of cocaine and 1 kilo of cocaine, respectively. Wisbey was sentenced to ten years, Hussey to seven.

Several other Train Robbers were touched by 'the curse', but in less spectacular ways. Despite a knee operation in prison, Bobby Welch was left permanently crippled. After years of pain, he finally had a leg amputated. Bruce Reynolds lost something far more dear to him while in prison: his share of the loot. Poverty-stricken, on release he tried his hand at drug dealing and was caught in possession of £5,000 worth of amphetamine and sentenced to three years.

William Boal wasn't even on the robbery, although he did sit in on some of the earlier planning meetings. A watch with traces of paint from Leatherslade Farm was said to have been found on him. He was sentenced to 18 years and died in prison of a brain tumour.

Which just leaves Ronnie Biggs. Popular mythology has it that Ronnie is the only 'lucky' robber, leading an idyllic life on the run after escaping from prison only one year into a 25-year sentence, imposed in 1964. So has he been untouched by 'the curse'?

In 1997 I was commissioned to work as a consultant on a documentary about the Great Train Robbery for Channel 4's *Secret History* programme. Together with a camera crew, I flew to Rio, where Ronnie had been avoiding extradition for 33 years. With me was an old friend of Ronnie's, Freddie Foreman, former member of the Kray Gang.

We met Ronnie in his basement flat in a rundown area of Rio that had seen better days. His reunion with Fred was emotional. The talk was all of hiding out in Fred's auntie Nell's flat, with a suitcase full of money hidden behind the sofa.

Ronnie looked well for a man of 70, especially considering the stroke he had had the previous year. At the sight of the camera crew, he seemed to come alive. Like the old trooper that he is, he launched into the well-rehearsed routine that has stood him in good stead through countless similar interviews over the years.

Later, I pulled him aside and asked him about 'the curse' and we went through his life since the escape. He had lost most of his money through friends who had betrayed him. Then there was the pressure of life on the run in Australia with his wife, Charmaine, and their three children. When the police caught up with him, he had fled to Brazil, leaving his family behind. His oldest boy was subsequently killed in a car crash and Ronnie didn't hear about it for nine months.

He had been arrested in Brazil and subjected to lengthy extradition proceedings. His marriage to his Brazilian wife, Raimunda, had saved him. He was allowed to stay, but had to eke out a living giving interviews and working as a tour guide. Life had been one long struggle to survive. In 1981, he had been kidnapped to Barbados by an English adventurer, but the courts took into account the illegal nature of his capture and returned him to Brazil. Then his wife, 11 years his junior, had died suddenly. Not exactly a blissful existence in paradise at all.

Ron was adamant, though. 'I adopted Brazil as my country and I've taken the good with the bad over the last 33 years,' he said, as I leafed through newspaper cuttings showing Ron lying by the pool, drinking beer and surrounded by local beauties. It had all been largely a creation by the media, though.

On the positive side, he introduced me to his Brazilian son, a fine-looking young man and former pop star in some of the good days. The family Rottweiler played by the pool between two parrots in cages. I mused that perhaps life hadn't been too bad in the circumstances. Brazil had been more than some vast open prison for him.

All at once, the camera crew were ready again. Ron climbed wearily to his feet, a resigned look on his face. 'What a way to have to earn a living,' he said. Suddenly, it came to me: was this Driver Mills's curse on Ronnie Biggs?

However, there was one final indignity to come. Seriously ill and in need of a crucial operation that he didn't have the money to pay for, Ronnie agreed to come back to England and give himself up. Somehow, the *Sun* tabloid had got in on the act. They enlisted the aid of Bruce Reynolds to travel to Brazil and come back with Ron. He was paid a large sum for his help.

Ron duly arrived in England, wearing a white T-shirt with THE SUN emblazoned on it. One could only reflect on the old man's state of mind after he had allowed himself to be talked into such a media circus. Further, those of us with experience of the Home Office knew that they would want their pound of flesh. His age and illness notwithstanding, they would want to make an example of Ronnie for all the years he had got away with it. There would be no mercy on their part.

Located in the top-security Belmarsh Prison with international terrorists and major drug dealers, Ron finally had his operation. It left him unable to speak and partially crippled. His ever-dutiful son constantly petitions the Home Office for his release on compassionate grounds, but compassion is in short supply where Ronnie is concerned.

So, still serving (at the time of writing) his 30-year sentence for a crime committed over 40 years ago, he sits mute and waiting for death in a top-security prison.

Yes, surely, this *is* Driver Mills's curse on Ronnie Biggs.

CHAPTER FOUR
ON THE SIDE OF THE ANGELS

With two assignments for *Loaded* now under my belt, I felt that I was beginning to understand something of the art of writing for magazines. Above everything else, as far as men's mags went, the subject matter had to be dramatic and exciting. Although not consciously attempting to do so, I did realise that my style owed a lot to so-called gonzo journalism. I understood this to mean when the writer/commentator interacts with the story and, indeed, becomes part of it. The Kentucky-born journalist Hunter S Thompson (1937–2005) was its most famous exponent.

This did not preclude me from writing in the same vein. After all, I felt it to be as a direct result of who I was (my notorious criminal background, that is) that I got most of the stories in the first place – that, coupled with an almost suicidal, self-destructiveness that took me into dangerous situations in the first place.

I also felt that it brought integrity and honesty to my writing. If someone was good enough to trust me with an interview, then the least I could do was to let them speak in their own words and not twist things or offer value judgements. Those would be left to the reader. No doubt I was still overly conscious of the criminal fraternity's characterisation of most journalists as grasses. I was determined to establish some trust.

I was aware that both gonzoism and honesty were given different degrees of freedom in different magazines. The *Loaded* experience had by no means been a bad one. By and large, they had published my articles almost verbatim, with relatively minor changes. Further, other than a few instances when it was a case of '*Loaded* did this' or '*Loaded* did that', they mainly credited me with all my actions.

However, I hadn't missed the fact that *Loaded* was just a minor part of a large publishing organisation. I didn't kid myself that, when push came to shove, if the powers-that-be determined that something needed changing or given a different slant, then that was exactly what would be done. And the first thing I would know about it was when I read the article in the magazine.

This was something that definitely worried me. If I had given my word to someone that I would give them a fair hearing, what would they think when they saw the article under my name with a completely biased slant to it? Would they accept the explanation that it had been done without either my permission or my knowledge? And what would that do for my fledgling reputation of integrity? With this in mind, as well as a desire to give myself as much independence as possible, I looked around for other magazines to write for.

I had met Eoin McSorley at several of the media bashes in and around Soho. He had read *Parkhurst Tales*, as well as my pieces for *Loaded*, and liked my writing. He was currently features editor for *Front* magazine, and he asked me if I would write for them.

Now *Front* was definitely the new kid on the block. A more recent creation than its longer-established rivals, it was still struggling for market share. At that time, it was selling between 150,000 and 200,000 copies a month. In order to attract attention and make a name for itself, it was brash, in your face and determinedly irreverent. If there had been a poor-taste award for men's magazines, then *Front* would definitely have been in strong contention.

However, I had been to their offices and was impressed by their down-to-earth enthusiasm and unpretentiousness. There had certainly been some at *Loaded* who had thought that they were minor celebrities in their own right. I sometimes got the impression that I would have to be careful not to put noses out of joint. There was none of that at *Front*. They were just a collection of working-class boys out to have a bit of fun and turn out a good magazine at the same time.

What impressed me most of all, though, was Eoin's assurance that he could guarantee me absolute editorial integrity. If I wrote it and they agreed that it could go in, then that was exactly the copy that would be published.

In the event, a story suddenly came up that dictated that what I wrote must be exactly what was published. In jail, I had become friends with a couple of Hell's Angels. Now they asked me to cover the funeral of one of their members who had just died. They trusted me to do a balanced piece. With the guarantee of editorial integrity firmly in mind, I took the story to *Front*. True to their word, they published it in its entirety. Here's the story.

ON THE SIDE OF THE ANGELS

The phone call had come from Moose, an old friend. We had met in Long Lartin top-security jail more than a decade earlier. Friendships fired in the furnace of the institution are often strong and enduring. Ours had certainly lasted well enough.

I followed directions and met him at 'Angel Farm', the clubhouse of the Hell's Angels Kent Chapter. A half-mile-long concrete path led across fields to a sprawling complex ensconced behind a high spiked fence. Moose opened a gate and let me into a yard where several Harleys were parked.

'Maz is dead,' were his first words, as we shook hands in the gathering gloom of late evening. He had died in a road accident the previous day.

I had never met him but I knew that Maz was the Angels' national spokesman when dealing with the press or the public, quite a significant honour in an organisation where all members are Brothers of equal standing. By coincidence, I had actually spoken to Maz on the phone recently, trying to arrange a trip to Arizona to interview the legendary Sonny Barger, founder member of the US Angels.

Moose led me into a long, low, barn-type building done out like a saloon. Several grim-faced Angels stood drinking at the bar. All wore their Angel colours, drum-tight over bulging muscles, tattoos much in evidence.

I had never hung around with the Angels, but I knew of them, mostly from the jailhouse. In there, and on the street, they were known to be proud honourable men, whatever their prejudices. If an Angel gave you his word, you could bet your life he would keep it. If he put his name to a deal, the deal would be done. And in this messed-up, jungle of a society that we live in, that's no small thing.

We all sat round a large table as Moose made the introductions. They were friendly enough, but their individual and collective grief was sufficient to charge the atmosphere with a feeling of impending violence. I was still wondering what it was all about and why I was here.

Cookie began on behalf of Kent. 'Norman, we've heard about you from Moose and some of us have read your books. We feel we can trust you.' He paused, I thought to control his grief, but it was rage that burst through. 'We hate the fucking press.' He screwed up his face in anger and looked sideways at his Brothers, who nodded in agreement. 'Whatever we do we can never be right. Very shortly we will be burying Maz and we don't want them taking the piss in any way. On behalf of Kent Chapter we'd like you to write an account of Maz and the funeral.'

What could I say? It wasn't an offer I couldn't refuse, because I really am my own man, whatever the cost. I felt, at first, flattered, then honoured. Again I reflected on the values of our society, of Queen's birthday honours and medals, often unmerited. There would be none of that for a man such as I, and none-wanted. I would settle for this vote of confidence from my Angel peers.

On the drive home, exactly what I had let myself in for began to sink in. I knew nothing whatsoever about Maz. What if he had been one of the wilder exponents of the biker lifestyle? Could I, in all conscience, write positively about that? No doubt all would be revealed to me on the day, a day I was now looking forward to with considerable trepidation.

It was bright, if somewhat overcast, as I drove Justin, my photographer from Front, towards Angel Farm and the funeral. There had been some initial resistance when I had mentioned that Front was backing the piece. 'Didn't they do that article on the "Outcasts"?' growled Cookie. The 'Outcasts' were the Angel's sworn enemies.

'I'm sure there was nothing personal in it,' I reassured. 'As far as I'm concerned you know exactly where you stand with Front. Once they agree on my copy, I can trust them not to change it behind my back.' I didn't want some smart-arsed backroom boy tacking on an irreverent piss-take that I would only see when the magazine came out.

It was still early, but already hundreds of bikers lined the dirt track alongside the clubhouse. Hundreds more milled about inside the grounds, their bikes parked en masse, shards of light glancing off highly polished metal in the early-morning sunlight. The several millions pounds' worth of custom-built Harleys were the Angels' collective pride and joy.

The men themselves looked every bit as impressive as their machines. If there were any small weedy Angels about, I couldn't see them. Hulking giants, muscles bulging, bedecked in full Angel finery, strode about giving each other their clenched-thumb handshake.

Every Angel in England was here, together with a score or so from Holland and representatives from several other European countries. Three South African Angels came with the Dutch contingent and there was even an Angel from Nova Scotia.

With them came their ladies. Of all ages, leather-clad and confident, they looked just as capable of riding the bikes as their men. And in fact they were. Most of them rode their own bikes.

Outside, along the dirt track, hundreds of other mourners congregated, with scores more arriving every minute. There were several other 'patch' clubs present, which even I, with my limited knowledge of biker politics, knew was unusual.

A dozen Satan's Slaves, wearing their colours, stood with their bikes in one group. Further down, a smaller group of 'Headhunters' lounged just a stone's throw from Pompey 'Road Warriors' and Wiltshire 'Lowlanders'. Maz must have had broad appeal to unite such different groups in mourning.

Then there were your normal, regular motorcycle enthusiasts, hundreds of them, all on various types of bikes. There were Jap bikes, Harleys, custom-built trikes that looked like something out of Mad Max and a rocket-bike with a built-on thruster that was clearly of the space age. Finally, at the far end of the track, a couple of dozen cars, jeeps and vans waited to take their place in the cortège.

Suddenly, the roar of engines and a cloud of dust announced the arrival of a new group. Leather-clad, riding bikes and trikes, they were similar to those already here, but for one, quite significant, difference. They were all women. I hadn't been aware that there was an all-woman biker club, but these were 'Women in the Wind', founded in the US in 1978, extant in the UK for the past 12 years.

Hard against the clubhouse fence was parked a large, flat-bed truck to which was hitched an equally large trailer. Both were piled high with hundreds of floral tributes. Some just saying 'Maz', others in the shape of bikes, they came from all over the *country and all over the world. H.A. Long Island, H.A. South Carolina, the Flying Deuces, Angels everywhere were saluting their fallen Brother.*

Quite incongruously, a blue and white striped police car inched its way through the crush to park opposite the truck. Two fresh-faced young coppers, one male, the other female, chatted away quite oblivious to the forces of the Apocalypse gathered around them. There was no fear and no hostility either. Maz was known, and it would seem, liked by both of them. They also had a relationship, of sorts, with the Angels. They made it clear that they expected no trouble. The funeral would be solely a traffic problem, not a public-order one.

By now I was quite puzzled. This man Maz was being mourned by people from all walks of life. In an age beset by 'isms', how could a Hell's Angel, a member of a club not known for its gregariousness, unite so many disparate groups?

So I went in search of him, or rather, what remained of him, the part that lived on in the minds of others. Quietly, discreetly, trying hard not to intrude on personal grief, I asked mourners about their recollections of Maz.

Dr Ian 'Maz' Harris, PhD, got his Doctorate at Warwick University. His later book, Biker, the Birth of the Modern Day Outlaw, *was based on his research. He had been a founder-member of the Kent Chapter of Hell's Angels and, when he had died aged 51, he had been an Angel for 25 years.*

In a club of rugged, free-thinking individualists to whom leadership was often anathema, Maz rose to become their national spokesman. He was a leading light in the organizing of the Kent Show, the biggest custom-built bike show in England and also the 'Bulldog Bash', the annual Angel party-cum-bike-show held in the Midlands. His whole life revolved around bikes and the free-spirited lifestyle he felt went with them.

On a personal level, he was warm and friendly, without either airs or graces. He was articulate and a great story-teller. But, over and above all these things, he was a writer! He wrote for the bike magazines Back Street Heroes *and* Heavy Duty, *among others. His columns, 'Radical Times' and 'Street Talkin'', celebrated bikes and the 'biker spirit'.*

He wrote on topics as diverse as engines, civil rights and pornography and, in so doing, had touched the lives of so many.

Cookie told me that thousands of e-mails had arrived from people who had been reading his stuff for years and felt that they knew him. They just wanted to say how sorry they were to hear of his death.

Bjorn, a close friend and fellow Angel from Sweden, said, 'I grew up reading "Radical Times". Maz was an inspiration to all bikers everywhere.' Which would go some way towards explaining why all of Kent's motorcycle police were on duty when several should have been off. They came in for free, out of respect for Maz.

Suddenly, like a giant clearing its throat, hundreds of bikes coughed, then roared into life. Justin, who had been scurrying about in a feeding frenzy of photography inspired by such an unusually visual subject, raced to take his seat on Moose's pillion. They jockeyed to take their place in the column of Angels that snaked slowly behind the hearse as it made its way out of Angel Farm.

On a day of death, everybody felt strangely invigorated. There was sadness, but pride and defiance too. Never mind what the straight world might say, they were on their way to bury a man honoured and beloved by them all. Whatever else they are, the Angels are a warrior caste. And woe betide anyone who would disrespect them this day.

With a thunder like an approaching Panzer division, the cortège turned on to the A2. The extent of the police operation to facilitate the funeral immediately became apparent. Traffic in both directions had been stopped. As the procession passed along the carriageway, police on bikes and in cars sealed off all tributary roads.

The surrounding countryside came to a halt as people came out of their houses and places of work to stand and stare in amazement. Riding several abreast, the column of bikers stretched back as far as the eye could see. One estimate put the number at 3,000. Most rode bare-headed as a sign of respect, a special concession on this special day.

As the cortège came into Crayford, it seemed as if the whole town had turned out. They stood in gardens and at the side of the road, quite silent, hats in hand.

St Paulinus Church and its graveyard was beautiful as only English country churches can be. Never before could a more *incongruous-looking crowd have stood within its precincts. Grim-faced and in total silence, the Angels and their fellow bikers sat in the church and stood among the graves as the service was relayed over loudspeakers.*

The Reverend read the eulogy between some of Maz's favourite music. 'Like a bird on a wire, I have tried in my way to be free,' sang Leonard Cohen.

Maz's sister, Jane, thanked everyone for coming, acknowledging in passing that she had always shared her brother with his Brothers in the Angels.

Then it was over. Like a film fast-forwarded, or pages flicked through in a picture book, we filed out of the church, gathered around the grave, said our 'goodbyes' to each other and headed off, lost in our own thoughts. Maz had touched our lives and, through that touching, there was now a sense of loss.

That he was a biker, a member of a so-called outlaw biker club, was neither here nor there. There would be captains of industry, knights of the realm, politicians of repute laid to rest with but a fraction of the respect paid to Maz Harris this day. You have your heroes, we will have ours. We know that Maz rides with the angels.

CHAPTER FIVE

FOR A COUNTRY FIT FOR DOGS TO LIVE IN

Although I considered that my writing for the magazines was going well, I never allowed myself to lose sight of the fact that my main aim was to publicise my books. At the end of each piece there would be a reference to either *Parkhurst Tales* or another title.

Purely from a financial perspective, the way the assignments were presently panning out, I couldn't have earned enough money to make it worthwhile, anyway. Each assignment was taking anything up to two weeks to research, plan and arrange all the logistics for. The trip itself would take from seven to ten days. Then it would take me a couple of days to write the story up from my notes. So it was highly unlikely that I could do more than one assignment per month. And, since each assignment paid only about £1,000, there was definitely no long-term future in it.

I had always been interested in politics and was an avid observer of the news. Looking around the world, I saw that there were literally scores, if not hundreds, of dangerous and interesting situations that would make for a good story. However, it was no use just going somewhere unless you had some kind of edge, some kind of contact. Furthermore, the magazine would want some evidence that you had a good chance of getting the story before they gave you a couple of thousand pounds in expenses.

Iraq was a place that definitely interested me. Apart from the fact that we and the Yanks were still bombing sporadically, there was an ongoing tragedy caused by the sanctions. Horrendous numbers of Iraqi children were dying for lack of basic food and medicine. If anyone else had been causing it, we would have raised it in the international arena at every opportunity. As it was, there would just be the occasional small article, quoting some United Nations report saying just how many kids were dying.

Sanctions against Iraq, first by America and later by the United Nations, were imposed as early as May 1990. By August, the International Red Cross admitted that the sanctions, which prevented food and medicines from reaching the country, violated international law. In 1993, UNICEF estimated that between 80,000 and 100,000 children had died as a direct result of the sanctions. By 1997, the people of Iraq were poorer than those of Bangladesh. Presently, only the US and Britain were adamant that sanctions should still be applied.

I had observed in prison just how callous and cruel the authorities could be, even to conniving at outright criminality. I did all I could to expose it in prison, which was precisely why they labelled me a troublemaker. Now I had the opportunity to do the same outside.

Further, a trip to Iraq would really put the cat among the pigeons regarding my right to travel abroad without Home Office permission. There was little doubt that they would notice I had been there – probably long before I arrived, too. I was sure the security services monitored all travel to and from Iraq. Bearing in mind I was doing an exposé on the government, it would be hypocritical in the extreme for them to pull me back into prison for breaching my life licence by travelling abroad without permission. But, as I was already well aware, the Home Office weren't above hypocrisy.

Now I had decided where I wanted to go, the next part was to work out how to get there. Apart from the fact that it was very difficult to travel physically to Iraq, I was aware that any journalist, or probably any non-Iraqi for that matter, couldn't just go to the country without permission from the Iraqi government.

I had read that George Galloway, MP, was one of the very few people who travelled regularly to Iraq. I spoke with his secretary and he gave me the telephone number of a Dr Amin, who was head of the Iraqi Interests Section which was located in Kensington.

I wrote to Dr Amin explaining that I was an English journalist who wrote for men's lifestyle magazines with circulations of anything up to a million. I pointed out that the British public were largely subjected to the 'American' view of Iraq which, more often than not, was erroneous.

I emphasised that I did not subscribe to that view. I went on to say that I had considerable sympathy for the plight of Iraqi children who were dying as a result of the sanctions and that it would be the object of my trip to publicise this to the full.

I included my address, telephone number, passport number, National Union of Journalists card number and my email address. I guessed they would do some checking. After all, being an Englishman whose government was still in a virtual state of war with Iraq, I could well be a spy.

I was in no doubt what the Iraqis did with spies, either. I had been friends with Tom Mangold, the noted TV journalist and BBC *Panorama* presenter, for many years. I had rung him at the BBC to ask him his advice about Iraq. It was he who told me about Farzad Bazoft.

On 17 August 1979, a huge explosion occurred 25 miles from Baghdad, which was clearly audible in the capital. For some, this confirmed that the Iraqi government were carrying out nuclear research.

The *Observer* sent one of its reporters, Iranian-born British national Farzad Bazoft, to investigate. Accounts differ as to his agenda: some say he was on an intelligence mission gathering soil samples for Britain and therefore working indirectly for Israel; others insist he was simply checking out a newsworthy story.

Either way, after driving back from the scene of the explosion, Farzad was arrested on charges of spying and sentenced to death. While in custody, he confessed to spying for Israel, but the Iraqi security forces are well known for torture. Everyone agrees that Farzad's confession was forced out of him.

There was an international outcry at the sentence. Jordan's King Hussein (one of Saddam Hussein's best friends in the Arab world) sent a letter asking for clemency and our then Tory Foreign Secretary Douglas Hurd pleaded to come to Baghdad to discuss the matter.

Saddam, however, insisted that Farzad must die and he was hanged on 15 March 1990. His body was unceremoniously dumped in front of the British Embassy and Iraq's Information Minister crowed, 'Mrs Thatcher wanted Bazoft alive. We gave her the body.'

The point wasn't lost on me that pressure from a powerful newspaper such as the *Observer* wasn't enough to save Bazoft; nor was a letter from the King of Jordan. All I had on my side was *Front* magazine, and perhaps a letter from the topless model Jordan.

Then there was the problem of my Jewishness. Well, it wasn't a problem for me, but it certainly could be for Saddam. Quite prominently at the front of *Parkhurst Tales*, it stated that both my parents were Jewish. Now that doesn't necessarily make me a member of Mossad, but it is just the sort of thing that could make a man like Saddam suspicious. Clearly, I would have to tread very carefully.

Anyway, it was all largely academic at the moment. I sent the letter off, thinking that would probably be the last I heard of Iraq. You can imagine my surprise when, a couple of days later, I got a letter from Dr Amin inviting me for an interview at the Iraqi Bureau in Kensington.

The rest was remarkably straightforward. I talked with Dr Amin for about 20 minutes, then filled out several forms with a young lady in reception. I was told that I would be informed of their decision in due course. To be frank, I still thought that was the end of it, but, about a month later, I suddenly received a letter instructing me to come to the bureau and pick up my visa.

I quickly found a travel agent in the Edgware Road who arranged trips to Iraq. There were two ways to go. I could either fly to Jordan, then make a two-day drive across the desert. Or I could fly to Damascus in neighbouring Syria and catch one of the two flights each week to Baghdad. This was the only plane that actually flew into Iraq and, as such, was highly symbolic. The Americans and the British were both imposing no-fly zones and cynics wouldn't have put it past either of them to bring the plane down 'by accident'. Then there were all Saddam's internal and external dissidents, who would most certainly have liked to bring it down.

However, I really didn't fancy the two-day drive across the desert. I guessed it would be arduous, quite expensive and rather hit-or-miss. I wanted to make sure that I got to Baghdad. With the Damascus plane, at least it was a direct flight.

I had a couple more vaccinations at BA's Regent Street clinic, against diseases even the Colombians hadn't heard off. Then I went directly to *Front*'s offices for a last-minute briefing with Eoin.

We discussed what he should do in case I got into trouble out there. There was no conversation, just 30 seconds of dead silence. Neither of us could think of anything at all worthwhile. As an afterthought, I asked that he keep Marsha informed.

Just as I was leaving, he suddenly came over all thoughtful and looked slightly embarrassed. I had to drag it out of him. He confessed that, while he thought it was a great assignment and highly dangerous to boot, the subject of thousands of dead kids was a bit dark for a lifestyle magazine. The upshot was a polite request for me to try to make it a bit funny!

Now I knew Saddam had been accused of many things, but I was sure he had never been accused of being funny. However, I did take the point. I would write the piece with a strong sense of the ironic, which is about as funny as it gets in Iraq. This is what I wrote.

No one was more surprised than I, when I finally received my visa for Iraq. Except perhaps the lady at the Iraqi bureau who had taken my original application about a month previously.

'Have you been in touch with Baghdad?' she queried. Now how would I? It's almost impossible to get through by phone and the only person I know there is Saddam, and we're not speaking at the moment.

I had already read extensively about Iraq, but, in search of further information, I rang my old pal, Tom, at the BBC. Tom had been everywhere and seen virtually everything.

'Don't drink the water, even the bottled stuff and be very careful,' Tom barked, 'they're a vicious bunch of bastards. Not the ordinary people. They're nice, like ordinary people everywhere. But Saddam's secret police are totally ruthless and quite evil.'

'But I'm a journalist, Tom,' I replied smugly.

'So was Farzad Bazoft of the Observer,*' retorted Tom, 'and they hanged him for spying.' Gee thanks, Tom, that's really put my mind at rest.*

While the Syrian Airlines plane was delayed for 90 minutes on the runway at Heathrow, the stewardesses brought round glasses of cool mineral water. It was only later that I saw the Arabic writing on the water bottles. Six hours later, while sitting in Damascus airport waiting for my connecting flight to Baghdad, I felt my stomach start to bubble.

Well aware of the British and US-enforced no-fly zones over most of Iraq, and conscious that this recently resumed flight was the only one operating in Iraqi airspace, I was already understandably concerned. The three very thorough baggage searches and my personal identification of my bag on the tarmac further alerted me to the very real possibility of a terrorist threat.

As the only European on board, I surreptitiously examined my fellow passengers. Wild-looking, hook-nosed Arabs in flowing robes sat cheek-by-jowl with old, female, Iranian pilgrims in black chadors, only their eyes visible. It did occur to me that I was the only one who didn't look like a potential terrorist. I was sure that just one 'Allah Akhbar' out of any of them would be enough to ensure instant cardiac arrest.

It wasn't long in coming. As we taxied for take-off a guttural voice called out from the rear. Immediately, the Iranian pilgrims answered in chorus. It was okay, they were only praying for a safe flight. But considering the dodgy state of my bowels, they might have warned me.

Saddam International Airport looked just as dilapidated as you would expect after standing idle for over ten years, all the clocks eternally frozen at 12.33. The arrivals board still bore legends of exotic destinations like Berlin and Bucharest, but now there were only these two flights a week from Damascus.

All the streets were deserted as we drove through the darkness to the hotel. To my enquiry about where all the people were, the taxi driver mimed that they were all asleep. How clever of Saddam to synchronise all Iraqi body-clocks so that everybody falls asleep at the same time!

The Melia-Mansur Hotel had once been five-star and the second best in Baghdad. It was still second best, but 'second best' is a comparative term. The expression 'faded grandeur' sprang to mind as I was shown to my room. Worn, holed carpets lined the corridor floors, stained wallpaper peeled from the walls, but I was past caring. My body longed for sleep, my bowels for a speedy encounter with a toilet.

In my room I triumphed in a brief skirmish with cockroaches, but baulked at washing my hands in the dark, brown water that ran from the taps. The final horror was soon to be revealed – no toilet roll!

That night I thrashed in the throes of fever. With my bed-sheets soaked in sweat I alternated between burning up and shivering with cold. I feared something serious. Could I have contracted one of those terrible tropical diseases you read about? I muttered a silent prayer, 'please don't let my dick shrivel and drop off'.

With Monday morning came my appointment with the Press Office. This would be crucial. They would decide what I could and could not do and I was determined to make a good impression on them. Not easy when half my concentration was on the whereabouts of the nearest toilet and how long it would take me to get there.

A five-minute walk took me to a shabby office block where the Press Office was located. I found my way to the director's office, where he sat with several colleagues. Stern faces, beards, moustaches and designer stubble were much in evidence. Supremely conscious of the fact they probably viewed me as, at best, the enemy and, at worst, a spy, I launched into my carefully prepared speech.

'I know all about America's role in undermining Iraq,' I thundered, leaning forward for effect. 'How they built you up as a counterbalance to the Shah of Iran, then, when Ayatollah Khomeini came to power in 1979, encouraged you to attack. Then, quite cynically, the Americans armed both sides until eight years of war had ruined both countries. Finally, with Iraq in dire straits, they got Kuwait to increase its oil production, further damaging the Iraqi economy. That was why you had to attack Kuwait.'

I sat back quite pleased with myself and carefully examined their faces. It was hard to gauge their reactions, what with the cultural differences and all. However, I was sure I saw thoughtfulness, grudging respect, admiration even. Not a bit of it. The director explained in fractured English that none of them spoke much English, so could I repeat myself to Mohammed, who was in the next office and was fluent.

Mohammed, another moustache-and-stubble guy, asked me for my proposed schedule. I listed: an interview with Saddam's sons, Uday and Qusay; a trip to Tikrit, Saddam's birthplace; a tour of the bunker at Amiriyah which was hit by US missiles in 1991 and evidence of the improved standing of Iraqi women, specifically, their fighting roles in the armed forces. A few photos of foreign women with guns always went down well in Front.

Mohammed said that he would forward my requests to a higher authority and told me to come back tomorrow.

As I left the Press Office I had my first real confrontation – with the weather. To say that it was like walking into an oven doesn't do it justice. The heat was like a wall that slowed all movement to a crawl. When the wind blew it was worse, because the wind was hot as well. Our hottest days in England rarely reach 27 degrees Celsius; here the temperature gauge regularly showed above 50. I slow-walked to the sanctuary of my air-conditioned room.

I must have dozed in the heat and the grip of fever. I awoke to the echoing sound of the mullah calling the faithful to prayer. He *must have had quite incredible stamina, for he kept it up for several hours. I briefly considered, then dismissed, the idea of going out onto the balcony and yelling for him to shut up.*

With my stomach still firmly in the grip of 'Baghdad Belly', food was the furthest thing from my mind. Instead, I decided to take a leisurely stroll in the hotel gardens. As soon as I appeared in the lobby, several swarthy, moustached flunkeys surrounded me. Where was I going? Did I want a car? They looked perplexed when I said I was just going for a walk.

The extensive gardens must have been quite beautiful once, but now cracked paving, broken lights and dry fountains complemented the look of the hotel perfectly. A handful of fellow guests strolled the pathways as wild cats scurried across the shabby lawns.

Having once been a career criminal, I now have a finely tuned talent for observation. I soon became aware of several large, moustached men in white shirts and dark trousers, sweating profusely, who came hurrying along paths, visibly slowing when they saw me and then, not quite knowing what to do with themselves. As a surveillance operation it was worthy of Inspector Clouseau. But clearly they were worried about me and didn't trust me. I would have to be careful.

On Tuesday morning Mohammed told me he had arranged an outing for me the following day. He would provide a driver and a photographer. He would be the guide. The catch was, it would cost me. The driver was 50 US dollars a day, the photographer was 100 dollars and the assistance of the Press Office another 50 dollars per day, whether I used it or not! And this in a country where the average government monthly salary was $4. It was quite a nice little racket they had running out of the Press Office. But what could I do? It was either pay, or no story.

Probably incensed by the rip-off, that evening I escaped from the hotel. I made as if to walk around the gardens, slid quickly alongside the car park and strolled briskly out of the gate. Wherever Clouseau's men were they definitely weren't with me. I was free, loose in Baghdad.

The evening sun was still oppressive, but at least I could breathe. The roads were clogged with the most run-down cars I had ever seen, all very old models, with dents discoloured by rust, and with cracked and broken windscreens. As they set off from the *traffic lights they resembled nothing so much as some vast demolition derby. Apart from a few, new four-wheel drives, the only other new vehicles on the roads were the big, red double-decker buses supplied by the Chinese.*

Armed troops were everywhere, outside buildings, in sentry boxes, crouched in bunkers and walking in groups. At virtually every intersection, armed police directed the traffic. But whatever their respective roles, they were totally oblivious to me. I walked unchallenged along streets and through alleyways, past buildings so decrepit I feared that, should someone slam a door too hard, half of Baghdad would collapse.

However, whatever Saddam's reputation for strong government, he obviously couldn't handle the local dustmen's union. Great piles of festering rubbish stood everywhere, even outside food shops. The shops themselves were generally well stocked though, but it was all cheap crap from China.

The people were surprisingly friendly, especially in view of the fact that we and the Yanks were still bombing them on a regular basis. But the Arabs have a great tradition of hospitality. Unlike us Brits. We're still rude to the Germans 60 years on.

I decided to change some money. One hundred dollars US brought me eight thick wads of Iraqi dinars and a carrier bag to take it away in. It used to be three dinars to the dollar, now it's closer to 2,000.

In one particularly poor neighbourhood, I saw children renting rides from a man with bicycles. Under a bridge, a small funfair with rides all pushed by hand catered to a crowd of children with their parents. On patches of waste ground there were impromptu games of football. The overwhelming impression was one of abject poverty. It was quite clear that the sanctions have hit ordinary Iraqis very hard.

They haven't stopped Saddam from building luxurious palaces and strikingly grand and dramatic monuments though. They stand, incongruous in their opulence, among the crumbling slums. Everywhere, giant depictions of Saddam stare down on passers-by. I learned that, at the New Year's Day military parade, there had been an impressive display of millions of dollars' worth of the latest armoured vehicles and missiles, together with thousands of well-armed troops.

The following morning I met Mohammed at the Press Office

and, together with the photographer, set off in the driver's old, black Buick. Mohammed informed me that we were on our way to see the Quds or Jerusalem Army, a group of women volunteers who were undergoing military training in order to liberate Palestine from the Israelis.

We arrived at Al Mustinsiriya University where they were based and met with instant confusion. There had been some mistake, because they only trained on weekends. So for any Mossad agents who happen to be reading this, Jerusalem's safe on weekdays.

We then drove to the bombed air raid shelter at Amiriyah, which had become a shrine. As I entered the low, squat structure I was met by Miriam, a young woman in a chador, who was to be my guide.

The inside of the shelter was quite well lit, courtesy of remembrance candles and a gaping hole in the six-feet-thick concrete roof. Miriam explained how the first missile had drilled its way through the concrete before exploding. The second missile flew in horizontally through an extractor fan and incinerated everyone who hadn't already been killed. As she spoke we walked past walls grimed with soot.

There had been 408 women, children and old men killed in the shelter, Egyptians, Jordanians and Iraqis, both Christian and Muslim. They had been sleeping in three-tiered bunks, with the children in the top row. When the second missile had exploded, burning children had been thrown upwards. Miriam stopped and pointed out charred remains of little hands and feet, still sticking to the ceiling ten years after the bombs had been dropped.

Further on we stopped at a wall where people had been burned, Hiroshima-like, into the concrete. Miriam pointed to the outline of a young woman and that of a child's leg from thigh to ankle. And there, peering out of the darkness at me, was the face of a young girl. She had vaporised, leaving just the pink skin of her face on the wall.

I'm tough enough, but I don't mind confessing that, as I walked out past photos of the young children as they had been, tears streamed freely down my face. Smart bombs? It's a shame the people who aim them are so fucking dumb!

Our next stop was at a museum dedicated to the reconstruction work that had been done to war-damaged buildings. I walked through vast dusty halls, past hundreds of display cases containing scale models depicting the buildings before and after repair. There were models of refineries, factories and bridges, but what surprised me was the number of schools, hospitals and mosques that had also been targeted. No wonder the Russians had referred to the Yanks as '20th-century barbarians'.

We drove around, stopping at a couple of locations so that the photographer could take some street scenes for me. Mohammed constantly hovered, controlling everything. Sometimes it was OK to shoot in one direction but not another, because that would take in sensitive buildings. In view of the number of assassination attempts there have been against Saddam, security was obviously still a major consideration.

As we couldn't see the Quds Army until Saturday, I had two days to kill. I hadn't been given permission to see anything else and the outings were proving to be so expensive my budget didn't allow for much else.

To take advantage of the 50 dollars a day I was paying the Press Office, I tried to engage Mohammed in conversation as often as I could. However, there was a whole range of topics that were off limits for discussion, so he wasn't a source of much information for me. After one conversation he did look thoughtful though. I had mentioned the idea of arranging a 'Live Aid'-style concert in Baghdad to emphasize the plight of Iraqi children under the sanctions. I suggested that I could try to interest some pop celebrities in England and, apart from a concert for the children, we could raise some money for much needed medicines.

I had been back in my room for no more than 20 minutes when the phone rang. It was Mohammed. He asked me to come to the Press Office immediately as something important had come up. I hurried over and was met by a very agitated Mohammed. It seemed that he had mentioned my idea to someone higher up and now a Minister wanted to speak with me.

I was ushered into the building next door and into a plush lift. I emerged into a carpeted hallway and entered a similarly plush office. Seated behind a large leather-covered desk sat a small dapper man with a thin moustache. With no preliminaries whatsoever, he asked me about my idea in perfect English.

I explained the principle behind 'Live Aid', adding that it raised not only money but also people's awareness of problems. It put pressure on governments to act. It could well lead to a lessening of *the sanctions. The Minister sat there, nodding all the while, but saying nothing. Right at the end he piped up. 'But what music will they be playing?' he asked.*

'Well, Western pop music, I suppose,' was my reply.

'Can't stand the stuff,' came the Minister's instant response, 'can't they play something classical?'

That really was the end of the conversation as far as I was concerned. I just couldn't picture Bob Geldof on third violin.

On the Friday I found a driver who was willing to take me to Babylon, 40 dollars no questions asked. We slipped out of the hotel early and were soon speeding out of Baghdad along well-maintained roads. But, in view of the fact that tarmac virtually seeps out of the ground here, perhaps well-maintained roads wasn't too great a feat.

Babylon, that great, mystical city of antiquity, was something of a disappointment. Only the foundations were original, the rest of the walls had been built out of new bricks. Any comfort I might have taken from the fact that Saddam had forbore to smother the place with great murals of himself was dispelled by the realization that he had had his name engraved on nearly every brick!

Saturday saw me at the University again with Mohammed, the photographer and the driver. Even on a weekend the campus was swarming with students, and so I took this opportunity to study them more closely. To a soul, they were a clean, wholesome-looking lot, not an orange punk haircut or pierced body-part in sight. In fact, they actually looked like they were there to study.

The women all wore long, ankle-length dresses, which must have been quite uncomfortable in the heat. I didn't actually enquire about specific sexual practices, but what with the climate, the dress and the religious restrictions, I feel confident in stating that there is absolutely no muff-diving whatsoever in the Middle East.

On a parade ground to the rear of the University we found the Quds Army. About 200 young women, aged between 16 and 30 and smartly dressed in well-pressed, sand-coloured fatigues, marched up and down under the direction of regular army officers.

It was explained to me that, in this first two weeks, they just learned to march. In the second two weeks they marched carrying guns. In the final two weeks they went to the army assault course to learn how to use the guns. Quite clearly, I was only going to be allowed to watch this simple marching.

As they marched the women sang, 'The enemy may have American weapons, but we have a genuine Tikritian hero.' Saddam comes from Tikrit, so no prizes for guessing who wrote those lyrics then.

Back at the Press Office I paid my bills, collected the official photographs and signed forms in triplicate. That night I took several sly shots of Baghdad after dark from my hotel balcony, then agonized for hours over whether anyone might have seen the flashes.

Sunday afternoon left me with a couple of hours to spare before I had to catch my evening flight to Damascus, so I got my taxi-driver to stop off at the zoo. The pride of lions in their cramped cage looked anything but proud, their manes decidedly moth-eaten.

The Bengal tiger wheezed as if it had been smoking 50 a day all its life. To an animal though, they were ignored by the few Iraqi visitors. They were all looking at me. The rarest live specimen in Baghdad Zoo is a tourist!

Passing a compound of wild asses, I chanced upon a line of cages similar to those holding the big cats. Peering inside, I noticed the occupants cowering in the corners. They were dogs, ordinary domestic dogs. Now I'm not an expert on breeds, but in one cage there were a pair that looked like Spaniels and, in another, some Terriers.

'What are these, Mahmood?' I asked, turning to the taxi-driver.

Mahmood looked suitably shame-faced. 'They get well-fed and looked after in here,' he confessed, 'out on the street they get shot and eaten by the soldiers.'

So there we have it then. If the fact that our sanctions have killed over 1.3 million Iraqi children doesn't move us Brits to anger, then perhaps this will.

For God's sake stop the sanctions. For a society fit for dogs to live in!

CHAPTER SIX
REBEL WITHOUT A PAUSE

On 8 March 1973, a massive car bomb exploded outside the Central Criminal Court, commonly known as the Old Bailey, in central London. Shortly afterwards, a second bomb exploded outside government offices just off Whitehall. The police found and defused a third car bomb parked outside Scotland Yard. Although telephone warnings had been given, one person was killed, 214 injured and massive damage was done to property.

The attack bore all the hallmarks of the IRA. There had been near-simultaneous bombings in Belfast and Dublin, and it came on the eve of an Ulster 'border referendum'. Some kind of symbolic act on the part of the IRA had been expected. The telephone warning, complete with an identification code, came as confirmation, if that had been needed.

Shortly afterwards, the police arrested ten members of the IRA unit responsible, as they sat on a plane at Gatwick, waiting to fly to Dublin. Mostly, they were young and inexperienced ex-students. Gerry Kelly, their leader, was 20, the Price sisters both 19, and there was a girl of 16. At their trial later, however, the judge remarked that it was one of the gravest crimes ever committed in this country and handed down life sentences to all involved.

I had noticed the bombings, but only to worry if family and friends had been caught up in them. Even then, it stayed at the periphery of my attention. I was three years into my own life sentence and my full concentration was on trying to escape. That, together with a natural rebelliousness, had ensured many long months in punishment blocks in solitary confinement and often on a bread-and-water diet, too. I lived in a world of pain.

Following an unsuccessful escape attempt and the ensuing riot at Albany Prison on the Isle of Wight, I was transferred to Wormwood Scrubs. This was a comparatively easy prison, with plenty of facilities and lots of time allowed out of the cell. Mostly, it was a jail for 'model' prisoners, first offenders and those who were no trouble to the prison authorities.

It seemed a strange move for a man like me, who had so recently been involved in so much trouble. But, then, there was method in the Home Office's madness. Sometimes they located a troublesome prisoner in an easy jail like the Scrubs to isolate him from other troublesome prisoners and so minimise his disruptive potential. Further, they hoped that the troublesome inmate would take to the good conditions and behave accordingly.

In my case, I decided to let the authorities think that I was settling down. However, although the Scrubs was a top-security, Category 'A' jail, there were weaknesses in its security that I had not seen in other top-security jails. I resolved to bide my time and plan an escape.

A major problem was that, in a jail full of model prisoners, virtually no one wanted to go. This is despite some extremely long sentences ranging from four right up to 30 years and life. That isn't to say that I couldn't have found someone willing to have a go, but they were either thoroughly untrustworthy and might have told the authorities, or they were naive and weak. I secretly schemed away while waiting for someone more reliable to arrive.

If 'the chaps' are a self-defined group of criminals who are stronger, more professional in their approach to crime and more trustworthy, then there were very few 'chaps' at the Scrubs. Most of these worked in the prison laundry. I knew or was known to most of them. I too got a job in the laundry.

A year passed and suddenly Ian, a close friend, arrived. He too had recently been in escape attempts and riots and the authorities were trying out exactly the same approach with him as they had with me.

I got him a job in the laundry with me and explained how far I had got with my planning. Through a corrupt civilian worker, I had managed to get my hands on an impression of a gate key. I sent this outside and had the finished key smuggled back in again. Now I could pass through any gate in the jail.

I had noticed that the prison Works Department sometimes left an extending ladder in the locked laundry over the weekend, chained and padlocked to a wall inside a store. The laundry was a one-storey building that lay across a yard, barely 20 yards from the long-term wing where Ian and I were housed. It would be possible to let ourselves out of the wing using the key and cross the yard to the laundry. There was a padlock that secured the laundry gate, which could be easily knocked off. Then it was just a matter of letting ourselves through the gate with the key.

Once we were inside, it would take seconds to knock the padlock off the chain that secured the ladder. Wormwood Scrubs, however, had two layers of perimeter security. First, there was a 20-foot-high wire-mesh fence. This had barbed wire at the top and trembler bells that sounded the alarm if they were shaken. Then there was an outside wall of similar height. Both were liberally festooned with CCTV cameras that were monitored in a central control room.

Quite clearly, once the ladder hit the first fence it would sound the alarm and we would have only a very short time to get over. It would be optimistic in the extreme to expect that the two of us could climb the ladder and have time to pull it up to use again on the outside wall. Patrolling guards with dogs would be on the scene too soon and would grab the bottom of the ladder.

However, the outside wall could be climbed with a rope and hook. There was abundant material to make the rope out of. This could be done beforehand and the rope hidden away in the laundry. The Works Department also had a locked store located in the laundry. This could be easily broken into and the tools used to make some sort of hook. In theory, it was an entirely feasible plan.

Ian immediately pointed out that the two of us would have more chance of getting away if we had two more people in on the escape. My reply to that was to ask where we would find two such people. Ian was much more gregarious than I, and mixed more extensively on the wing. He suggested a young guy called Malcolm and Gerry Kelly.

I knew something of Malcolm, but only because of all the trouble he had been in at other jails. Still only 20, he had done many months of punishment for rebelling against the warders. Criminally, though, he was very naive and had never stolen anything in his life. He was fanatical about politics, and was a libertarian. He was sentenced to ten years for fire-bombing his local town hall. Malcolm was brave enough and certainly trustworthy.

Gerry Kelly was another kettle of fish entirely. Physically unimposing, he still had the slim, bespectacled, owlish look of the student he had so recently been. However, I had to agree with Ian that he was probably brave enough and could definitely be trusted not to betray us to the authorities. As far as the criminal pecking order on the long-term wing was concerned, both were virtual nobodies. But, as Ian pointed out, you didn't have to be one of 'the chaps' to qualify for a place on our escape. They were friends of Ian's rather than friends of mine, so I told him to ask them if they were interested.

Early planning meetings immediately revealed a gulf between our respective ideologies. Apart from organising the escape, Ian and I had agreed to provide a hiding place in London until we could leave the country. This would be needed because getting out of Britain would take a couple of weeks to organise.

Ian mentioned that, before he had been arrested, he had been looking at a 'bit of work' involving the armed robbery of a main Post Office sorting depot. He said that the prize could be as much as £100,000. Ian suggested that the four of us rob the depot to provide us with much-needed money to go on the run with.

There was an embarrassed silence. Malcolm spoke first, stating quite unequivocally that it was against his principles to steal. Probably encouraged by this, Gerry added that this was also his position. He went on to say that he was just a bomber and that others did the robbing. Temporarily confused by this concise definition of the division of labour within the IRA, I could only mutter that he could always give his share to the organisation, but he wasn't to be swayed. They were both on board for only the escape.

As things turned out, I was overtaken by events. A prisoner had been killed in the punishment block. Questions were raised in the local press. To keep up the pressure, many of the inmates of the long-term wing took part in a sit-down protest. I was a leading organiser of the protest. For my pains, I was shipped out to another prison, as was Malcolm. Ian and Gerry, though, carried on with the escape. It was to prove interesting, as we'll see shortly.

Over the years I had occasionally seen references to Gerry in the press. I was aware that, on release from prison, he had joined Sinn Fein, the political wing of the IRA, and was currently an elected member of the Northern Ireland Assembly, the devolved government involving all parties to the conflict in Northern Ireland.

So, just as I had transformed myself from a violent gangster into a writer and journalist, so, it would seem, had Gerry turned from a 'man of war' to a 'man of peace'. I thought that it would make for a good story for me to go to Belfast and do an interview with him, picking up where we had left off some quarter-century earlier.

Eoin, who came from the Republic of Ireland himself and most probably had considerable Republican sympathies, thought it was a great idea. He commissioned me to do the piece for *Front*.

There were a couple of immediate problems. First, I hadn't been in touch with Gerry for nearly 25 years. I would have to find a way of doing so. Second, how would he remember me? We had been comrades rather than close friends and he most certainly hadn't agreed with my professional pursuit of crime. Last, there was the *Front* factor. How would he react to doing an interview for a lads' mag?

The first problem I solved by phoning the Sinn Fein office in Belfast. I was soon put through to Gerry Kelly's secretary, Margaret. I explained who I was and what I wanted to do. I said that I wrote for an English men's lifestyle magazine with a circulation in the hundreds of thousands. I added that the theme of the article would be that we had both transformed ourselves into 'men of peace'.

All this was perfectly true. What I didn't mention was *Front*'s name, in the hope that the lads'-mag phenomenon hadn't yet reached Belfast. Margaret asked me to phone back the following day.

When I did so, Margaret told me that, of course, Gerry remembered me and would be pleased to do an interview. I would have to come to Belfast, though, as none of Sinn Fein's elected MPs had taken up their right to sit in the House of Commons.

I came in to land at Belfast International Airport late in the evening and it was nearing midnight as my taxi pulled up outside the community centre in the Falls Road that I had been directed to by Margaret. The articulate young Irishman who was manning the upstairs reception desk was obviously expecting me. He informed me that certain members of the community put guests up for bed and breakfast. It was relatively cheap and provided an opportunity for the visitor to get a feel for the local community. This is what had been organised for me.

It was a five-minute taxi ride to a street half a mile further up the Falls Road. As we pulled up at the gate of a terraced house, a short middle-aged woman hurried down the path to meet me. She introduced herself as Anne and, grabbing my bag, bustled me into the house.

The house was spotlessly clean, if unostentatiously furnished. Anne made me a cup of tea and we sat at a kitchen table together. Even sitting down, she was filled with a boundless energy. Over the next hour, she regaled me with stories from 'the Troubles', in many of which she had played an active role. She emphasised that she had never been a member of the IRA or taken part in any 'terrorist' activity. But there had been many other ways the local community had supported their men and women who had been members.

Anne was a great talker and funny with it too. With a liberal use of expletives, she made even dramatic incidents sound humorous, without ever once sounding crude. It became clear to me that women like Anne had been the backbone of the fight for justice in Northern Ireland. Without her and thousands like her, the IRA could never have reached the point they had now.

All of a sudden, I was dead tired. The travelling and the lateness of the hour had combined to make me nod as I sat at the table. 'Come on, off to bed with you now,' Anne barked, startling me awake. She ushered me upstairs to my bedroom and, promising me breakfast when I arose in the morning, wished me goodnight.

Breakfast with Anne was a case of more of the same, but it was never boring. Her fund of interesting stories seemed endless. From time to time, neighbouring women and their children popped in and out. Anne was a virtual surrogate mother to several kids. I had noticed that she had no children of her own and there seemed to be no trace of a man about the house. Also, there was a carefully disguised sadness about her that she put on a brave face to hide. But I didn't pry. No doubt she would tell me her circumstances if she thought it relevant.

My appointment with Gerry Kelly was for the following day. The Press Office sent their apologies, but explained that there were important meetings scheduled for today. So I had a whole day to kill. Anne indicated that I could accompany her on her daily round if I so desired. It seemed a great way to learn more about the local Catholic community and Republicanism in general. That would help me to put people like Gerry Kelly in context.

Halfway up her street there was a small community centre and gardens. These had been built with the help of a grant from the European Community Fund. Anne mentioned that, as peace began to break out, every household had also received a £10,000 grant for improvements from the same fund.

The community centre performed a multitude of functions, from serving as a simple meeting place to sorting out local people's problems. It was all done on an informal basis, using volunteers. So there was none of the antagonism common to such places in mainland Britain, where the local authority was viewed as the 'them' as opposed to 'us'.

In fact, the whole phenomenon of the local community spirit was amazing, especially to a Londoner like me, coming from a city where one might never speak to a neighbour, although having lived next door to them for ten years.

As I walked down the street with Anne, people would call out and come over to talk. People were forever popping in and out of each other's houses. She invariably introduced me as 'Gerry's friend from England'.

Gable ends decorated with Republican wall art leaped out of their gloomy working-class surroundings: here, a gigantic mural celebrating the life and death of hunger striker Bobby Sands; there, a roll call of IRA men and women killed in 'the Troubles'. I reflected that, in most communities, the dead stayed only in the graveyard. Here, in Republican West Belfast, they were alive and living in the community.

Republican graffiti, though, wasn't the only kind. I noticed several instances of 'Fuck the IRA' and other less-than-complimentary slogans painted on walls. I thought that it had been done by the Loyalists. 'No, it's the fucking yobbos,' Anne corrected. Like any other urban community, it seemed that West Belfast suffered at the hands of teenage joyriders, vandals and their ilk.

As the organisation responsible for policing their community, the IRA had taken on the responsibility for this problem. Some of their methods had been very direct. Generally, they were supported in this by the majority; however, some yobbos and their families obviously felt otherwise.

I had intimated to Anne that I would like to meet Roy, another old IRA friend from prison, while I was here. Roy was much more in the 'Irish rascal' mould than Gerry and I could expect a grittier low-down on what it was really like on 'the street' from him.

Within half an hour, I was given the address of an old warehouse several streets away.

Roy was expecting me and we hugged each other warmly. We had shared some tough times in jail. Now, though, we were both out on the street and very pleased to be so. We had both weathered the experience well.

The first 20 minutes was spent asking about old friends. Then we got around to talking about the peace process. Although he spoke positively about it, he was quite cynical. 'The Loyalists know we've won, because we're outbreeding the bastards,' he laughed. I took this to be a reference to the fact that the Catholic community, where contraception was largely eschewed, had a much higher birth rate than the Protestant community, where it wasn't.

On the subject of the yobbos, Roy was quite matter-of-fact about it. 'Some of them are a fucking nuisance and make people's lives a misery,' he said. He also added that many of them were on drugs that they bought from the Loyalist gangs in East Belfast.

'Some people say that the IRA deal in drugs,' I said, looking Roy right in the eye.

'We shoot drug dealers,' replied Roy, quite deadpan and staring straight back. It was 'point taken'. The idea of the IRA selling drugs in their own communities was never really accepted by me. Knowing the strong principles of people like Gerry Kelly, I knew it would never be allowed.

That evening there was some kind of Republican celebration scheduled. It was a celebration of the hunger strikes and those who had been involved in them. There were parades and marches up and down the Falls Road, at the side of which had been built a mock-up of a prison cell. Various IRA men took turns to spend time symbolically in the 'cell', just wrapped in a blanket.

I walked with Anne through the packed streets and, even though I was the only Englishman there, I never felt under any kind of threat. The locals blamed the British government for their problems, not the ordinary person in the street.

Anne was everywhere. Shaking hands with this group and having a joke with that one. Often I was left for a while with a group of women from her street. Suddenly, one of them put her hand to her mouth in surprise and muttered an involuntary, 'Oh, my God, it's him.'

'For fuck's sake, don't let her see him, she'll fucking attack him,' cried another as they milled about in confusion.

I looked in the direction they were looking and saw a big rangy guy of about 50, standing with a group of men next to the mock-up of the prison cell. Suddenly, I was back in prison mode. I had come to like Anne, and the 'chaps' rules' state quite clearly that, should any man worthy of the name be in the company of a woman who is menaced by another man, then he must fight.

I looked more closely at the man in question. He was about the same age as I was, but a good six inches taller and three to four stones heavier. Yet, in seconds, I was contemplating rolling about in the dust of the Falls Road with him. Coupled with the fact that he was quite obviously a local IRA hero and was standing with several of his mates, the prospects were daunting to say the least.

I was just wondering how I would explain it all to Gerry in the morning when, suddenly, the problem solved itself. As the group of Anne's friends rushed over and engaged her in earnest conversation about where they were all going next, the big guy and his mates drifted off in the other direction.

The following morning I set off early for my meeting with Gerry. A 20-minute walk along the Falls Road brought me to the Press Office. Lots of bars and grilles covered the doors and windows. I pressed the bell and waited patiently.

The door opened almost immediately and an attractive young woman, her face wreathed in smiles, motioned me inside. I gave her my name and showed her my press card. 'Oh, we're expecting you,' she said chirpily. 'You're Gerry's friend from England. He won't be long. Please take a seat.'

I sat in a small reception area and passed a few minutes reading the posters and newspaper cuttings hanging on the walls. I looked up quickly as a group came in, recognition dawning as I saw a familiar face. As the tall heavily bearded man walked up to me, my mind struggled to accept that Gerry could have changed so much. I instantly rejected the notion though, because I had seen recent photos of Gerry and he looked nothing like this.

The puzzle was soon solved when the man introduced himself as Gerry Adams. I had seen the leader of Sinn Fein many times on TV (that was where the recognition had come from). He obviously knew who I was because, as we shook hands, he said that Gerry would be along in a minute.

The door opened again and suddenly Gerry was standing before me. The passage of nearly 25 years had added several pounds to his tall frame, but his still-youthful, well-nourished face belied his 47 years. We had never been close prison pals and Gerry had never subscribed to the criminal ethos, so there was no embracing and slapping of backs. There was a certain gravitas to Gerry Kelly now, a component, no doubt, of his present role as a politician. He greeted me warmly, though, while shaking my hand quite formally, almost ritually.

He ushered me into his office and asked me if I would like tea. As we waited for the girl to bring it, he asked me how I was and where I was staying. In truth, the pause before the interview proper gave me time to consider my approach. I wanted something more than just a formal interview. Any journalist could get that and, no doubt, Gerry did a dozen of those every day. He was friendly enough and his open, easygoing nature came across quite clearly. I would have to hope that, as we got into the subject matter, a more intimate Gerry would emerge.

When I told him I was staying with Anne, up the Falls Road, he looked interested. He told me how she had everybody's respect, that she had great spirit and had been a tireless fighter for the cause over many years. I told Gerry about how she had been showing me around and introducing me to people. When I got to the episode involving the previous evening, I asked who the man was that Anne's friends had been so keen to keep her from seeing.

Gerry looked thoughtful for a moment, then serious. 'It's a great shame, Norman, a tragedy, really. Another way that the Troubles have wrecked lives and families. That man was Sean M—. He was one of the original hunger strikers and an IRA volunteer over many years. He was married to Anne. She travelled all over the country to visit and support him. However, through his countless legal actions against the government, he became very close with his solicitor. She was a younger, quite well-to-do woman from the South. They fell in love and, when he got out, he divorced Anne and married her. Anne took it quite badly. Apart from anything else, it was a very public humiliation. It was a bad business altogether.' For a moment he was lost in thought, gazing into the middle distance.

At that point, the arrival of the tea made for a welcome interruption. As we settled down with our respective cups, Gerry asked me what it was I wanted from him.

I explained the theme I had in mind, that we had both once been 'men of war' and were now 'men of peace'. The story would be one about what we had been through to get here. I mentioned that a good starting point might be when we had last met. I had just been shipped out of the Scrubs, leaving Ian and Gerry to carry on with the escape.

It was a good conversational ploy, because, within seconds, Gerry was lost in the details of that adventure those 25 years previously.

'It came as a shock, of course, your being moved. Luckily, though, we knew where you'd hidden the key. We stole two warders' uniforms from the laundry and altered them to fit Ian and myself. How is Ian, by the way?' He paused as the memory of his old friend intruded.

I explained that, partway through his 25-year sentence, Ian's mind had snapped and he had never recovered. He lived in much-reduced circumstances in North London now. I still saw him frequently, but he wasn't the same man.

'It happened to many of ours, Norman, and it's always a great tragedy. Please give him my best regards when next you see him. Now, where was I? Oh, yes. One Saturday afternoon, with several of our friends looking out for us, we changed into the uniforms in Tommy's cell down on the "ones" [ground-floor landing]. You know, it was close to the end of the wing. We came out and had to walk past all those prisoners watching TV, before we could let ourselves out of the gate at the end of the wing. Of course, several people recognised us. A couple actually got up out of their seats, probably to go and tell the warders. But our friends made them sit down again until it was all over.

'Anyway, we crossed the yard to the laundry with no problem. Ian quickly knocked the padlock off the gate with a hammer and we let ourselves into the laundry with the key.'

'Where you found the ladder,' I interjected quickly.

'Hell, no!' said Gerry animatedly. 'That was the first thing to go wrong.' He was caught up in the story now and had relaxed considerably with me. This was precisely what I had intended.

'We broke into the works store and there was no ladder. They must have left it somewhere else that weekend. So we had to improvise. We broke struts off the big laundry benches and nailed them to a pair of stepladders. It wasn't ideal, but we thought it would do the job. Then we let ourselves out of the laundry again and ran at the fence.'

He paused momentarily, as the memory of that fear-charged moment was with him again. They were running blind. There could have been a dog patrol, with two warders and two dogs just around the corner, and they would have run smack into them. But there was no way of knowing that. This part was left purely to chance.

'But our luck was in,' he continued. 'Wherever the dog patrols were, they weren't in that area. We slammed the ladder up against the fence to make good contact. We knew that the slightest touch would set the alarms off anyway and we wanted to get up first time. But, as I went up, I saw a dog patrol come running round the corner. I'd just reached the top when they got to the bottom of the ladder. They pulled it and it snapped and Ian, who was only halfway up, fell to the ground. There was nothing I could do for him.'

He looked directly at me, then paused, just as he must have paused in the heat of the moment, perched on top of the wire-mesh fence all those years ago. A man as loyal as Gerry would have considered the plight of his fellow escaper and friend. But, as he said, there was nothing he could have done and, in fact, Ian himself had confirmed as much to me.

'Ian shouted for me to carry on, so I dropped to the floor, between the fence and the wall now. Over in the corner, where the two walls met, a cable hung down from the CCTV camera. I knew that I could reach it. It took a couple of tries, but at last I grabbed it. I pulled myself up and scrambled on top of the wall.'

'So all you had to do now was to drop down and run to the car we'd arranged to be left in the hospital car park,' I observed.

'No, that was the final thing to go wrong,' responded Gerry. 'I had estimated that I would take less than a minute from the time I got over the fence to the time I climbed the wall, but I'd taken more than three times that. Now there were 20 warders between me and the car.'

'So you enjoyed the view while it lasted?' I added.

'I certainly felt more free than I had for a long while,' said Gerry, smiling broadly.

'So what happened next?' I asked.

'I climbed back down quickly enough and they took me over to the segregation block and beat me up.' He screwed up his face at the memory.

'We should have warned you about that bit,' I said, laughing. 'Now I don't feel nearly so bad about missing the escape. So where did you go next?'

Gerry was laughing too now. 'To Long Lartin, but not for very long,' he continued. 'The IRA had declared a ceasefire and the fate of my co-defendants and myself had become part of the negotiations with the British government. It was all very hush-hush. They were saying one thing publicly about not negotiating with the IRA and doing something quite different in secret. The Price sisters had already been sent back to Ireland. They were still only young girls, really, and their health was very poor. Hugh Feeney and I weren't long behind them. We were taken to Heathrow and flown to Belfast. We spent a week in the old Crumlin Road jail, then we were granted political status and put in Long Kesh, what the British called "The Maze".'

'But thanks to me you had a bad case of permanently itchy feet,' I said, laughing.

Gerry laughed with me. 'I was always going to try to escape, Norman, with or without your initial encouragement. You see, as a member of the IRA, I saw myself as a prisoner of war and it was my duty to try to escape. In 1977, I tried to escape from a military hospital. In 1979, I tried again at Long Kesh, and also failed to get away from another military hospital in 1982.'

'I suppose that having political status meant that they couldn't do much to punish you. There was no remission to take away,' I observed.

'No, but Thatcher did something much worse,' replied Gerry animatedly. 'She was determined to portray us as common criminals rather than political prisoners, so she took away our political status. It was something we couldn't take lying down. We had to make a response. Fortunately, we'd been planning a big escape from Long Kesh for a while.

'It was never going to be easy, because "the Kesh" was Europe's most heavily guarded prison. Warders manned the inside and the British Army guarded the outside. Each of the top-security H blocks could only be opened from the outside, with a key held at the gate.'

Gerry paused, no doubt to fortify himself mentally against the memories of the dramatic event, before launching himself into the story again. 'We smuggled in guns and knives and took over the wing. Then we grabbed the next shift as they came on. Now we waited until the meals lorry came to the wing and we grabbed that. By now, of course, many of us were dressed in warders' uniforms.

'Mind you,' he continued, 'it wasn't as simple and as smooth as I've just described it. Already, a warder had resisted and been shot in the head. Then, as we drove the meals lorry towards the gate with all the lads in the back, a warder coming on duty recognised a couple of us in the front and pulled his car in front of the gate. At the last minute, we managed to ram the lorry through a side gate and then a pitched battle broke out between us and the warders in the gatehouse. That's when the warder was killed. Although he was stabbed, he actually died of a heart attack. He'd had a heart attack previously.'

'I wouldn't have fancied your chances of proving that if you'd come to trial in an English court,' I remarked.

'No, neither would I,' continued Gerry. 'It was all very unfortunate and not intended. We wanted to get away with as least fuss as possible. Anyway, 38 of us got away, 11 were recaptured almost immediately and several more were caught over the next few weeks. I got clean away. At first I was on the run in the border areas. Then I went abroad. I was free for just over 30 months, then a special Dutch unit arrested me in Amsterdam.'

'I suppose there are worse countries you could have been caught in,' I broke in. 'The Dutch are very fair in their interpretation of international law, aren't they?'

'Not *that* fair,' responded Gerry. 'In fact, they were very pro the British government. However, they refused to extradite me on the basis of my conviction for the Old Bailey bombing on the grounds that it was a political act, but they still sent me back. Then it all became very strange. In Ireland, I was placed on remand over charges arising out of the escape. Then one morning the prison governor summoned me to his office. He was trying hard to be civil, but you could see that he was very annoyed about something. Suddenly he got out a big, official-looking parchment and began to read from it in very old-fashioned language. The gist of it was that I was being given a free pardon for my role in the Old Bailey bombing and my life sentence was set aside.'

'I've known men in English jails who've lodged appeals for 20 years and never got that,' I said in surprise.

'Yes, I suppose I was very lucky, Norman. And my luck continued to get better. For my role in the escape I was sentenced to only five years and sent back to "the Kesh". As I had already served a couple of years on remand I only had about 13 months left to do. So I immersed myself in studying politics. When I got out in 1989, I joined Sinn Fein, rather than the IRA. It was an option open to Republicans who wanted some kind of life for themselves, as opposed to a life on the run all the time.'

'So the "man of war" really did turn into the "man of peace", Gerry?'

'It was a time for peace, Norman. In 1990, I was involved with Martin McGuinness in conflict resolution. We were negotiating with Loyalist gangs who were killing Catholics. At about this time, the British government insisted that, rather than being appointed by Sinn Fein, us negotiators had to be elected. In 1996, I was elected to a negotiating body called "The Forum". Within two years, we'd helped to produce the "Good Friday Agreement". In 1998, I stood as a Sinn Fein candidate for the Legislative Assembly, the devolved government for Northern Ireland, and was elected.'

'So it's "Assemblyman Kelly" now, is it, Gerry?' I asked, laughing.

'Plain Gerry will do from you, Norman.' He was laughing too.

'You've come a long way from Wormwood Scrubs all those years ago. Any regrets, Gerry?'

He looked thoughtful for a moment. 'Lots of regrets and I wouldn't know where to start if I had to list them. For the Nationalist community, it's always been viewed as a war. And in a war there are always casualties, on both sides. I regret all the dead and all the injured on both sides. All we can hope is that some good will come out of it now and Ireland will finally find some peace.'

We had been talking for quite a while now and I was rapidly running out of questions. I remembered one last thing, though. 'Talking of peace, President Clinton visited recently to assist the peace process and you spent some time talking to him. Do you feel he was sincere, or was it a cynical move on his part to try to influence the Irish vote back in the US?'

'Clinton was very well briefed, Norman, and he's used his influence in a very positive way. He's opened up the White House to us in a way that no other US president ever has. Not even Eamon De Valera [a former Irish prime minister and president] was invited to the White House, but Gerry Adams has been in and out of the place regularly.'

At this point the phone rang and, suddenly, Gerry was doing a down-the-line interview as part of a nationally broadcast, live radio programme. I listened to him speak, articulate, knowledgeable, the consummate politician now. Then it was the unseen Unionist's turn. I watched Gerry's brow furrow as he shook his head in frustration. Then he stared wistfully out of the window as if wishing himself far away. And he *was* far away as far as I was concerned: I had lost him to his electorate, which was as it should be.

Seizing my opportunity, I tapped him on the arm to get his attention and motioned towards the door to signify that I was leaving. He quickly shook my hand and mouthed a silent 'Goodbye'.

Gerry Kelly, Nationalist politician, Irish rebel, had certainly come a long way since the last time we had met.

CHAPTER SEVEN

THE COCAINE FACTORY

Several months had now passed since my trip to Colombia to do the FARC story. Through that time I had stayed in regular contact with Danny, both by phone and email. Apart from the fact that I now considered him to be a friend, I was always on the lookout for new and interesting stories. And Colombia was a country so rich in pathos that there seemed to be such stories everywhere. The problem, of course, was to get sufficiently good access to be able to cover them.

Bearing in mind the fact that, in most people's minds, Colombia is synonymous with cocaine, it was inevitable that I should be looking for a good cocaine story. One thing that had really surprised me on my release from prison was just how widely the drug culture had spread. In 1970, there was no such culture. A few people took pills of various types and others smoked grass, but it was very much a fringe-group activity. Now, drugs were everywhere.

Cocaine seemed to be especially upwardly mobile. Whereas previously the fringe drug culture had been largely a working-class phenomenon, cocaine seemed to know no social boundaries. In fact, because it was so expensive vis-à-vis other drugs, it was very much the narcotic of choice for the middle and upper classes. Certainly, in my meanderings around the media pubs, clubs, restaurants and bars in Soho, it seemed to be offered around with such regularity as to be almost the norm.

So a story set in Colombia about cocaine production would excite the interest of a wide audience. I had asked Danny several times about just such a story and each time he said that he would see what he could arrange. It was no problem for him, or for anyone else for that matter, to make a good drugs connection in Colombia. Colombia was the world's foremost producer of cocaine and, if it wasn't exactly acknowledged as its national product, then it certainly underpinned its economy. There was massive corruption at every level.

So if I had just wanted to buy cocaine, no matter in how big a quantity, that would have been no problem at all. Provided that my money was good and they thought me to be a trustworthy guy who would keep his mouth shut, there would have been a queue of dealers lining up to serve me. As it was, the exact opposite was the case. Not only wasn't I going to part with any money to buy so much as a gram of the stuff, but I was also going to spread the tale all over the pages of a magazine. Quite clearly, there was very little that was attractive in this deal for the average Colombian narco-trafficker.

Just as I was beginning to think that I should forget about the cocaine story, I received a phone call from a very excited Danny. 'I've done it, mate. I've cracked it,' he shouted down the phone. It took a few seconds to calm him down, and then he told me that he had managed to find a Colombian journalist called Edgar, who could take us to a farm where the cocaine was grown and processed.

Now, if Danny had a fault, it was that he could be overoptimistic at times, especially when he had a vested interest in the outcome. I tried to tie him down to specifics. Who was the guy? Could he be trusted? Why didn't he do the story himself? I bombarded Danny with questions.

Whatever he was, Dan was no fool. He knew how to pitch something with the best of them. 'Look, Norm, this ain't Camden town, you know. You can't get a written guarantee that someone'll give you this story. This is Colombia, a seriously fucked-up country. There's always going to be an element of chance. But I think that he's genuine.'

He had me. I had already seen something of the country and I knew that any venture whatsoever was always going to be something of a leap in the dark. I was going to have to put my reputation on the line with some magazine, though. From a quick costing with Dan, the story would cost over £3,000 in expenses. They wouldn't thank me if I came back with nothing. However, Colombia was such a dramatic and visual country that I was sure I could come back with something worthwhile.

Now I had to decide whom to pitch the story to. I had a good working relationship with *Front* now and, out of loyalty, I should really offer it to them first. Further, they would take my word for it that I could get the story and would give me a large degree of autonomy. With *Loaded*, I would have to 'sell' them the story and they would have insisted on sending their own photographer. I certainly didn't want that. In an attempt to keep costs down, I had asked Danny if he could find a suitable Colombian photographer. That would save £500 for an airfare and his rates would be much cheaper.

Danny said that he had just the man. Jorge was a professional photographer, who would also put me up in his flat in Bogotá, so saving money for a hotel. Working out the costings, I had already figured that I would probably have to underwrite some of the expense myself, so I was trying hard to keep costs to a minimum.

Eoin was excited when I told him about the story, although he did blanch somewhat when I mentioned how much I thought it would cost. He asked me if I could guarantee the story, and I had to be honest and say no. I did assure him, though, that I wouldn't be taking his money if I didn't think there was a very good chance of my coming back with the goods or dying in the attempt.

By now I had established a high degree of trust with him and he knew how fiercely committed I was when I went after a story. He laughed at my melodramatic remark and said, 'We don't want you getting killed for us, Norm, but if anyone can get this story I suppose it's you.'

With that compliment ringing in my ears, I started to make preparations for the trip.

First, I had to make a 'pitch' of an entirely different kind. In view of what had happened before, the word Colombia was like a red rag to a bull as far as Marsha was concerned. Not only was she still very pissed off at my not arriving in time for her birthday, but also she hadn't enjoyed the story when she had read it in the magazine. There were the issues of Lucero, the beautiful FARC guerrilla, and Danny and Trent's visit to the brothel. Several apologies were followed by several wicked oaths to stay away from all Colombian women and not to go within shouting distance of any houses of ill repute whatsoever. This was all quite straightforward for me, as I had no interest in pursuing either. My full concentration would be on staying alive.

Discount the dangers as I may, this latest trip would be infinitely more dangerous that the trip to see FARC. Then, I had been in the hands of only the one guerrilla group, one with a finely tuned sense of public relations, too. The chances of their killing me out of hand for merely covering what went on in their jungle capital had been quite remote.

The cocaine story was a different kettle of fish entirely. If what I had heard was true, then virtually all parties to the conflict dealt, in one way or another, in cocaine. The group that controlled the particular territory where the coca leaf was grown taxed the trade, whether this was FARC, ELN, the paramilitaries or the Colombian Army. None of these would take kindly to the notion of an English journalist coming into their territory and publicising the existence of farms openly producing cocaine.

Then there were the Americans. They were currently in the process of giving Colombia over $1 billion as part of Plan Colombia, ostensibly to eradicate coca production. While they might welcome a piece exposing FARC's or ELN's involvement, they certainly wouldn't be pleased with something that showed the involvement of their allies, the Colombian Army, and the latter's allies, the paramilitaries. I would have to be very careful indeed.

Danny met me at Bogotá Airport and was beside himself with excitement about the coming trip. Although he had been living in Colombia for over 20 years now, he had never been to the places where we would be going. He was adamant that no one had ever done this story before, to go down into the jungle and photograph and report on a working cocaine factory.

Perhaps that should have told me something. Either that it was too impractical or too dangerous. However, I was committed now; I had taken *Front*'s money and accepted the assignment. I would have to follow through, no matter what.

The first disappointment was Jorge. He was a pleasant, roly-poly sort of guy in his late thirties, who lived with his girlfriend, a much larger lady of a similar age, in her small but clean flat just a stone's throw from the presidential palace. I guessed that the armed guard on the gate of the unpretentious block had more to do with the level of local crime than it did to its proximity to the presidential palace.

The disappointment was that Jorge wasn't really a photographer. He had been a TV cameraman for a national network until he had been laid off over two years ago. He was very polite, eager and willing, and you could tell that he desperately needed the money. However, even from my limited knowledge of photography, it was a profession quite distinct from that of cameraman. But it was too late to look for someone else and both Dan and I had cameras and yards of film. So if, between the three of us, we took several hundred photos, at least a couple should turn out OK.

We were due to travel to the town of Barranca to meet Edgar. It was a jungle town insofar as *every* place outside the plateau city of Bogotá was down in the jungle. Travel would be by plane, as most of the jungle roads were often impassable. Further, absolutely none of them was policed, except by the local guerrillas or militias, and they were a law unto themselves, so anything could happen.

The following afternoon, the three of us presented ourselves at Bogotá Airport for our flight to Barranca. If I had been surprised that internal Colombian flights were so cheap, then I soon found out why. The battered, twin-engined 28-seater Fokker had obviously seen long service. All the passengers turned to look at Danny and me as we boarded, the only two Europeans on the flight.

I suppose the 180-mile flight to the north of Bogotá was uneventful, unless you counted the roller-coaster ups and downs as the light plane was buffeted by the warm jungle updrafts, uncomfortably reminding me of my first flight in a Fokker on my earlier visit to Colombia.

Edgar was waiting for us as we arrived. A tall, well-built, handsome guy in his late thirties, he had the impeccable manners of most Colombians that we had met. He quickly ushered us into a taxi, remarking that you had to be very careful with taxis as some of them were operated by criminals who would kidnap and rob you.

El Pilaton was a decent enough hotel. We booked two double rooms and then went to a nearby restaurant, where Edgar filled us in on some background details. Then came the second disappointment. It seemed that Edgar wasn't really a journalist. He said that he had worked as a journalist for 15 years, but for the last two years he had been a bouncer in a local nightclub. Now I knew that journalism was by no means an exclusive profession – I was living proof of that. But the transition from scribe to bouncer threw a lot of doubt on exactly what type of journalist he had been in the first place.

Seeing the look on my face as Danny translated, Edgar hastened to reassure me that the story could be done and that, in fact, he had been wanting to do this current story for 15 years, but the circumstances had never been right and he had never found anyone who wanted to do it. I pondered the implication that no one had been stupid enough to try.

Further details about our current location were something less than reassuring, too. Edgar informed us that Barranca, a town of 370,000 souls, was claimed as home turf by all the parties to the conflict. At different times, FARC, ELN, the paramilitaries and the Colombian Army had all held sway here for a while. At the moment, no one group enjoyed absolute power, but all were fighting to do so. Last year there had been 700 murders and 1,000 disappearances. Now the authorities didn't bother to report massacres involving fewer than ten people.

In any other set of circumstances one could only have concluded that Edgar was joking. But his delivery was deadpan and absolutely matter-of-fact. As we got up to make our way back to the hotel, he added, almost as an afterthought, that it was best that we stay close together, as very few Europeans ever came to Barranca and there was a very real chance of being kidnapped. As a throwaway line, it really took the prize. As I lay in my hotel room, I couldn't help thinking, If that's what he was *willing* to tell us, what has he held back?

Disappointments were coming thick and fast now. The next arrived with breakfast. As I sat opposite Danny in the hotel dining room I could tell something was very wrong. The normal boisterousness was gone and his complexion was the same hue as the milk he was pouring on his cornflakes. 'I'm scared, Norm,' he suddenly blurted out. 'I know this country and things are very dangerous here right now. The boatman who Edgar had hired to take us upriver has pulled out because FARC and ELN are fighting in that area.'

I knew that we were going to have to make the rest of the journey by boat, because roads just didn't run through the jungle. The hotel was situated on the bank of the river. The dirty brown water flowed swiftly past the dining-room window where we sat. As I gazed into the middle distance, I cursed Hollywood for making us all live filmically now. I couldn't help thinking about *Apocalypse Now* and Martin Sheen's boat trip into the 'heart of darkness'.

Danny suddenly brought me out of my reverie. 'Edgar's managed to get us another boatman, Norm, but he says it's very dangerous and that's why I'm scared.'

I wouldn't have described my own state of mind as 'scared', rather as 'concerned but committed'. If I set my mind on doing something, I tended to accept the dangers and just focused on achieving it. But the way Dan was going on, my state of mind could soon change to 'scared'. 'Look, Dan, I'm scared, too, mate, but I've taken *Front*'s money now and I'm committed to go through with it.'

Danny's reaction was characteristic. Suddenly, he burst out laughing. 'I didn't say I wasn't going, Norm. I'm just saying that I'm fucking scared.'

That made me laugh, too. Danny was brave enough. He had told me that he'd run with West Ham's 'Inter City Firm' for a while, and you can't be a faint heart and cope with that level of football violence. He had the loyalty that went with it, too, and the more I got to know him, the more I liked him.

The atmosphere changed somewhat as Edgar joined us at the breakfast table. For the worse. Over his toast, he presented me with his scale of charges. It would be $300 to take us to our first stop, a jungle village some 80 miles upriver. Then it would be another $200 for the next leg to another village. He was just in the process of detailing the amount for the next leg, all pointed out on a little map he had spread out on the breakfast table, when I stopped him abruptly.

Anger flared as I waved my hand to silence him as internationally as I knew how. 'Danny, you tell this prick that I'm not some kind of fucking idiot.' The anger was clear in my voice now, and in my expression too. Edgar sat back abruptly. 'I want one price for the whole trip, start to finish. I can see what's going to happen. We'll get to the last stage and it will be some sort of $1,000 to get to the prize. By then I'll be in for several hundred dollars anyway, so I won't have much choice. Tell him, one price for the whole trip, or we call it quits now.'

You could tell that Edgar was impressed. He had been nodding in agreement through my tirade without ever understanding one word I said. But he didn't have to. No doubt he was a sharp cookie and knew all the moves. Now he knew that I knew them too. Apart from anything else, it was essential that I establish some sort of understanding with him right from the start. Now, at least, he knew that I wasn't a mug.

We agreed on the round sum of $1,000, an absolute fortune by Colombian standards. But, as he so rightly argued, he was risking his life for us. By now, Jorge had joined us at the table. As he heard the final stages of the agreement, his glum look perfectly matched the one Danny currently had on his face. I was paying them $700 each. However, my irate state was enough to preclude any negotiations for an increase in their pay.

Edgar was all smiles now. He leaned across the table and shook my hand and I thought I saw a new respect there. I was frantically using all my prison-learned skills of summing a man up. I was reasonably sure he wasn't an evil bastard. If I had got an inkling of that I would have had to watch him very closely indeed. There was always the possibility of his luring us somewhere and killing the lot of us for all the money.

In this new spirit of camaraderie, Edgar suddenly pulled a small box out of his pocket and offered the contents around. They were small pills of two distinct types. He explained that one was an anti-malaria tablet and that we should take it because the river was infested with mosquitoes. The other was a muscle relaxant. It seemed that the constant battering of the boat by the river over the four-hour trip could seriously bruise your back. The experienced river traveller always took a muscle relaxant.

We collected our bags from our rooms and, with Edgar leading, trudged down the muddy bank to the boat, or, to give it its correct name, the canoe. The term boat smacked of something substantial, and there was little substantial about this craft. Basically, it was a 15-foot-long flat-bottomed punt with an outboard motor at the back. That it regularly functioned as a punt was evidenced by the long pole held in the hands of the boatman as he welcomed us aboard.

The boatman, an elderly black guy, was all smiles as he steadied the boat with the pole while we settled into our seats. Or rather, benches, for these were bare wooden boards without a trace of cushioning. Muscle relaxants or no muscle relaxants, I could still see my getting out at the other end with a sore bum.

As we settled in, the boatman's assistant, a teenaged boy, scurried about helping to stow our bags. With an absolute minimum of fuss, the boatman pushed the boat away from the shore with his pole and started the outboard motor. Soon we were speeding along at about 30 miles an hour.

Now I was starting to enjoy myself. This was the start of the adventure proper. I reminded myself that, whatever the outcome of the assignment, this would be the experience of a lifetime. Barely two years previously, I had been sitting in a prison cell. Now I was speeding into the heart of the Colombian rainforest in pursuit of a cocaine factory.

I had instructed both Jorge and Danny to take lots of photos of anything of interest. The three of us sat with cameras at the ready. That was when I discovered that, stimulating as I had first thought the boat ride to be, there was very little of interest to see. For a start, there were no roads, no bridges, no buildings of any kind, no telegraph poles, no animals and no people. And, since both banks were lined by tall reeds, all you could see in every direction was a brown-green wall that served to obscure everything else.

I was soon bored. The few birds we might have seen were frightened off by the roar of the outboard, which, as the river narrowed, seemed deafening. Then there was the percussive drumbeat of the bottom of the boat striking the water as it skimmed across the waves. This was aggravated by the boatman's crisscrossing of the river to avoid the shallows. Resist it as I might, whatever position I adopted it still sent shockwaves all the way up my spine. Now I could appreciate the value of the muscle relaxants. My romantic conception of river travel was rapidly undergoing a marked transformation. Already I longed for the boat ride to be over.

But, as Edgar was quick to inform us, we had just over four hours of this before we got to our destination. This was another thing I was discovering about Edgar. Although, at first sight, he didn't seem to be a morbid chap, he was an absolute fund of disturbing information. All conversations had to be conducted at a shout, to be heard over the roar of the outboard, so there was no ignoring what he was saying. Either he was bored too and was talking to pass the time, or he saw it as part of his duty as tour guide. However, he told us in quick succession that the river was teeming with piranha, some of them so large they could bite your hand off; there were also lots of alligators and crocodiles, some of which could grow to 20 feet or more; and there was the ever-present danger of colliding with sunken logs as we sped along the river. I briefly contemplated the prospect of some scaly, armoured behemoth pulling me from the canoe, as his smaller brethren, all snapping teeth and flailing fins, tore chunks of flesh from my bones. I resolved that the first Spanish phrase I must learn would be: 'For fuck's sake, shut up, Edgar!'

Half an hour into the journey, the river suddenly widened again and there, on the bank about 200 yards away, was some kind of military checkpoint. Two soldiers wearing army fatigues, crouched over a heavy machine gun. 'Don't let the soldiers see the cameras,' shouted Edgar, in a determined attempt at a whisper. 'If they think we're journalists, they might turn us back or confiscate the cameras.'

You would have thought that, with so little else to occupy them, the soldiers would have taken the opportunity at least to search the boat and question us about where we were going. For, if Europeans were scarce in the jungle towns of Colombia, you could bet your life they were virtually nonexistent on the rivers. But not at all. Without even standing up, they glanced down into the boat, checking, I guess, that we weren't carrying weapons. Then they waved us on.

On the bank, perhaps 50 yards past the checkpoint, was the wreckage of a crashed plane. It was a small two-seater job that looked relatively intact, except for the tail section, which had broken off and was lying separate from the rest. Edgar said that it was probably a narco-trafficker's plane that had been forced down. Soldiers or no soldiers, I just couldn't resist the opportunity to photograph the first interesting thing we had so far come across. Shielding the camera with my body, I took several surreptitious snaps of the downed plane.

The next three and a half hours seemed to pass exceedingly slowly. Occasionally, a straw hut would break the unchanging backdrop of the wall of vegetation. From time to time, a native fisherman would stare at us as we sped by. The monotony of the unchanging surroundings, the roar of the engine, the buffeting from the boat, the heat and the mosquitoes all combined to make an experience that was little better than purgatory. The only moments of interest were when the river narrowed to such an extent and the shallows became so difficult to pass that the boatman and his assistant both got out of the boat and, waist deep in the opaque water, guided us through by hand. My thoughts firmly with the crocs and the piranhas, I wondered out loud if the time would come when we too would have to do the same. I took little comfort from the fact that Edgar didn't see fit to reply.

It was during one of these periods, when the boatmen were out of the boat and the outboard noise was just below the pain barrier, that Edgar decided to share one of his gems with us. He remarked that he had been kidnapped a total of five times by the various armed groups.

Discussing it later, Dan and I were of the considered opinion that he had left it rather late to tell us and, seeing that he had left it so very late, why did he bother to tell us at all?

Eventually, the river widened out again and there before us was El Bagre, our destination. You could barely call it a village, just a collection of wood and straw huts clustered along the river bank. As Edgar had explained to us, it was a point controlled by FARC. It was one of them who would direct us to the *cocina*, or coke kitchen. They didn't call them farms or factories.

We made our way up the bank and Edgar introduced us to Comandante Alphonso, who was the senior FARC guerrilla in charge. Alphonso was a very laidback black guy. He said he would phone HQ and find out what had been arranged for us. Still in a very laidback manner, he cautioned us that if we were spies we would be shot.

Minutes later he told us that a FARC boat was on its way to take us on the next leg of the journey, as there were no *cocinas* in the

Above: Outside FARC's office in the Farcland guerilla capital of San Vicente, Colombia.

Below: The Colombian media setting up for a televised interview with FARC second-in-command, Raul Reyes, near San Vicente.

On assignment in Brazil for a Channel Four documentary on the Great Train Robbery, with Ronnie Biggs *(middle)* and Freddie Foreman of the Kray gang *(left)*.

Hell's Angels at Angel Farm clubhouse, Kent, waiting for the funeral of their national spokesman, Maz, to begin.

Floral tributes to Maz from all over the world.

The ancient city of Babylon, re-built by Saddam Hussein, with the Ishtar Gate in the bottom photo.

Above: One hundred US dollars worth of Iraqi dinars.

Below: Domestic dogs were locked in cages in Baghdad zoo for protection. Out on the street they would be shot and eaten by the soldiers.

Above: With Northern Ireland assemblyman, Gerry Kelley, in his Sinn Fein office, Belfast.

Above: More art in Shiels Street, expressing solidarity with the Cuban revolution.

Below: Wall art in Springfield road, near the Catholic/Protestant interface.

immediate area. I settled down in the shade to wait, all the while observing daily life in El Bagre.

The sun was exceedingly hot and the humidity made breathing difficult at times. So all activities were conducted at a very leisurely pace. There were about 30 villagers in all and among them I saw two more guerrillas patrolling slowly between the huts. Alphonso told us that the paramilitaries had attacked El Bagre two weeks previously. A FARC guerrilla had been killed and ten villagers massacred, while the paramilitaries had lost ten of their own. It seemed hard to believe in a place that looked so idyllic.

From time to time, boats stopped at the bottom of the bank. One of the guerrillas would walk down and check the cargo, money would exchange hands and then the boat would be on its way again. Mostly they were carrying clearly visible drums of gasoline and bags of cement. Other cargoes were hidden under covers. Edgar explained that it was all connected with the coke trade. The gasoline and cement were used in the production process and the hidden cargoes were the finished product. All cargoes were taxed by FARC before being allowed to go on their way.

Occasionally, other people arrived and came to sit around a hut that served drinks and snacks. Their city-smart shirts and slacks made them stand out quite clearly from the villagers. Danny was quite an authority on the coke trade himself. He pointed out two well-dressed, serious-looking guys sitting together by the snacks hut. 'They're both from Cali,' he said. He pointed at two other similar guys sitting a short distance away. 'And they're from Medellín. That's something you wouldn't have seen a couple of years ago. They'd have killed each other on sight. But the big cartels have been broken up and there are hundreds of smaller cartels and people have learned to cooperate.'

Dan went on to explain that these guys were here to buy the coca base produced in the *cocinas*. They would pay about £600 a kilo for it. Back in their home cities, they would process the base into its crystalline form and its price would increase to about £1,200 a kilo. Quite amazingly, though, they wouldn't take so much as a gram back with them. The actual bags of coke they bought and paid for at El Bagre would be exactly the same ones delivered to them by FARC in their home cities!

All of a sudden, the soporific effect of the heat was causing my eyelids to droop and I felt an irresistible urge to sleep. I found an empty hut that must have been used as a store and fell asleep immediately.

When I awoke a couple of hours later, Danny was standing outside, ''Ere, come and have a look at this, Norm,' he urged. 'See what you've been sleeping next to.'

I stumbled outside, blinking in the bright sunlight. The hut I had been sleeping in was divided in half by a wall. Danny was pointing to the inside of its other half. Stacked against the wall were about three dozen clear polythene bags containing large off-white granules. 'You've been sleeping right next to 40 kilos of coca base, Norm.'

If nothing else, it was an excellent photo opportunity. I fetched a clean *Front* T-shirt from my bag and put it on. It was a black one with *Front* printed on the front of it in big yellow letters. Then, holding several kilo bags of coke in my arms, but with the word *Front* clearly visible, I got Danny to take a dozen or so photos. I guessed that these photos alone would be worth the trip to the boys back at the magazine.

For a while I sat watching some women of the village washing clothes in the river down by the bank where we had landed. Due to the heat I had been going through clean socks at an alarming rate. It caused some amusement among the women when I joined them to wash some socks out in the river water. I reasoned that, in the heat, they would be dried out before we went on our way.

Ever mindful of Edgar's crocs, alligators and piranha, I was paying more attention to what was going on in the nearby waters than I was to the actual washing of the socks. I didn't relax till I was hanging them on a line stretched between two huts. Suddenly, there was a loud explosion. I cringed and ducked with everyone else. All eyes turned to focus on a young city-dressed guy standing next to a group of playing children. A pistol was lying on the ground between his feet. Clearly, it had dropped from his belt and accidentally gone off. I watched as the nearest guerrilla walked across and roundly chastised him.

Almost immediately there was a flurry of activity down by the riverbank. A canoe pulled up carrying four heavily armed guerrillas in jungle fatigues. They trudged up the bank, the bright sunlight glancing off the machine guns and bandoleers of bullets they were carrying.

Two things surprised me. First, they were ELN guerrillas. ELN were supposed to be fighting with FARC at our original destination, yet here they were comrades and friends. Secondly, they were all so very young. They were also very friendly. Edgar did the introductions. Ernesto, their leader, was still only 20 and had been training to become a doctor before he had joined the guerrillas. I asked him, through Danny, why he had joined.

'When you see the paramilitaries come to your town and massacre people, you know it could be your turn next. It is only common sense to fight,' he said with passion.

Although friendly, too, Elena said little. She was barely 17 and clearly quite shy, but there was something more. It was as if she had retreated from the world. When we got Ernesto on his own, he told us that her whole family had been massacred by the 'death squads'. That was why she had joined ELN. He added that she was a fearless fighter and offered the opinion that it was very sad, because it seemed that she was searching for death.

By now, Danny, in his own inimitable way, was on excellent terms with all of them. He had Ernesto laughing heartily and even Elena was smiling. Next thing, he had their M16s and Kalashnikovs off them and he and I were holding them over our *Front* T-shirts for another set of photos. When they asked what we were doing here, Danny told them about our mission to find a *cocina*. Ernesto said that, if we couldn't do it through FARC, we should come to their base at a nearby lagoon in the morning and they would try to help us. I got Danny to take full details of exactly how to get there. I wanted to give myself other options, because I was becoming worried now by the lack of results at our current location.

It was as they were leaving that I suddenly realised that the boatman who had brought us to El Bagre was nowhere to be seen, and nor was his boat. Edgar said that I shouldn't worry, because his job was only to bring us here. River travel was the only way to get about here and it would be the easiest thing in the world to get another boatman to take us where we wanted to go.

Then the senior FARC *comandante* everyone was waiting for arrived. He was a serious-looking, no-nonsense sort of guy in his forties, wearing the regulation jungle fatigue and the equally regulation heavy black moustache. He moved about with an air of authority, clearly used to being obeyed. The pace of the three local FARC guys quickened visibly, as they hurried about to his barked orders.

Even with Edgar's influence, the best we could achieve was a place at the back of the queue behind the guys from Cali and Medellín. Quite clearly, the important business of the day was coke business. I watched as local growers and vendors brought their bags of coca base out for the inspection of the city guys. Quality was discussed and price negotiated. Money was handed over and delivery details given for where the coke should be delivered to. All the while, the senior FARC *comandante* supervised proceedings.

With our turn came our latest and biggest disappointment. We found out that the only reason the *comandante* had come to El Bagre was to do the coke business. He said that there were too many things going on in the area for him or FARC to accommodate our wish to see a *cocina*. And he said it in a manner that brooked no argument. Almost before we knew it, he was back in his canoe and speeding away up the river.

So what did I do now? I looked at Edgar enquiringly, and his gaze could hardly hold mine. The reality was that I was deep in the Colombian jungle and I was no closer to finding a *cocina*. Edgar suggested that we go to see Ernesto at the ELN base in the morning. 'What's the matter with now?' I demanded aggressively, the prospect of failure looming like a spectre before my eyes.

'It's almost six p.m. and FARC shut the river at six,' said Edgar sheepishly.

'What?' I barked.

'It's a curfew, Norm,' added Danny. 'After six p.m., nothing moves on the river and anything that does gets shot at by FARC.'

Well, that was straightforward enough. Whatever our next moves were going to be, the sure thing was that we were going to spend the night at El Bagre.

There was no such thing as a hotel, of course, just a wooden hut partitioned off into absolutely basic rooms. Luckily for us, there was one room left. Unluckily for Jorge and Edgar, it had only two beds. To be honest, I would have tossed a coin to see who slept where, but Edgar, overcome with guilt no doubt, volunteered to sleep in the cane chairs near the café. At the same time he volunteered for Jorge, too.

When I saw the room, I realised that he hadn't made much of a sacrifice. I don't know what impressed me the least: the two hammocks slung between the rough wood walls, the open gaps for windows or the bare earth floor. Before leaving us for the night, Edgar just couldn't resist imparting one last gem of wisdom. 'Make sure you sleep with your shoes in the hammock with you, under the mosquito netting,' he called out. 'Otherwise poisonous scorpions, snakes and spiders could get in them in the night and sting you when you go to put them on in the morning.'

I knew I was going to have difficulty falling asleep. I was roasting in the heat, suffocating in the humidity and my right arm was on fire from a dozen mosquito bites. Now, as I swung perilously in the unstable hammock, a sweaty trainer nestling snugly under each arm, all I could think of was the big bristly tarantula, poised at this very second to launch itself upwards and bite my unprotected bum through the hammock canvas. I briefly toyed with the idea of waking Dan up and asking him how high the Colombian spiders could jump, but I knew he wouldn't thank me for it.

I must have lain there for a couple of hours, listening to the sounds of the jungle. The myriad rustlings, chirpings, buzzings, hissings, slitherings, croakings, hummings, screechings and growlings – and Danny's snoring acting as a backdrop to the sudden sharp death cries, as nature's creatures fell upon one another in an orgy of mass slaughter.

Just as I was finally dropping off from sheer exhaustion, there was a piercing shriek ending in a throaty gurgling that brought me fully awake and nearly pitched me out of the hammock. I heard Dan stir and I called out in a breathy whisper, 'Dan, what the fuck was that?'

There was silence for a couple of seconds, over which I could hear the continuing gurgling. 'Sounds like someone slaughtered a pig,' said Dan and, with a grunt, turned over and fell asleep again. I lay there wondering what sort of idiot slaughtered a pig in the middle of the night.

The following morning I wasn't in the best of moods. I had just spent the most uncomfortable night of my life and I had awoken to find that toilet arrangements were basic in the extreme. Residents took turns to fill a bucket from a large vat of river water, then wash in the bucket. I improvised slightly by filling several buckets with the relatively cool water and tipping them over my head. Bliss, utter bliss! But only for about half an hour, when the cycle of sweating and overheating began again.

We ate breakfast at the café, then the four of us trudged back down the bank to where another boatman was waiting with his motorised canoe. The ELN base was located at a nearby lagoon called San Lorenzo. We sped along narrow rivers that were little more than streams, turning sharply round tight bends and sending our frothy white wake crashing into the reedy banks.

I had promised Marsha I would phone her every day. I knew that a little detail like being in the middle of a tropical rainforest would carry little or no weight with her should I not do so. There had been no phone at El Bagre, so I told Danny to ask the boatman to stop if there was a place with a phone.

The canoe slowed as we suddenly came to a junction where four small rivers met. The boatman pointed to the bank and spoke to Danny. 'He said that there's a small village over there called Four

Mouths and it's got a phone,' said Dan in a tone that sounded not at all pleased.

'So let's pull over for a minute,' I replied, puzzled. This was good news. In a few minutes, I would be talking to my dearly beloved and getting myself off the hook for another day.

'It ain't that easy, Norm.' Dan's tone was still grim. 'The boatman says that the "head cutters" have been active in this area recently and they may've attacked this village.'

I digested the information and conjured up two images: one was of a death squad comprising bloodthirsty cutthroats; the other was of an irate Marsha. It was no contest really. 'Fuck 'em, Dan. I've got to phone Marsha, so let's put ashore, eh.'

There was a large hut situated right on the shoreline, so we coasted in close by. Behind it, through the trees, could be seen similar huts with a narrow earth road between them. All was deathly quiet and it seemed as if no one was about.

It was only at the last moment that we noticed the painted slogan daubed on the side of the hut in large white letters. Danny translated, but I already knew that the letters AUC stood for 'Autodefensas de Colombia', the preferred name of the paramilitary death squads. So we now knew for sure that they had been here. The burning question was, were they still about?

The five of us advanced slowly up the narrow earth road, stepping around household articles that had been pulled from the huts and left. The inside of every hut had been ransacked and unwanted items smashed. Here and there fires had been started, as evidenced by the blackened timbers and piles of ash. Other huts had had their corrugated tin roofs pulled off. Two dozen or more chickens foraged among the ruins. Still there was no one to be seen.

Not one word had been exchanged between us since we had landed. Treading carefully to avoid making too much noise, we were listening intently for signs of life.   Although we all must have been aware that we were entering a potentially dangerous situation here, it was as if we were being drawn inexorably onwards by our desire to find out what had happened.

For myself, I saw an opportunity to save a failing assignment. In the absence of a cocaine story, photographic evidence to reveal this latest massacre to the world would suffice. That was why it was worth taking a risk. Mentally, I steeled myself against the discovery of tortured corpses and severed heads on poles.

At its end, the narrow dirt road broadened out into large roughly rectangular open space that must have served as the village square. In the middle was a wooden hut with the remains of telephone wires running to it. The window openings were all blackened with smoke and the roof had collapsed. Wordlessly, I wished goodbye to my phone call to Marsha.

On the side of another hut was some more painted writing. Once again the letters AUC stood out clearly. Danny translated. 'It's a warning. It says, "This is what happens to the enemies of the AUC."' He looked directly at me. 'We better get out of here, Norm, just in case they're still around. These aren't people to fuck about with. They'll kill you as soon as look at you.'

It was enough to bring all of us to our senses. It was almost as if I had been sleepwalking through the village. The full implications of what could happen should we bump into this group finally hit home. Without actually breaking into a run, we hurried back to the boat.

Just as we were pushing off from the bank, an old man emerged from the trees. Edgar got out and went over to speak with him. The conversation was brief and he came rushing back, motioning for the boatman to push off as he climbed in. 'The paramilitaries were here just over a week ago,' he gushed. 'They killed ten villagers and the rest have fled. There's only this old man now. He's lived here all his life. He says he's sad and lonely.'

The old man stood in the trees, watching us as we disappeared up the river. I stared for a long time at the forlorn figure, musing that this was the real face of Colombia's civil war. A civilian population at the mercy of right-wing death squads, in league with the Colombian Army and indirectly supported by the US.

The river narrowed again and under overarching trees perhaps 50 feet ahead was a jungle-fatigued guerrilla in an outboard-powered canoe. He immediately set off with us in pursuit. At times it was almost like a chase, as we twisted and turned around sharp bends.

Until now, all the journey had been in the gloom of small rivers overhung by a canopy of trees that served to keep most of the light out. Suddenly, the river opened out into a large and most beautiful lagoon. Golden sunlight danced on impossibly blue waters, as countless thousands of multicoloured exotic birds swooped and called. It was breathtaking.

We crossed the lagoon and docked near the small group of huts that was San Lorenzo. The four ELN guerrillas we had met the day before were sitting among the trees with several of their colleagues. We pressed them on their offer to show us a *cocina* and they said they would have to ask their commanders further up the river.

A ten-minute canoe ride took us to The Point, a fortified bend in the river that served as an ELN command post. We were introduced to Comandante Julian and Comandante Aguado, the two most senior ELN commanders in the area. Both were friendly and helpful, but, in practical terms, there was little they could do personally to show us a *cocina*. However, they did say they would make some enquiries. Quite bizarrely, I then found myself discussing the finer points of Marxist ideology with them, while we awaited an answer.

All the while I was watching the comings and goings of the boats on the river. Many had the telltale cargoes of gasoline and cement. All were stopped by the ELN and all were taxed. Noting my interest, Comandante Julian suddenly asserted that the ELN were not involved in the cocaine trade. They taxed only the cattle and gold trades. Bearing in mind I realised I had seen only timber structures since I'd been in the jungle, I forbore to ask what all the cement was being used for then.

I snoozed for a while in the shade of a large tree and awoke to find Danny exercising a previously unknown talent as a film director. Having decided that the guerrillas weren't actually doing a lot just sitting about in the shade, Dan had decided to get them on manoeuvres for a photoshoot. He had several in a slit trench pointing guns aggressively and several more were in an attacking formation down by the jetty confronting half a dozen more who were bursting out of some bushes. Meanwhile, he and Jorge were snapping away like crazy with their little cameras with both *comandantes*, Julian and Aguado, looking on benignly.

Our answer, when it came over a badly crackling radio link, wasn't helpful. ELN in that area couldn't help us find a *cocina*, but they would send us upriver to a FARC post, where there was a commander who could.

Once again we headed upriver in the canoe. A 90-minute trip took us to Yanque, another collection of huts, but this time set atop a steep hill. The most welcoming aspect for us was the Coca-Cola sign. We sat in the village café, greedily guzzling exquisitely cold soft drinks.

By all accounts, Comandante Yasid was the most senior FARC commander we had met so far. He was a young, intense, yet friendly guy, whose fledgling beard and moustache only served to emphasise his youth. He was introduced as the commander of the whole 24th Front.

As Edgar waved his hand expansively to indicate the extent of Yasid's kingdom, I could only muse that never had one so young been in total charge of so many trees.

In a country that was at the forefront of cocaine production, it seemed amazing that, despite travelling across hundreds of miles, we had never been near or by a *cocina*. And that was exactly the situation now. Yasid said that there wasn't one in the area, but he knew of one near a village called Agua Sucio.

However, there were a number of problems. The direct route was by water to a large town called San Pablo, and we could get a jeep from there. San Pablo, though, was a paramilitary stronghold and anyone arriving from FARC-held territory was liable to be shot on sight. I had been following the conversation carefully through Danny's translation and, as we got to the stage of Yasid's telling us the alternative, I followed his pointing arm as it indicated a massive green-swathed mountain in the middle distance. Danny was suddenly uncharacteristically tight-lipped.

'Go on, then, Dan. What's the alternative?' I urged.

'Yasid said that it's a five-hour trip by mule over that mountain,' he pronounced grimly.

By now, it was all becoming thoroughly ridiculous. I had expected some unusual situations, but a close encounter with a mule hadn't been among my expectations.

'And we're not used to riding mules,' added Dan, stating the obvious. 'An hour's ride will cripple us.'

'I've got too much respect for my bollocks to spend five hours on a fucking mule,' I exploded. 'We're going to San Pablo by boat.'

The boatman thought otherwise, though. It was only the obscene sum of £100, a small fortune by local standards, that managed to change his mind. I didn't much care for the way he crossed himself as we set off, but at least we were going by the direct route now.

We arrived at San Pablo just as night was falling. The four of us booked into a small scruffy hotel, then went in search of supper. Of all the places I had been so far, there was definitely a different feel about this place. People looked at us furtively and there was an air of fear. It didn't help our collective paranoia when we noticed a guy on a motorbike who was following us everywhere. We ate quickly in a restaurant, then retired to our rooms for the night.

Breakfast brought another drama. The guy with the jeep, whom Edgar had hired to take us beyond Agua Sucio, had backed out. At daybreak,

600 paramilitaries had driven up the very road we were due to travel on to attack ELN positions in the biggest operation in years. The whole area had suddenly become even more dangerous than usual, ergo, no jeep driver.

Seeing the expression on my face and having already felt the force of my anger on several occasions now, Edgar was apologetic: 'I did warn you before we started that in Colombia nothing remains the same. Everything changes.' And, to give credit where it is due, he *had* warned me. He had also warned me about something called 'locombia', a corruption of *loco*, the Spanish word for mad, and, of course, *Colombia*. The word itself meant a particularly crazy Colombian state of mind that ran through all things. This latest situation was classic 'locombia'.

All was forgiven, though, when, barely half an hour later, Edgar showed up with another guy with a jeep. Just outside San Pablo, our big red Toyota jeep was stopped at a heavily fortified army checkpoint. Whatever Edgar said to the soldiers, it was enough to get us through. Further on, special government anti-guerrilla troops waved us to the side of the road and Edgar talked us through again. A glaring irony that wasn't lost on me was that this was the road that 600 paramilitaries, the death squads, had travelled up just a few hours earlier. So much for the fiction that the regular army doesn't collude and cooperate with them, I thought.

We passed a burned-out command post that had belonged to FARC. The driver told us that ten guerrillas had died here only the previous week. From here on, a road that had been merely impassable to cars became a four-wheel-drive obstacle course. The good news was that, where the paramilitaries had turned off, our route carried straight on. We forded five rivers and drove around and over fallen trees, deep ruts and boulders. Agua Sucio just wasn't worth it. Fortunately, this miserable collection of huts was just another stop on the journey. We topped up with cool soft drinks and were soon on our way again. Finally, we breasted the brow of a steep hill and stopped. Our bone-shaking ride had lasted over three hours.

The present stop was for Edgar to take a pee. Just before disappearing into the undergrowth, he pointed out to me the farm buildings nestling in the lee of the hill below. The sweep of his hand took in the thousands of coca plants that covered the surrounding hills. Among them he pointed out the *raspachinos*, or pickers, working in the blazing sun.

He cautioned me about taking photos, saying that good manners demanded that we ask his permission first. Well, I'm afraid that by this stage I was clean out of 'good manners', and something called 'enlightened self-interest' was firmly in their place. I hadn't come all this way, risking life and limb, for some farmer to say I couldn't take any photos. I could take the best story in the world back to *Front*, but in the absence of photos it would be as nothing.

I too walked off into the undergrowth, making as if I were going for a pee. As I gazed through the lens of my thoroughly ordinary camera, I wondered what all the fuss was about. The collection of scruffy sheds in the distance could have been anything, anywhere in the world. If it really was a coke farm, then it certainly didn't look it from where I was standing.

As it turned out, the farmer was hospitality personified. He was at pains to emphasise that he was only a poor man and the obvious poverty on his farm attested to that. When asked why he grew coca, he pointed to his six children. He said that there weren't any alternatives for him. If he grew the food plant yucca, it would be too expensive to sell by the time he got it to market, because of the distance and the cost of transport.

Certainly, the economics of cocaine production at this end of the market weren't impressive. Coca was a hardy plant that would grow virtually anywhere. However, it still had to be fumigated by hand two to three times before each of the three harvests each year, to protect it from insects and worms. He usually employed 30 *raspachinos*, working 11-hour days, six days a week. For this each was paid around £8 per day, with free board and lodging.

The gasoline and cement to produce the coca base had to be brought in by boat, and this was subject to taxing on the way. He paid a flat tax of about £18 per hectare to the paramilitaries who controlled the area and a further £60 per kilo tax on each kilo of coca base produced. Finally, he would have to sell the base to the paramilitaries for about £600 per kilo. These were the very paramilitaries who operated out of San Pablo under the protection of the army!

The farmer said that we could photograph what we liked, as long as we didn't photograph him or the faces of his workers. That could bring the wrath of the paramilitaries down on them. He absolutely refused all offers of payment. I was already deeply impressed by the simple Colombian courtesy and hospitality I had experienced.

Before we embarked on the guided tour, though, there was one final ritual to be observed. After taking a boiling pot off a nearby stove containing coca leaves, the farmer poured each of us a cup of coca tea. He said that it was good for everything, including illnesses and allergies, and would give us energy.

It wasn't for me, though. I had long ago promised myself that coke wouldn't have me in any way, shape or form. Further, abstinence had become almost an article of faith for me on this trip. I felt that, if I lived clean, then I might just get the story. And, as for the extra energy, on most days I tripped on my own adrenalin, anyway.

With two *raspachinos* as extra guides, we climbed the slopes covered with coca bushes and the two different types were pointed out to us. Both types of leaf looked identical to me, apart from the fact that the Peruvian coca leaf was much darker than the Colombian one. We were told that it also yielded four crops a year against three for the Colombian.

The actual *cocina* was on the summit of a small hill. Basically, it was a long shed with no walls, just six upright beams to hold the roof up. Inside, two large black plastic sheets were spread out on the rough earth floor. On the first, a worker was chopping a vast pile of leaves into small pieces with a garden strimmer. On the second sheet, the chopped leaf was covered with cement powder, sprinkled with gasoline, then trod in by men wearing wellington boots. Once it was well mixed in, it was shovelled into large black plastic drums, which were topped up with gasoline and left for two hours.

The next stage involved letting the liquid drain out of each drum into another drum below. Permanganate was added and stirred well in. The mixture was then left to stand for another two hours, when the coca paste could be seen in the form of a white viscous precipitation at the bottom of each drum. The farmer told us that his *cocina* turned out approximately 15 kilos of base a week.

All through the guided tour, Danny, Jorge and I had been photographing everything that was remotely interesting. I was sure that we had several hundred photos between us. Together with the farmer's description, I had what I had come for. The worry that exercised me now was whether, since everyday Colombian life was so problematic, I would get back safely with the photos. Edgar emphasised that nobody had ever photographed a working *cocina* before.

I wanted to leave immediately, but the farmer asked us to join him for lunch. In the circumstances it would have been churlish to refuse. I ate with a tranquillity belied by my internal mood. I consoled myself with the thought that the trip back couldn't be nearly as fraught as the trip out.

The ride back to San Pablo was without incident. The army roadblock had gone and there was no sign of the paramilitaries, either. I paid the driver off, musing that too many trips like today's would see his new jeep a wreck in no time.

Back at the hotel, the first priority was a cool shower and a change into clean clothes. I took the rolls of film with me everywhere. Afterwards, I went to reception to get a cold drink from the fridge. Four young guys were by the reception desk. They gave me a hard stare as I came in. It was one of those 'Who are you looking at?' stares that were so commonplace in London. Back there I would probably have responded in kind, but, quite strangely, because personal interaction was so polite and unthreatening in Colombia, I had relaxed considerably. However, it registered subliminally as I returned to my room.

Within minutes, raised voices could be heard coming from reception. As I came out of my room, Danny was already in the hall. We hurried towards the reception area. The four young guys had Jorge and Edgar backed up against a wall. Both were white as sheets and literally shaking with fear. 'They're taking us away,' cried Edgar to Danny. 'Please help us.'

It was in situations like this that Danny was worth his weight in gold. He quickly engaged the four guys in conversation and soon had them laughing. Within seconds all the threat went out of the situation. It transpired that they were paramilitaries and they had heard that we were in town and wanted to know what we were doing here. They had thought that we were Americans.

Danny explained that we were English and made some deprecating remarks about Yanks that had them laughing again. He told them of our mission to photograph the *cocina*. They left, still laughing and seemingly satisfied.

Jorge and Edgar, though, were definitely not laughing. Still shaking, Edgar said that they were definitely on the verge of being taken away and killed. He emphasised that we must get out of town right away. 'We must leave right now or we're dead' were his exact words.

It wasn't exactly panic, but we had our bags packed and were in reception paying our bill in no time at all. The owner was relieved to see the back of us. He had been following developments from inside his office and was as white as Edgar and Jorge.

At a trot, we made our way down to the river and accepted the first boat available without bothering to negotiate the price. Soon we were heading upstream towards Barranca. If I had thought that we were now safe, Edgar soon disabused me of that notion. 'They will phone ahead to their comrades. We must get out of Barranca as soon as possible,' added a still shaken Edgar. Ever mindful of the 700 dead and 1,000 missing last year alone, I could only agree with him.

We docked at Barranca and Edgar spent a couple of minutes finding a properly registered taxi. We paid him the £80 he wanted to take us to Bucaramanga. Three hours later, we were in the Melia Confort Hotel, five-star, safe and secure.

After the almost constant excitement in Colombia, England was something of an anti-climax. My reunion with Marsha wasn't nearly as fraught as I might have expected, despite several missed phone calls. I figured that, whatever else she might do, she wasn't about to cut my head off and stick it on a pole. However, I did refrain from planting the idea in her mind.

My arrival at *Front*'s offices had all the sense of occasion of a returning hero. Eoin must have been considerably relieved. This had been a comparatively expensive assignment and he had gone out on a limb to OK it. But when he saw the photos and listened to the story he was delighted.

The following month's issue saw my *cocina* story prominently displayed inside, over several pages. The pièce de résistance, of course, was the photo of me in a *Front* T-shirt holding several kilos of coke in my arms. Eoin told me later that that particular issue had increased the month's circulation by 80,000.

Even the BBC showed an interest. They put an account of the trip, together with several photos, on their news website, where it remains to this day under the head EYEWITNESS: INSIDE A COCAINE FACTORY.

I was now quite a 'hot' magazine journalist and, although it wasn't the situation that every door was open to me, I could at least consider writing for more prestigious media outlets. Not that I was ungrateful to *Front*, but, quite obviously, I didn't want to spend the rest of my career writing exclusively for them. The problem with a triumph, though, was that it always raised the question of what to do for an encore. I already had my next story, though – and had already done it.

CHAPTER EIGHT
THE NUMBER OF THE BEAST

As a child I was afraid of the dark. The margins of my nights were always peopled with werewolves, vampires and demons. But we grow out of these things, don't we? With adulthood comes the realisation that such intangible creatures have no basis in reality. With the advent of day, they melt away like the early-morning mist.

Shortly before my 19th birthday I was sentenced to six years' imprisonment. I was sent to Wakefield Prison in Yorkshire, a top-security jail the local people call 'The House of Horrors'. Among the 700 adult prisoners, there were men like beasts: multiple murderers, serial rapists, torturers – their crimes almost defied belief. To my horror I discovered that vampires, werewolves and demons *do* exist.

No, not in actual physical form. The appearance of these men never changed one iota. But, when they slaughtered and mutilated humans, sometimes drinking their blood and devouring their flesh, their psychological persona was identical to that of the vampire or werewolf. Who could say that they weren't possessed by the demon spirit?

It isn't known whether little Luis Alberto Garavito was afraid of the dark. However, what we do know is that he certainly had enough horror to deal with in broad daylight. He was born, the first of seven children, to a poor family in Quindío province, Colombia, on 25 January 1957. There is evidence that his father was a brute who regularly beat him, to such an extent that the boy would literally shake in his presence. At age 13, he was raped by a male family friend. In view of what was to follow, one can only conclude that, although not rigidly deterministic factors in their own right, these events must have played a part in his later development.

At age 25, he started raping young boys. They were all 'street kids', children of the very poor. Their ages ranged from six to fifteen and they were invariably good-looking boys with light complexions.

Garavito's approach was far from haphazard. Often he would spend days befriending the boys. To aid him in this and to lower their suspicion, he used a variety of props and disguises. Sometimes he would dress and pass himself off as a priest. On other occasions, he would pretend he was a teacher, a seller of lottery tickets, a vendor of religious artefacts and a tramp. Parts of the subterfuge were the wigs, beards, walking sticks, plastered arms, neck braces, crutches and glasses he used. A naive, unsuspecting child would be taken right in.

Then he would get them to walk with him into the vast sugarcane fields that were everywhere in that region. Here he would bind their hands and rape them. Between 1982 and 1993 he raped more than 300 young boys.

Although his modus operandi always remained the same, after 1993 there was a development that was pure fiend. He still disguised himself and lured the boys in the same way. Their hands were still tied behind their backs, with the same-coloured string each time. But now he would slash them with knives and burn them with lighted cigarettes. The more they fought and screamed, the more he tortured them. Garavito revelled in their agony.

He would force them to kiss him, then he would rape them. In a penultimate act of savagery, he would cut their throats with such force as virtually to decapitate them. Finally, he would cut off the penis and place it in the boy's mouth.

Garavito was so prolific that bodies were soon found all over, not only in Quindío, but also in the surrounding provinces. If the crimes themselves weren't quite unique enough, he 'hallmarked' them further by using the same-coloured string each time, and he always left an empty bottle of Cacique rum at the scene. Yet no one realised that it was the work of one man.

To put these events into context, though, Colombia is a country racked by a 35-year-long civil war. Every single day, there is widespread murder and destruction; every day a massacre somewhere of innocent civilians, caught up in the battle between the guerrillas and the government. In the midst of such mayhem, civilised governance has gone by the board. 'Street kids' as a class are not well looked after, anyway. In many cases Garavito's victims weren't even reported missing, because so many children just run away from home. Often they become an urban menace, robbing and stealing at will. In Bogotá, death squads calling themselves '*limpiadores*' or cleaners, try to solve this problem by murdering 'street kids' wholesale. The police are even suspected of involvement. It is a national scandal that there isn't more of an outcry about it.

Locally, though, in Quindío province, some of the kids were missed. Protest marches were organised, calling on the authorities to do something about the disappearances. There were headlines in local newspapers calling for an inquiry. Among the suspects were child prostitution rings, *limpiadores*, drug traffickers, paedophiles, organ traffickers and black-magic groups. To try to calm public anger, the police actually arrested several tramps and drifters. However, the murders continued.

By all other indicators, Garavito's life was unremarkable throughout this period. He worked as an accountant in Bogotá, a handyman, then as an employee in a fast-food restaurant. He was living platonically with two women, both of whom had young sons, without ever molesting the boys in any way. He was viewed as unusual by some though, being nicknamed 'Goofy' and 'El Loco'.

By now, the murders had mounted into the hundreds, but still the authorities didn't realise that they were looking for one man. The official view was that the murders were too many and too widespread. Incompetence at the top was more than matched by incompetence at the bottom. They actually had Garavito, sometimes using false names, in custody several times before releasing him due to lack of evidence. In June 1996, he was arrested under his own name at Tunja, Boyaca, following the disappearance of a young boy. They released him due to lack of evidence the following day. The next day, they found the boy's body, but Garavito was long gone.

Finally, in 1997, the Colombian authorities grasped the enormity of the horror they were faced with. Literally hundreds of young boys had gone missing, with most turning up murdered in the most horrible ways. However, they still didn't accept that they were dealing with the work of one man. After some investigation they came up with a list of ten suspects. Garavito's name wasn't on it!

In November 1998, 25 bodies were found in one month, all killed in exactly the same way.

Invariably, though, those who serve evil are subject to a quirk of fate that is instrumental in bringing about their downfall. It is almost as if nature itself were crying out for justice, which then comes in the form of peculiar misfortune. In February 1999, at the scene of his latest crime, Garavito fell asleep, drunk (he was later to claim that he was drunk during all his crimes). As he slept, somehow he set himself alight, burning his left arm severely. In a drunken panic, he ran off, leaving behind his shoes, glasses, trousers, a sum of money and, of course, the usual coloured string and empty Cacique bottle. The police traced the money to where it was issued, forging a positive link to Garavito.

At long last, in March 1999, the authorities finally acknowledged that the killings were all the work of one man and that the man was Garavito. They formed a special task force to look for him.

Fortunately, fate intervened again. On 22 April 1999, Garavito was at the scene of his latest crime. He had lured a boy of 12 into the sugarcane fields near Villavicencio. As Garavito tortured him, the boy's screams alerted a man who was sitting in a nearby field, smoking some of the local 'grass'. He ran to investigate and detained Garavito after a brief struggle.

The police arrived just as the crowd that had gathered was about to lynch him. He was arrested under the name of Bonifacio Morera Lizcano and charged with the attempted sexual abuse of the boy. They sent details of the case to the central police authority, as they were required to do by a circular that had been issued ordering them to report all sexual attacks on young boys. They were in the process of releasing him when the special task force got to hear of the case.

For the next six months, Garavito's arrest was kept a closely guarded secret. Enough mistakes had been made already and the authorities were preparing their case carefully. Then, in October 1999, Garavito was charged with multiple murder.

For seven hours, he protested his innocence. Suddenly, he vomited, fell on his knees and begged God's forgiveness. Then, in a confession eight hours long, he admitted to murdering 192 young boys in the seven years from 1993. At his lodgings, the police found newspaper cuttings concerning each murder and bus tickets placing him in the area at the time of the crime. Most importantly, they found a secret diary that Garavito had kept, recording in gruesome detail exactly what he did to each boy!

A further, remarkable aspect of the case has been his memory. With amazing accuracy he has produced detailed drawings of the scene of each crime, leading the police to recover a total of 157 bodies. He says that his sole aim now is to reunite the grieving parents with the bodies of their children.

Naturally enough, the authorities were eager to learn what manner of man could carry out such a widespread slaughter of the innocents. On careful examination, Garavito proved to be singularly unimpressive. Barely five foot six tall, he has a metal plate in his right leg, which causes him to walk with a limp. His left eye is noticeably smaller than his right. Dr Oscar Díaz, the examining psychiatrist, found no trace of any recognisable mental illness and therefore declared him to be, from a psychiatric point of view, quite normal!

Among his confessions, Garavito did put forward some kind of explanation for his actions. He said that, at the time of each offence, he felt himself overwhelmed by a 'strange force', which he found impossible to resist. He readily admitted that, should he be released, he would not be able to stop himself from doing the same things again.

After his confession, Garavito embraced religion and he regularly prays with a priest. His sense of guilt seems to be real, for he has twice tried to kill himself. In the absence of a death penalty in Colombia, he has so far been sentenced to 1,200 years in jail, with many more cases pending.

This much I had learned from reading press reports about the case. As I was visiting Colombia anyway, I wanted to have alternative stories I could turn to in the event that the actual story I was working on couldn't be done. In the present case, it was the 'cocaine factory' story and, not only had I done it, I had done it in just over five days. This left me with a further seven days 'in country' before my return flight. Rather than sit about partying with Dan, I resolved to try to find out where Garavito was being held.

It was remarkably easy. Jorge's girlfriend, Anna Santa-Maria, was in the fortunate position of being a government civil servant, working in a ministry in Bogotá. The 'fortunate' part was that, of all the other sectors of the Colombian workforce, the civil service stood the best chance of being regularly paid their wages. This gave them a social status over and above what it would have been otherwise.

Among her friends, Anna Santa-Maria numbered a presenter and director of news at state television called Julia Navarette. Julia was regularly to be seen reading the nightly news. She had covered the story for the network of all the young boys being murdered and of Garavito's arrest. A quick phone call was made and I was told that we would be meeting Julia that evening for drinks.

Julia was an attractive dark-haired woman in her thirties, whose photogenic looks and articulacy lent themselves perfectly to her chosen profession. Unfortunately, like the overwhelming majority of Colombians, she spoke little or no English. However, she was very friendly and consummately professional. She had presented many of the reports about Garavito and his crimes and had always felt that more should have been done on the subject.

Danny introduced me to her both as a magazine journalist and someone with contacts at the BBC. I stated that I was interested in Garavito with a view to doing a documentary for the BBC. This, in fact, wasn't too far from the truth. For many years I had been friends with the noted *Panorama* journalist Tom Mangold. We had met while he was doing a documentary on prisons and had corresponded and remained friends ever since. After my release, I had regularly consulted with him and his colleague at the BBC, Toby, regarding various TV projects. They were always on the lookout for suitable material.

Using the 'BBC' word was like uttering a magic incantation. In a world of rapidly deteriorating standards, the Beeb seemed to stand out as a beacon of fairness, accuracy and professionalism. Without ever having to prove a connection in any way, or even having to show my NUJ card, it opened doors that otherwise would have remained firmly closed.

We spent a delightful evening with Julia and members of her extended family at a restaurant in the suburbs of Bogotá. Seated around several tables in the cooler evening air, the company was extremely good, as was the food. The subject of Garavito seemed to fascinate and repulse the average Colombian in equal measure. They were only too well aware that, as a country, they held the dubious distinction of coming first on all the major crime and violence indicators. They took no pride whatsoever in the fact that now they had the world's worst serial killer.

Julia knew more about the subject than most. She had covered the growing outcry over the disappearances, then the manhunt and, finally, the arrest and trial. This had added to her already impressive list of contacts among Colombia's police and judiciary. As we parted, she announced that she had arranged a meeting for Danny and myself in the morning with the national director of the Fiscalia.

I was immediately both impressed and concerned. If I hadn't already known then, Danny would have soon told me that the Fiscalia was the premier law-enforcement agency in Colombia. It was a cross between the American FBI and our own Crown Prosecution Service, with an emphasis on the former. All the rest of Colombia's law enforcement might be something of a Mickey Mouse operation, but not the Fiscalia. Rumour had it that they had been trained by the CIA.

As one can imagine, I wasn't concerned only about my journalistic antecedents, or rather, the lack of them. There was always the small matter of my extremely serious criminal antecedents. These would certainly be held by Interpol and thus be only a mouse click away. Even with the most cursory of checks, the game would be up. It might not be enough to get me deported, but it would attract a lot of attention to me. I still had to get back to the UK with all the crucial photos for my 'cocaine kitchen' story. I didn't want to jeopardise that in any way.

Danny thought that it was all hugely amusing, just another interesting episode in that spaced-out reality that passed for his daily life. I did manage to force one major concession out of him though. For the duration of our visit to the Fiscalia, he would leave his little tin and its powdery white contents at home!

Noon the following day saw Danny, Julia and me seated around a table in the fortress-like building that housed Bogotá's Fiscalia. As someone with vast experience of top-security set-ups I was duly impressed. The high concrete walls, with state-of-the-art electronic surveillance paraphernalia draped everywhere, spoke of an organisation that was very much 21st century. My passport sufficed to get me through all the identity checks and screenings. Secretly I prayed that it would be enough to get me out again.

Pablo Elias Gonzalez was the national director of the entire Colombian Fiscalia. With him was his head of press, Alexandra Buitrago, and the forensic scientist who had investigated every scene of crime in the Garavito case, Dr Helga Quevedo. It could hardly have been a more high-powered meeting. I truly was flying by the seat of my pants.

Danny was introduced as our interpreter and it was certainly the universal lack of English that saved me. All questions were routed through him and any that could have been even slightly compromising were duly ignored and put down to having been lost in translation. Anyway, the Colombian tradition of politeness and good manners prevailed throughout. I further noticed that there was a healthy degree of openness in the way they conducted their business of governance, an object lesson to our own secrecy-obsessed Home Office.

There was another factor, of course, that of politics. It seemed that the national directorship was an elected post and that Señor Gonzalez was soon to stand for election again. Clearly, he felt that a prestigious documentary by the BBC, featuring himself prominently, would do his chances no harm whatsoever. However, there was also a genuine belief that this was an important case, with strong implications for other cases of its ilk, and that not enough had been done on it.

An animated discussion followed. They showed me a computerised file comprising their entire records on the Garavito case and printed me off a copy! They also gave me an 'in-house' video showing, among other things, scenes of crimes, Garavito in custody, mutilated bodies and arresting officers. Most importantly, Dr Quevedo was due to visit Garavito at the prison where he was being held at Villavicencio in two days' time. Arrangements were being made for us to visit Garavito with her.

An amazing relationship had sprung up between Garavito and Helga, a shy girl barely out of her teens. Since his confession, Garavito had turned his back on the world, refusing to meet with anyone but Helga and the priest. He was especially incensed by Colombian journalists, who had referred to him as a monster. Helga regularly visited to try to determine the location of further bodies. Garavito would hug her to him and cry. It was Helga who would ask Garavito to see us and to take part in the documentary.

Early Thursday morning, Danny, Julia and I set out on the three-hour drive to Villavicencio. Helga was going by plane. As on any road outside Bogotá, we could expect to be stopped not only by police and army checkpoints, but also by guerrilla ones. The latter eventuality would mean certain death for Helga. The guerrillas always shoot members of the Fiscalia on sight.

We descended from the chilly heights of Bogotá, through stunningly beautiful mountain gorges, to the tropical plains on which Villavicencio lay. Everywhere a confusion of greenery thrust itself skywards in an explosion of fecundity. In a country so blighted by human death it was as if nature itself were showing that it had the power to regenerate.

Villavicencio was hot. As long as the car was moving, cool air poured in through the windows. But as soon as we stopped, however fleetingly, sweat would spring wherever cloth met flesh. We quickly found the local Fiscalia building and were instantly grateful for its efficient air conditioning.

The local director, Carlos Arturo Torres, had obviously been briefed by his national director. He assured us that we were to be afforded every assistance. He informed us that Helga was arriving shortly and that we were all expected at the prison at 2 p.m.

Shortly afterwards, Helga arrived with the local chief of detectives. He was a short, stocky, tough-looking guy in his late thirties who had obviously been around. He had that naturally suspicious nature that, no doubt, makes for a good detective, coupled with something of a sixth sense. He picked up on me immediately. A couple of times I caught him looking at me thoughtfully while I was talking to someone else. Mentally, I made a note to be careful around this guy, lest I raise his suspicions further.

We all repaired to a local restaurant as guests of El Director. The food was sensational, the conversation lively. Once again I was spared probing questions by my lack of Spanish.

In a three-car convoy, we descended on the prison. There was immediately a problem, but I was expecting it. Prison guards are the same the world over. I'm sure there is a multinational somewhere that manufactures the basic model, probably in association with Microsoft. The gist of the matter was that they didn't give a flying fuck who we were. It wasn't visiting day and we didn't have a valid visiting order. So we couldn't see Garavito, who obviously wasn't their favourite prisoner anyway.

Impasse! But suddenly help arrived in the form of the senior prosecutor for the entire province. Dr Janet Espinosa was a statuesque, middle-aged woman in a flame-red evening gown that she had obviously been wearing at the function she had so recently left. Perhaps El Director had phoned her for help. Dr Espinosa didn't suffer fools gladly and, clearly, she felt that she was confronted by fools. Like sheep behind the shepherd, we followed in her wake as she forced a bridgehead through the assembled ranks of the guards and past the main gate. Here, in the no-man's-land between the inner and outer walls of the prison, battle commenced.

Various lower-order officials duly appeared and entered the fray. Overweight guards, carrying machine guns, pistols and riot sticks like small trees, milled about in confusion. Dr Espinosa was magnificent. Wielding her mobile phone like a short sword, she cut through the various levels of bureaucracy. One final telling phone call to someone extremely senior in Bogotá seemed to do the trick. But first we would have to leave until the paperwork was done.

Danny, Julia and I had been watching quite passively as the battle raged around us. Now, as I turned to leave, I asked Danny about the inscription over the gate leading to the inner prison proper. Danny translated it as saying, 'Here enters the man, not the crime.'

'Is that where Garavito is?' I asked Julia through Danny.

'No, he's over there,' she replied, pointing.

I followed the direction of her finger and saw a small, squat, one-roomed building that seemed to have been added almost as an afterthought to a one-storied white-painted administration office that stood barely 30 paces away. It had been built of concrete blocks and left unpainted. The whole thing looked decidedly temporary. The one window was heavily barred but unglazed. In the opening stood Helga and the figure next to her could only be Garavito. He had been watching us all the time.

We had been so close to him that now I didn't want to leave. However, there was no option. We withdrew to a café that stood opposite the jail and spent a fraught 20 minutes waiting for the next development. In the event, it was a compromise. 'They will allow you to see him, but only for ten minutes,' declared Dr Espinosa.

As we entered the jail again, two things that Helga had said kept coming back to me. 'Call him Alberto, not Luis. His father always called him Luis and it upsets him.' And, 'You mustn't show that you're afraid of him.'

The first warning I would strive to remember, but the second wasn't relevant at all. I had met too many crazy and dangerous killers in my time in jail. Most of these had chosen fully grown adults as their victims, yet I had stood my ground. In fact, a child killer like our Alberto here would have stood a very good chance of being severely bashed in many of our long-term jails. And more likely than not by me, had I had the good fortune to bump into him. So, of all the emotions that were exercising me at that moment, fear wasn't one of them.

Whatever was going on inside of me at an emotional level, though, at an intellectual level it was absolutely clear that I had to be professional. I truly felt that, in many ways, I was ideally suited to get into Garavito's head. Handled properly, he would be a fount of information on what drives serial killers. This information could be crucial in other investigations. It would take a while to win his confidence, but over time I was confident that he would more clearly describe this 'strange force' that overwhelmed him at the time of each killing.

I approached the barred window and put out my hand. Garavito reached through and shook it. As he rattled away in Spanish I was frantically trying to size him up in the short time I knew was available. Nondescript was the word that sprang to mind. He was the janitor of your apartment building whom you spoke to only in passing; he was the driver of the school bus. The handshake was weak, his eyes vacuous and empty. If he was a driven man, then the demon that had driven him was noticeably absent today.

According to Danny's translation, Alberto was very interested in the proposed documentary. He cursed the Colombian press for calling him a monster. Clearly, he felt that the BBC would be more circumspect. He stressed that he didn't want to be exploited.

All the time, Helga hovered in the background. I had been so focused on Garavito that I hadn't noticed anything else. Suddenly, I became aware of the dozens of canvasses that stood on easels, chairs and tables and were spaced about the room on the floor. Mentally, I gasped. They were quite breathtakingly beautiful. All were oil paintings showing in exquisite detail the flora and fauna of various jungle scenes. In the middle of each was the corpse of a young boy. This was how he was working with Helga to locate missing bodies. Garavito's recall was phenomenal. Each painting had proved accurate down to the last detail.

The juxtaposition of the two extremes of beauty and horror was spellbinding. With Garavito in the foreground and Helga drifting in and out of the paintings, it was all quite surreal. I was sure that, in such a setting, a documentary would prove to be mesmerising.

Suddenly, Garavito started to jig about and sing. The unexpected movement snapped me out of my reverie and caused me to jump. I instantly regretted it. I was determined to show no weakness to this man. Around me Helga, Julia and Danny were all smiling broadly. Quite clearly I was missing something.

Danny explained to me that the jingle Garavito was singing was from a popular Colombian TV soap called something like *Betty the Ugly*. Garavito had put his own words to it concerning himself. If nothing else it alerted me to the fact that our Alberto was something of a narcissist.

All too soon the visit was over. Garavito reiterated his intention of cooperating with the documentary and, in fact, signed a note to that effect which Danny had quickly drawn up. My enduring memory is of him standing among his paintings and waving as we retreated to the gate.

We assembled in the café opposite the prison again and this time we were joined by the director of the prison. Lieutenant Colonel Manuel Martinez had been 30 years in the police before assuming his present post. Strangely for someone in his position, he was a pleasant avuncular man, whose time-worn face seemed forever wreathed in smiles. He had never seen the like of Garavito. 'He is a stone in my shoe,' he confessed. 'It's a full-time job just keeping him alive. If the other inmates got hold of him they would kill him. So would some of the guards.'

Dr Espinosa joined us and proved to be a fount of information. As the senior prosecutor of the province, she had been the first to question Garavito. She maintained that he told her that the true number of his crimes was 1,800 murders and 3,000 rapes.

She further remarked on the significance of the area in which Garavito was born. Armenia, the capital town of the comparatively tiny Quindío province, has the highest number of Satanic groups of any town in Colombia. The previous year, Armenia was devastated by an earthquake. The local people said that it was God's punishment.

Back in Bogotá, I was jubilant. Not only had I managed to do the cocaine-factory story, to the delight of Eoin and *Front*, I now had a potential TV documentary for the BBC as well. I immediately phoned Tom Mangold and filled him in on all the details. I fully expected to be coming back the following week with a TV crew.

Tom's tone was doubtful. 'What language does he speak?' he queried.

'Well, Colombian Spanish, of course Tom.' I couldn't fathom why he was being so obtuse. All was soon to be revealed though.

'That's the problem, Norman. We had a good line into an Indian serial killer but he only spoke Urdu. If they don't speak English the Beeb aren't interested.'

So, even though I had been the only journalist ever to be allowed to meet with Garavito and had a world exclusive for a documentary, no one was interested in doing it. I cursed the realities of the media world I was still only discovering.

On the plane back I measured the numerological significance of Garavito's name. Using the system A = 6, B = 12, C = 18, D = 24, etc., I summed the letters of 'Garavito'. I got the number 558. If you further sum 5 + 5 + 8, you get the number 18. The significance of 18 is that it is the sum of three sixes.

And as we all know, 666 is the number of the Beast!

CHAPTER NINE

BE CAREFUL WHAT YOU WISH FOR

Just try to imagine this. You and five of your friends are going away for the weekend. You get off the train at the ferry terminal and the port police take you aside. They put each of you in a separate room and say that the local police are coming and they want to talk to you.

The local police arrive and immediately start screaming at you that you're dirty murdering bastards. Bombs have gone off in your home town, killing dozens and maiming hundreds. You protest that it's nothing to do with you, but the police say they don't care, because you're going down for it anyway.

Over the next three days, they beat, threaten and torture you all until some of your friends can't take it any more. They sign statements admitting guilt. At the subsequent trial, you're all convicted of mass murder and sentenced to life imprisonment. It takes 16 years for you to prove your innocence!

On the night of 21 November 1974, the IRA's mainland bombing campaign reached an unprecedented level of murder and mayhem. There have been claims that warnings were given, but the stark facts are that at 8.18 p.m. a blast ripped through the Mulberry Bush bar in central Birmingham, killing 10 people and injuring 40.

Two minutes later, a second bomb went off in the packed basement bar of the Tavern in the Town. That blast killed 11 and injured 126, mostly young people.

There was a massive outpouring of public anger and revulsion at the outrage. It was accompanied by a fierce backlash against Britain's Irish community. Consequently, the police were under immense pressure to find the culprits and get convictions. Six Irishmen, domiciled in England, were beaten, tortured and made to sign confessions that were eventually to get them life sentences.

A long drawn-out campaign was started by the men, who subsequently came to be known as the Birmingham Six by the media, to prove their innocence. It was only after the intervention of the Labour MP Chris Mullin, followed by two ITV *World in Action* reports, that they were released. They had served 16 years!

I believed the Birmingham Six were innocent long before they were finally cleared on appeal and released. Not that it was a subject that occupied my attention in any meaningful way. Every jail has its complement of innocent men. For the rest of us trying to survive the tragedy that our own lives had become, it was nothing important. If we thought of them at all, it was that they were 'poor sods'. At least we had done something to merit our sentences.

On my travels from one top-security jail to another, no matter how the regimes might differ, there was always one constant. At recreation time and exercise time out on the prison yard or sports field, the IRA prisoners would always congregate together. The most senior IRA man in the jail would automatically be the commanding officer, for these were men who considered themselves to be prisoners of war, not convicts. He would 'hold court' with the other IRA men. Although they did mix quite widely with other prisoners at other times, these meetings were solely for IRA members.

I was with all the Birmingham Six in various jails and at various times. Never once did I see them sit with the IRA. The real IRA men would tell us that the Six weren't and never had been members. To many English prisoners, that was too fine a distinction to make, so they shunned them anyway. They wandered, lonely, tormented and ghostlike, across a human landscape blighted by tragedy and suffering.

I had been in Gartree Prison with Paddy Hill, one of the Six. I was there for only three months, yet never spoke to Paddy or even noticed him. Innocent or not, that was the degree to which he had become a faceless person in the human warehouse that is our long-term prison system.

After my release, though, I did see quite a lot of him. Paddy had formed an organisation called MOJO (Miscarriages of Justice Organisation) to fight for miscarriage-of-justice prisoners still incarcerated. Much of the journalism I was doing was related to criminal-justice issues. I also got involved in the cases of other innocent men. It was inevitable that we would meet.

I was always impressed by Paddy's concern for others. He gave of himself tirelessly for countless campaigns, usually started by the innocent person's family. And there was no 'grandstanding' with Paddy. He wasn't after recognition, or even thanks. He genuinely identified with the person's predicament and wanted to do all he could to help.

As an experienced and skilled observer of the human condition, I couldn't help but make certain assessments about Paddy. They were so starkly obvious. Although neither nasty nor vicious in any way, either by word or deed, he seethed with a barely suppressed anger. At times, it exercised him to such an extent that he could hardly keep still.

Once he started talking about miscarriages of justice, it would all pour out of him. He would fulminate and rage against the system in an uninterrupted torrent of pure bile. Sentences would be run together, liberally littered with foul language. If it was a cathartic release, it certainly didn't leave him spent and at peace. The anger and pain inside of him seemed utterly bottomless.

He readily confessed to bouts of uncontrollable rage, coupled with periods of deep depression. He slept only intermittently for a few hours each night. Often he would feel trapped in his apartment and would go for long walks at all hours of the day or night. He couldn't relate at all to people. It had caused absolute chaos in his family life. Unable to relate to his wife or children, he had left them. This caused him severe feelings of guilt.

So, even though he had physically left the prison sentence behind, it had not left him. Its mark was on him for every second of every day of his life. As someone who had experienced an extended period of extreme hardship and suffering myself, I had made something of a study about how people dealt with such things. I spoke to Eoin about doing an interview with Paddy Hill for *Front*, and he was very much up for it. For the magazine article I edited and structured the interview to make it easier to read. But here I will let Paddy speak to you himself, verbatim.

Norman: Paddy, can I just take you back? I know it will be painful. First, was there a book?

Paddy: I wrote a book, *Forever Lost, Forever Gone*.

N: So, Paddy, you'd never been nicked before in your life?

P: Oh, no, I'd been nicked before. I had a criminal record, violence, gang warfare, slicings and all that. GBH, wounding with intent to commit, et cetera, all part and parcel of coming over here and growing up in Birmingham. It was a very racialist city and very gang-oriented. The problems that I encountered when I first came over were not really mine. Most of my problems were my younger brothers and my sister, people picking on them. We were a big family, six of us and I was more than capable of taking care of myself.

And of course, coming out of the backstreets of Belfast, I'm the first person to admit that I was a vicious little bastard. But was a very happy-go-lucky guy, er, I was involved in taking and driving away. I loved motorbikes. I was only a kid, 15, just left school in '59, then brought over to Birmingham.

To be honest, I didn't want to come over, but I had so many family over here, uncles and aunts and cousins et cetera, so we ended up coming over because there was nothing in Belfast for us, no work et cetera, usual thing. And my father had just come out of the British Army after 30 years' service in '59 and the reason he left, he was in the Territorial Army and he was an unarmed-combat and weapons instructor for the British Army, but they wanted to make him the resident SM and they wanted us to move to Hollyrood Barracks, and anyone who knows the geography of Northern Ireland, that's like going into the lion's den, and of course we weren't going to come out of the Ardoyne into there so my father came out of the British Army, but my older brother and the second eldest of six joined the British Army and came over here. Then my dad came over, then me mum. Then they came back over to Belfast and took us all over. And, of course, I lived in different parts of Birmingham and ended up in a place called Summer Lane.

At the time it was probably the poorest area of Birmingham. It's where all the poor Brummies ... and a lot of them had Irish connections, marriage, et cetera, Scots and, as I say, I just fell in love with it. And of course I ended up meeting a girl and I fell in love with her and got married and by the time I got married I'd, for want of a better word, made a bit of a reputation for myself, and everybody knew to leave the family alone and that was it, like.

There was me and three mates and we all looked after each other, you know. There were four Scots fellas and three Irish.

There were seven of us and the biggest one was five feet four, and we were all, like, vicious, but we looked after each other and our families and that was what it was all about. And I'm very proud of the fact that, even though I've got a criminal record, none of my brothers have. I sent them all to college. They became master tradesmen. One of them's a master carpenter. Another's a master builder, et cetera, and none of them's ever been in trouble. I took all the trouble being the oldest one there. I thought it was my job and, if someone had to go to jail, I was prepared to go to jail and I did it.

N: It was old-time values.

P: Exactly, and that's the way it was in the old areas. Everybody stuck together. And by the time 1974 came around I was a happily married man. I had five daughters and, of course, I had a son. He was the youngest of the six. And to all intents and purposes my world was complete. We'd always wanted a son and my world was complete. And of course in 1972 in Ireland things had escalated and the Provisional IRA, which had just been set up then after the civil-rights thing in '60.

After that was set up, someone in the army command at home in the IRA made a decision to take the war to the mainland. And in and around the Midlands between 1972, which culminated in the Birmingham pub bombings in November 1974, there was probably about 60 to 70 bombings that had occurred in and around a 30- to 40-mile radius of Birmingham. And of course during all those attacks, up till then, the only fatalities was one person dropped dead down in the Old Bailey bomb from a heart attack, and the only other fatality was a bomb-disposal expert in Birmingham who tried to defuse a bomb. And of course everybody knows that most of the IRA's deaths in those days were what were called 'own goals', because the method of bomb making then was very crude compared to the technique they have today.

That has become so sophisticated over the years. And then in 1974, in August, the whole pattern of bombing in this country changed for some unknown reason, and before that bombs that were planted – there was always adequate warning for the areas to be safely cordoned off. And until mid-'74 the exact locations were always given. There was never any obscurity about them – they were precise and exact. And, due to that saving grace, there were no people that were injured or killed before then.

But then the whole pattern changed and we had the M62 coach bombing, which a young English girl, Judith Ward, was convicted largely due to evidence given by the same people who fitted me up. Of course, shortly after that came the Guildford and Woolwich bombs in the October.

N: When was the M62 bomb?

P: That was in August '74 and then there was the Guildford and Woolwich in October '74. And of course, in between there was other bombs in and around the country. But the next major one was the Birmingham pub bombings. And the revulsion that that sent around the country was – I must confess I have never read an account in a newspaper, anything, about the Birmingham pub bombings. By the time I got access to the newspapers it had sort of disappeared from ... you know. And the only news that was in the newspapers then was the fact of us going to court every Thursday on remand.

N: So you were actually on your way over to Ireland when you were arrested?

P: I was. On the night in question, in 1974, in November. James McDade, a young Irishman from Ardoyne in Belfast, who I grew up with, who comes from the same area as me. And of course, one of my co-defendants, Jerry Hunter, we all lived together in Birmingham, we worked together, although I didn't see much of McDade – he was a loner. But Jerry Hunter and myself were very pally – we worked on numerous painting firms and what have you. And Johnny Walker and Richard McKilkenny, we all came from the same area, Hughie Callaghan. And we knew James McDade and, of course, when he blew himself up … I didn't find out until the Sunday. I thought at first it was a Scots fella because of the way it was being pronounced. And I found out on the Sunday and I found out Jerry and them were going to go home for the funeral and, of course, I made my arrangements as well, because I had an aunt, my aunt Mary, who reared me in the Ardoyne. We lived next door to my aunt and my granny. So I was going home to see my aunt and also, as I said at my trial, I would have paid my respects to Mr and Mrs McDade on the death of his son and, of course, at that particular time and even up to the present moment, people in the upper classes in this country, especially judges in the courts, they have a very hard time understanding Irish culture. They don't seem to understand and never wanted to understand that, in relation to funerals, funerals are probably the biggest business in Ireland and they are carried out with such reverence et cetera, and as I try to tell people when I am speaking at universities and public meetings, if I had a choice to go to a funeral or a wedding, I would take the funeral. And the reason why, if it was a drink and you like the craic, and at that time I did, if you go to a wedding, the wedding only starts on the Saturday and finishes on the Sunday and that's it. But, if you go to a funeral, the funeral lasts for a week. And everybody sits around telling yarns. It's a non-stop craic for three or four days while the body lies in state at home. And, of course, I would have gone to McDade's funeral, not as the prosecution put up at the trial that we were going to honour a big IRA hero et cetera. Bullshit! It goes to show how ignorant the judges are and the upper classes are in this country in respect of the IRA or anything Irish. In relation to the IRA, they never display any form of heroism for anyone. They don't have any other rank other than one and the only rank they have is the quartermaster. In our trial they put us up as: Johnny Walker was a brigadier, there was lieutenants, there was fucking captains, you name it. And Billy Power who had only joined, who had only joined the IRA a half-hour before, according to the prosecution, and he became a lieutenant instantly. People like us laugh because we have to, but it's so stupid, but this is the sort of things that were portrayed at our trial.

N: At what stage did you realise that you were in trouble?

P: I remember I had very mixed feelings, because people were under the impression that we were arrested. We were never arrested. When we got to Heysham boat station I met a cop there who, a detective constable of Heysham port security, he was from Morecambe police force. He questioned me. I had a wonderful time with that man and his sidekick, a superior officer, a Sergeant Watson, and I was involved with two police forces. The one the Morecambe police force and the other the West Midlands Serious Crimes Squad. In relation to the Morecambe police force, I have only one complaint against them. And that complaint is in respect to the way they closed ranks and didn't come forward to tell the truth about us being tortured at the police station. They admitted off the record you could hear the screaming and they knew that we were getting battered and tortured something terrible, but none of them come forward and still have not today. But in respect of my treatment in the hands of the Morecambe police, they couldn't have treated the royal family any better. I have nothing but the utmost respect for them. And with Detective Constable Willoughby I had the craic with him, and on television that was portrayed that there was some sort of hue and cry and big police blockade on the ports. Bullshit! There wasn't even a cop on Heysham port security when we got there, and, when we come through the door on to the concourse, there were half a dozen plastic tables laid out with two cops on each, and I walked up to one of them and he asked me where I was coming from and I told him where I was going, Belfast, et cetera, and he asked me to step into the office and I asked him where it was and he pointed behind him at a Portakabin and he asked me a number of questions: where I was coming from, where I was going, my age, normal routine, because I'd been in the hands of the police. He asked me if I owed any fines, but I said I paid them. I told him that I had criminal convictions, but wasn't wanted by the police. I told him I was clean, have been for years. We had a great craic and we come out of there and was talking about the football match the night before. He walked me along the concourse and took me up the gangplank of the boat and we stood there talking for about ten minutes and he wished me a good voyage. And he came back on the boat about a half an hour later and took me off and told me that the officer in charge wanted to talk to me. That there had been some explosion in England. And when I come off there I went over to the security offices and went in and it was then that Sergeant Bell had informed me that bombs had gone off in Birmingham, and I'll never forget his words. He told me, quote, 'Excuse the pun, Paddy, you know how things get blown up out of all proportion, but this is serious. Bombs have blown up and there have been over 200 people injured and there's 14 killed, but I can tell you it's serious.' I said, 'I understand, sir.' And he asked me if I had any objections to seeing Birmingham police. I said, 'No, what time's the next train back?' He said that there was no train till the morning, but not to worry because Birmingham police would come down and take a statement from me. But would I mind going down to Heysham?

N: So where are the others?

P: I was taken into a little office, so I think they are getting the same treatment. But I'm clean so I don't give a fuck. I waited about ten minutes, got in a car with two policemen and drove down to Morecambe police station a few miles away and got there about two o'clock in the morning, pissing down with rain and it was a brand-new police station. That's the thing I remember better than anything.

It was glittering like a jewel in the fucking desert, you know what I mean? I got out the car and walked up the steps of the station and as I walked up those steps I never dreamed for one second, Norman, that those were the last steps of freedom I'd take for sixteen and a half years. I walked into the police station and Sergeant Willoughby came in after me and told the desk sergeant that I was waiting to be interviewed. And he said, 'You can put your feet there, Paddy.' And I sat right next to the door for three-quarters of an hour and the desk sergeant got up twice and left.

I could have got up and walked out of the police station any time. A short time after, Willoughby came back with a detective sergeant and we went into an office and I made a detailed statement about my movements for 48 hours.

N: Which, as an experienced criminal, you wouldn't have done?

P: I give them my home address, phone number, everything, gave them the information with respect to my criminal record, when I got out of jail the last time, et cetera, et cetera, and I gave them a full detailed statement and they went away and I'm sitting there, and they came back at half past six in the morning and they told me they checked me out, et cetera, et cetera, and that everything I had told them was 100 per cent correct, including the fact that I was with the others and that we had stopped at Crewe to change trains and that I'd bought the teas and coffees. And I'm sitting in the custody area on a little bench, reading a book that one of the cops had given me. And I remember the door opened and I've got two uniformed cops in sight. One of them was Scots and we're having a great craic. We'd been slagging each other off about the football and the boxing and the door opened and I looked up and these two guys walked in and they had bundles of clothes, shirts and jackets in their arms and they dumped them behind the door, and I could feel that they were glowering at me and I happened to look up and I could feel the vibes coming off them. And I looked outside the door and there was another guy, only he had a .38 Colt Smith and Wesson shoulder holster with a gun in it and he had one on his hip and I remember thinking to myself, Fuck me, some poor bastard's in for a rough ride. And I never dreamed for one second that it was me. And then, about half past seven, I'm sitting on the bench and I knew I'm in trouble then.

There was a cop, about six feet two, 17 stone, with a military look, and he's standing over me rubbing his hands. And I was a lot heavier then, Norman, about 14 stone, 46-inch chest and 19-inch neck. I was like a little bull. And he said to me, 'See you, you little bastard, you dirty, murdering, little Irish fuck-pig.' And he spat right in my face. And I went like, 'What the fuck are you on about?' And he pushed me down in the chair and said, 'You'll find out soon enough, you dirty, little murdering cunt.' And he spat in my face again and walked away.

And that's when I realised I was in trouble. I never realised I was in serious trouble until the Saturday. They'd been battering me all day the Friday, Saturday. Just how much trouble I realised about half past six on the Saturday night. I was brought back after my second interview. They'd been at me from about a quarter to nine in the morning to five thirty. I try to tell people this and people find it amazing, but I have never, ever been questioned about the Birmingham pub bombings in my life, not even by the West Midlands Serious Crime Squad.

N: So they'd already made up their minds, eh?

P: Two cops told me, quote, 'We know you didn't do it. We don't give a fuck who done it. Our orders are that we're to get the confessions and the convictions and to use any means possible. It keeps the public off our gaffer's back and our gaffer off our back.' Unquote.

He pulled a piece of paper out of his pocket. He picked me up by the hair and lifted me up and shoved the piece of paper under my nose and said, 'Read that, you fucking murdering bastard, read it. That's our orders: get confessions and convictions, signed right to the top. We can do what we like, we can take you out and shoot you if we want. You're going to jail, end of story. You can have it the easy way or the fucking hard way, and the easy way –' He picked up the statement form and said, 'Sign under the caution, sign the bottom right-hand corner. We can fill it in. You can have it the easy way or the hard way.' And I said, 'I ain't—' And that was as far as I got. They knocked me off the chair and kicked me up and down the floor again, and this carried on until half past five on the Friday. And of course, at intermittent times, they were telling me that my co-defendants were making statements admitting that they'd done this, and that I was the bomb maker. I was the explosive expert, et cetera, et cetera, and of course, I didn't believe any of this. I knew the old fucking police routine. And they took us back down to Birmingham and tried to throw me out on the motorway and put guns in my mouth in the car, broke all me teeth. And that's why I had to have special implants. I had no gums or nothing – my gums were busted. And they battered me again on the Saturday morning. They kept me awake all the Friday night with guns, terrorising us. And then the Saturday morning took me out and photographed me, fingerprinted me. Took me upstairs about seven o'clock in the morning and then they were battering me from then until one o'clock. I remember a cop looking at his watch and saying it was five to one and they were going to go for their dinner.

I was out in the cells area and they came back about three o'clock and they carried on battering me to about half past five, six o'clock. They said they were going to go for their tea and they would be back afterwards.

And that afternoon they told me that Billy Powers had made a statement and he'd said this, that and the other. And they brought this statement, but they wouldn't let me see it. They read bits and pieces of it, you know. They also told me that my ex-wife had made one, saying that I was in the IRA and all this, but I knew it was all a load of bollocks, because I wasn't in the IRA. When I got back to my cell I bent down and whispered through the vent, you know the old prison routine, but they threatened to batter us more if they heard us whispering through the vent, and it was Billy Power. And I said, 'Billy, the cops say that you've signed a statement. Please, Billy, son, tell me it isn't true.' And Billy Power just bursted out crying and he said, 'I'm sorry, Paddy Joe, but I couldn't take any more, I can't take it.' And I said, 'Don't worry, son, it will be sorted out when we get to court.'

But I knew then that it was all over. And, as it turned out, we didn't go for trial, we were already convicted. All we went for was to be sentenced. They talk about a fair trial and all that. When we finally got out they refused to put the cops up on trial even though there was more evidence – we had concrete evidence – to show that they had falsified everything. And they refused to put them up on trial.

The magistrate said that they wouldn't get a fair trial because of all the adverse publicity. Adverse publicity! Well, even before we were charged on the Sunday, we had the Assistant Chief Constable of Birmingham on television that weekend, with our photographs and everything, and we hadn't even made a court appearance yet. And our photographs are on television and he's telling the whole world, 'We caught the people who done the bombings, they're covered in gelignite, these are the people who planted the bombs, et cetera, et cetera.' Adverse publicity!

N: Did we ever meet in jail, Paddy?

P: Yes, we met in Gartree Jail. I got slung out of Gartree five times and they had to bring me back because no other jail would take me. I spent the first four years in Gartree, in the block practically, working on my case, and I spent most of it in solitary, and it was only in – what? – 1985, when the *World in Action* programme came out, that they started getting off my back, you know what I mean?

N: So, when you first got out did you immediately get involved in the protest movement for other people?

P: Oh, yes. Before I got out, I had been with Jimmy Robinson of the Bridgewater Four, also Brian Parsons and a number of other people, and I told Jimmy – I was naive enough – I told Jimmy that I'd give him the first year of my life. Nine months after us, the Tottenham Three were cleared, but immediately after that the gate came down.

During the first year I was out, I picked up a number of cases along the way. Since I've been out I've been involved with about a hundred people. I'm glad to say the vast majority have gone to the Court of Appeal. Two weeks after I got out, I got £50,000 as an interim payment. I'd like to say I spent it, but I squandered it. I had no valuation of money.

No one spoke to me since I left jail. The last one to speak to me was the Appeal Court judge, who said we were free to leave and that's the last person of officialdom who spoke to me.

N: Paddy, at least I had the consolation of knowing I did what I did to get in jail, but you didn't have that.

P: I could never come to terms with it. I used to walk up and down that fucking cell every night and I kept asking myself over and over again, 'What the fuck am I doing here? Why am I here?' And even today I say, like the way the courts have done it, no charges against the police. In the last ten years, approximately 300 people have been released by the courts, wrongfully imprisoned, and they've probably served between them about 3,000 years, and nobody's done anything wrong, not one police officer has stood on trial.

N: And this is why you formed MOJO?

P: Well, since I've come out I've been campaigning on my own. I got £300,000 in interim payments and the only thing I've bought myself is a flat in Muswell Hill – cost me £100,000 – and I've spent about £100,000 or more campaigning for people here and all round Europe, America, et cetera. And I've always paid my own way, never been paid for anything. Even when I go to speak, I'd pay for myself.

I was spending a couple of hundred pounds a week and it ended up, last year, well, I'm on income support. I'm getting deeper and deeper in debt, but what I want to do is set up a network of MOJO offices. However, under the new legislation that has been introduced by Jack Straw [then Home Secretary], he now states that the officer in charge of the case will be the officer who decides what is and what is not evidence, that officer will also be the officer to say which of the evidence, if any, he wishes to disclose to the defence, and also, after five years, paperwork of the case will be destroyed. Everyone knows that, in respect of miscarriage-of-justice cases, under the present system that is being run by the government, mainly the Criminal Cases Review Commission, the way the system runs, everyone knows the two biggest things in miscarriages of justice. One is very bad legal representation. The commission and the government say that 65 per cent of people wouldn't be wrongly convicted if they had decent legal representation. The other big thing is nondisclosure with regard to legal representation. What it means is that the cops can go into court and get away with saying anything they like. People say that the system hasn't learned anything. I tell people that that's the biggest, stupidest remark they will ever make. In actual fact, the system has learned a hell of a lot. Under the new legislation, they've learned how not to get caught so easily.

N: The whole experience seems to have affected you very badly. What are the worst things?

P: The depression. My major problem is depression. The doctors told me that I had been living in a depressed state for so long that it was now normal for me. They recommended to the Home Office that I get five years' deep psychological counselling. Post-traumatic stress and Vietnam syndrome were both mentioned. The anti-depressants didn't work. The only thing that did work was to smoke loads and loads of cannabis. If I travelled to a new place, I didn't want to go out and kept bursting into tears all the time. I had no appetite. I couldn't sleep. I felt angry and frustrated all the time.

N: You've been out for 12 years now. Is this getting better or worse?

P: That old cliché of time being a wonderful healer is a lot of bollocks. If you're lucky, it helps you to come to terms with it a bit better, but it doesn't heal fuck all.

In 2003, Marsha suddenly decided that I had wasted far too much time gallivanting about the world on what she thought to be pointless assignments and that I should now do something positive with my life. She suggested that I should do a master's degree in criminology. I already had a BA Hons, which I had passed in prison. This didn't impress Marsha one bit. She had two honours degrees and two master's degrees and was on the verge of getting her doctorate. By comparison, I was something of a dunce.

I did argue that, at 58, I was a bit too old to start a career in criminology. Marsha's answer to that was that people of 80 regularly took and passed various degrees. It did interest me, though. I was very knowledgeable about criminal matters and I did think that, perhaps, I could bring a new perspective to the discipline. All it would cost me was three and a half grand of my money and nine months of my life!

Initially, the powers-that-be at Surrey University refused to accept me. They seemed to be troubled by the small matter of my murder and manslaughter convictions. I contemplated arguing along the lines that for many years I had been working on mastering the *practical* side of criminology; now I wanted to move on to the theoretical. However, one man's irony is another man's sarcasm. Instead, I got my MP, my probation officer and the head of a prisoners' rights group to phone up and complain.

It was a pushover. Terrified of being seen as politically incorrect towards any minority, even one as esoteric as ex-murderers, they accepted me, with the proviso that all the other students should be warned about me. It was just as well that I had developed a thick skin over the years. I wouldn't have cared if no one had talked to me. In the event, everyone in the social sciences department was very friendly.

The criminology course was in its first year. There were five students: I and four women. Assessment for the degree came in two parts. The first was based on assignments, the second on a piece of original research, a thesis. The subject matter for my thesis came to me right away.

Through associating with Paddy and getting involved in miscarriage-of-justice issues I had met several other wrongfully imprisoned men. There is a prison term used to describe someone whose mental state is in considerable disarray. We say that they are 'shot to pieces'. All of the wrongfully imprisoned men I had met were *thoroughly* shot to pieces.

I had wondered why they should be like this when the vast majority of guilty men who had done very long sentences had survived in much better mental condition. I decided to make this the subject of my thesis. If it had been an article for *Front*, no doubt I would have called it SHOT TO PIECES. In social-science jargon, it didn't have quite that ring, becoming, 'Coping strategies and enduring psychological trauma in some miscarriage of justice victims'. Here is the 'Conclusion'.

> There is abundant evidence that human beings are affected by their environment, whether it be by the mechanism of 'dynamic interchange' (p. 5) as described by Ittelson, Rivlin, Proshansky and Winkel (1974), or by some less interactive method. And if they are going to be affected by any environment, then they are most surely going to be affected by prison, that harshest of human environments so eloquently described by Toch (1979, 1992). However, the point at issue here is how deeply the individual will be affected, and will the effects be lasting and, perhaps, irreversible?
>
> There is much in the literature to support the argument that significant psychological damage can be caused by a prison sentence. However, once a rigorous scientific methodology is applied to the results, there is little evidence to show that it will endure after the inmate leaves the institution.
>
> Zamble and Porporino (1988) predict that, 'most men will return to some approximation of their behaviour before imprisonment' (p. 148). Following their review of the literature, Walker (1993) and Gearing (1979) agree.
>
> My own experience and that of the three lifers I interviewed for the control group also strongly support this position. Jack equates the experience to that of his school or army days. When Peter thinks of the prison years he just thinks of the good times. For John it was 'an education you can't buy'. For my part, I still have many prison friends with whom I regularly talk about the old times and manage to laugh.
>
> As traumatic as the experience was at the time, it has left no lasting, harmful effects. There is no sleep disturbance, fear of crowds, traumatic association, difficulty with relationships, or any of the other conditions that seem to afflict the 'miscarriage of justice' group. If Peter now considers himself to be a 'well-

balanced, reasonable guy', then perhaps this description fits all four of us. The experience is behind us.

The same cannot be said for the six men in the sample group. There are the grave diagnoses by the many psychiatrists they have seen between them, and, especially, those of Dr Adrian Grounds. Apart from this, Paddy Hill, Raff Rowe, Michael Davis and John Kamara all show clear signs of dyscontrol and disequilibrium. According to Menninger's categories, they are not coping. If we include self-intoxication and narcotisation, neither is Bob Maynard.

Similarly, none of this group fits neatly into Goffman's categories of coping strategies. The closest is Goffman's 'intransigent line', but this is 'typically a temporary and initial phase or reaction, with the inmate shifting to situational withdrawal or some other line of adaption' (p. 62). However, the inmates of the 'miscarriage of justice' sample group maintained their 'intransigence' for the 12, 16 or 20 years of their incarceration.

When we come to examine the coping strategies of the control group vis-à-vis the sample group we see significant differences. All the control group settled down comparatively quickly in their sentences. Even I abandoned my escapes and 'prison activist' role after ten years. This means that the four of us had many years of stable, if monotonous, prison routine before we were released.

Further, we all enjoyed the support of prison friendships. Peter says, 'I couldn't have made it without the support of my fellow prisoners.' Jack talks about how he 'got support from other inmates and found them to be good fellas'. John speaks of other inmates taking him under their wing and I had support from the Londoners' criminal network.

Paddy has referred to the support he got from other prisoners, but in his own words he was, 'in and out of blocks, 40 moves and lie-downs, thrown out of Gartree nine times'.

This also involved a considerable period of solitary confinement. John Kamara did 16 years in solitary. Raff and Michael spent long periods in isolation in the punishment block. This lifestyle is not conducive to either forming or maintaining friendships in prison. I, and the others of the control group, enjoyed the social support of friendships that often lasted several years.

Then there is the enormous damage that solitary confinement does to the psyche.

'Miscarriage of justice' victims typically do far longer spells in *solitary than normal prisoners, so this in itself could be a contributory factor to their experiencing enduring psychological problems on release.*

I, and many other prisoners who were 'career criminals', also had the support of a sustaining ideology. I believed that the distribution of wealth in society was unfair and a spirited man would, of necessity, come into conflict with the law. Imprisonment then becomes an unwelcome, if not entirely unexpected, result of this outlook.

McKorkle and Korn (1954) reflect something of this view when they say, 'In many ways, the inmate social system may be viewed as providing a way of life which enables the inmate to avoid the devastating psychological effects of internalising and converting social rejection into self-rejection. In effect, it permits the inmate to reject his rejectors rather than himself' (p. 58 in Goffman). Needless to say, the innocent 'miscarriage of justice' victim does not have the support of this or any other inmate-sustaining ideology.

Another factor is the effect of being different, being 'innocent' in a world of guilty men and how much this set them apart from their fellow prisoners. From my own experience, in the cynical world of long-term prisons, there is little sympathy for 'innocent' men. If anything, they remind other prisoners of that especially traumatic early period when they themselves were fighting to prove their innocence. They failed and have moved on. They are settled down, doing their time and don't need to be reminded of it. Raff's remark, 'I made no friends in prison' is deeply disturbing. I have never, ever heard of anyone before who never made a friend in prison. It is symptomatic of all that is wrong about the way he forced himself to do his time. There is little doubt in my mind that the way the sample group forced themselves to do their time, the isolation, etc., is a major, contributory factor to the subsequent enduring psychological damage. However, it isn't the whole story. There is a final trigger.

Maynard and Dudley are the two 'miscarriage of justice' victims who spent the longest in prison. Yet, on the face of it, they have suffered nothing like the enduring psychological damage that the other four of the sample group have. So, if the contention of this paper is that a further effect of suffering a miscarriage of justice is enduring psychological harm, what is it that is different in the cases of Maynard and Dudley?

At first sight, Maynard and Dudley could have been members of the control group. They quickly settled into the prison routine, without recourse to disobedience and rule breaking. It could even be said that Dudley fits Goffman's category of 'colonisation' by using his painting ability to take the maximum advantage of privileges available.

Both were committed criminals in so far as they had extensive criminal records and had served significant jail sentences. Both were supported by networks of friends in prison. In Dudley's words, 'It was no hardship going into prison ... you know the routine.'

And like the control group, they have emerged from prison with little obvious psychological damage. They have reintegrated themselves into their social milieu in a comparatively short time. There is some underlying bitterness, but nothing like that of the other 'miscarriage of justice' victims. Neither is there traumatic association with all things that remind them of prison. On interview, both were relaxed and as 'normal' as any of the control group. There was little to distinguish them from men who had never been in prison.

When pressed for an explanation of how he had re-adapted so well, and with so little obvious psychological damage, Maynard suggested that it was a function of his having been a professional criminal. As a professional criminal he had expected to go to prison.

He even went so far as to say that, had he been framed for the sort of crime that he had actually committed, though not been caught for, he could have fully accepted it. Dudley certainly shared the 'professional criminal's' outlook too.

So perhaps that was it, then. Even though Kamara had done a four and a half year sentence for armed robbery and Rowe and Davis had both served short sentences for minor crimes, perhaps it was the fact that Maynard and Dudley had considered themselves to be professional criminals (with all the mindset that went with that) that prevented the latter pair from suffering enduring psychological harm. I wasn't really convinced.

Then I realised something that had not fully registered with me before. Both Maynard and Dudley had been released from prison in the conventional way that most long-term prisoners are released. They had gone through the whole procedure of open prison, town visits, working outside, home leaves, working on the hostel scheme and finally release. It was after they had been released that they had been cleared.

Talking of the release procedure, Cohen and Taylor (1972) say, 'there is much attention in ordinary prisons to preparing the inmate for this transition: vocational training, halfway hostels, pre-release programs'. They also refer to, 'the psychological "bends" the men will face as they re-surface.'

Apocryphal tales abound of the old lag who has served all his sentence in a closed prison only to refuse to leave on the final day due to an inordinate fear of freedom itself.

There are very few 'frills' in prison. The prison authorities do not waste money on things that have no proven, practical worth. The pre-release procedure is expensive in terms of both staff time and prison resources. It is there for a good reason.

When I am asked what my first day of freedom was like after more than 20 years inside, I always ask in return what day they are referring to. Is it my first 'town walk' with the Governor; my first 'town walk' on my own, my first day 'working outside'; my first day with my mother on home leave or even my first day on the hostel scheme? It most certainly wasn't that last day when they finally signed the paper and let me go.

For the average long-term prisoner, freedom is a lengthy procedure rather than an event.

For 'miscarriage of justice' victims it is an event, and a cataclysmic one at that. Except for Maynard and Dudley, all were taken from their cells in a closed prison and released within hours. What a supreme irony it would be if the very thing they had yearned for, for so many years, immediate freedom, was the very thing that did them enduring psychological harm!

So, be careful what you wish for!

Anyone wishing to read the thesis in its entirety can find it on my website at http://www.parkerstales.com.

CHAPTER TEN

SEE AND BLIND, HEAR AND DEAF

Living inside the long-term prison system year after year, one couldn't help but become something of a criminologist, albeit an amateur one. The talk is inevitably about crime, its nature, causes and trends. Further, with each influx of the newly convicted comes the latest news of what's really happening out on the street. So we were always well informed.

Throughout the eighties, into the nineties and right up to the present day, you could not fail but to notice the phenomenal rise in gun crime. Shootings in general and murder by shooting used to be comparatively rare crimes, and then seen mostly in the big cities such as London, Manchester and Glasgow. Suddenly, shootings and murder by shooting were everyday occurrences, almost everywhere.

Other than positing a theory that people in society had somehow become more homicidal generally, it was agreed that the answer lay in the changing nature of crime itself. Specifically, the burgeoning growth of the drugs trade. The dynamics of the drugs trade were mostly quite different from other types of crime. With the latter, criminals usually worked in small groups, which kept themselves to themselves. You didn't 'work' with people you didn't know and trust, and it was largely a cash business. Either you stole cash, or you stole goods and were paid for them in cash.

With drugs, though, people who had the money and the organisational ability to smuggle drugs into the country didn't necessarily have either the ability or the inclination to sell the drugs on in smaller quantities. The more people you dealt with, the more chance there was of coming to the notice of the police.

Middlemen had to be used. Very few of these middlemen had the cash to pay for the drugs upfront, so they were given them on credit. Similarly, these middlemen would sell on in smaller quantities to other middlemen, again mostly on credit. It is a fact of the drugs trade that the only group who usually pay cash for their drugs are the users themselves. So we are talking here of a business that is largely run on credit.

Often, large sums of money were involved. Equally often, the middleman's cut for selling on is comparatively small. Needless to say, there is a considerable temptation not to pay. Quite obviously, in an illegal business, one can't sue at law. So a high level of intimidation, either actual or implied, has to be used.

There is much demand for violent men in the drugs trade. Even so, this violence was always kept at a reasonable level before. To have to shoot or kill someone to recover money that was owed could only attract the attention of the police. Further, the penalty for such violence was usually very much greater than that for dealing in the drugs themselves.

There was always the odd nutter, but a 'consensus' level of 'reasonable' violence emerged. In the eighties, all this started to change. First, shootings proliferated for comparatively small sums of drugs money. Then, as a gun culture of violent men emerged, shooting for reputation or respect emerged. This was especially so among black criminals, where the level of shooting was highest and where they were often for quite trivial things. The 'white' drugs trade was considerably less violent.

We often talked about this to our black friends and acquaintances in jail. Unanimously, they pointed to a new element that had emerged within black criminal society, an element that we white criminals had been totally oblivious to. This was the influx of Jamaican criminals into Britain. These Jamaicans, or Yardies as they were called, worked exclusively within the black community. Or, more correctly, they preyed exclusively on the black community, for they had no moral or ethical code and were thoroughly predatory by nature.

They were also phenomenally violent. This came as something of a surprise to us. We had noticed, but only in passing, the influx of Jamaican criminals into prison, much the same as we had noticed the influx of the Nigerians, Chinese and Colombians. These Jamaicans seemed generally to be cheerful and unthreatening. Our black friends warned us that this was only because they were so much in the minority and didn't have access to guns. Back home in Jamaica, they were homicide personified.

With my interest in countercultural groups, it was inevitable that I do something on the Yardies. Following my recent triumph in the industry with the 'cocaine kitchen' story, I had become something of a 'hot' writer. Having worked regularly for both *Loaded* and *Front*, I had had my eye on working for *Maxim*, the market leader. So now looked like as good a time as any, especially as Bill Borrows, features editor at *Loaded*, had now moved from there to *Maxim*. With his help, I pitched the Yardie story to them and they went for it.

Due to my early warning about them in the prison, I was now well aware of the Yardies as a criminal phenomenon. As well as the many apocryphal tales from my black friends, there were the many well-documented accounts in the world's, if not the British, media. It made for a fascinating, almost unbelievable, story. The word Yardie is a peculiarly English term used to describe Jamaican criminals. In reality, Yardie just means a recent arrival from Jamaica. Bearing in mind that the vast majority of Jamaicans are law-abiding people, this then is a significant slur on Jamaicans everywhere.

The Rude Boys, or rudies, originated from among the multitude of unemployed youth in West Kingston, Jamaica, around the late fifties. If they had an ideology, it was one heavily influenced by American popular street culture. Rabidly anti-authority, fearless and extremely violent, they had their own inimitable style in both music and dress. They organised themselves into posses or crews in order to take for themselves what the state had so consistently failed to provide for them. Their attitude was that it was better to live fast and die young than to become a slave for life to the 'Babylon' system, a reference to the biblical city of sin. Crime rates in Kingston soared off the scale.

After Jamaica's independence from Britain in the early sixties, two main political parties contested for power. In reality, the Jamaica Labour Party (JLP) under Edgar Seaga and the People's National Party (PNP) under Michael Manley differed little in either ideology or policy. So, in order to get the vote out for their political cause, grass roots activists both parties recruited the rudie gangs to their respective banners.

Thus was political patronage first established. It became institutionalised in the form of 'garrison constituencies'. These were ghetto areas that had been terrorised and subjugated by the local rudie posse into voting for one party or the other. Rewards and sanctions were both tangible and immediate. Residents of those areas that had supported the victorious party were given jobs, housing, public services and other benefits. Areas that had supported the losing party got literally nothing.

Over time, the leaders of these posses, called *dons*, became the political partners of the politicians and the posses became private political armies. The successful politician would channel money and other largesse to the ghetto don, who became a *de facto*, if unelected, community leader. He would both make and administer the local law and generally provided those services to the local community that the state should have provided.

Election times were particularly bloody affairs, often descending into small-scale civil war. Murder rates rose into the hundreds as political tribalism replaced democratic party politics. At roughly the time that the posses became politicised, Jamaican farmers discovered a new and rapidly expanding market for their 'ganja', or marijuana, in the United States. Although the JLP had introduced quite draconian punishments for even minor possession and use of ganja, it had never curbed its widespread popularity across the island. Now production was increased to supply this new foreign market and it soon became a multimillion-dollar industry.

In order to protect their ganja plantations from rivals and the police, the farmers/drugs bosses recruited the rudie posses as their personal armies. With money in plentiful supply and ganja often bartered in the US for guns, the posses soon outgunned the Jamaican Constabulary Force (JCF), or police, who regularly had to call in the Jamaican Defence Force (JDF), or army, to support them. As if the situation weren't already very serious, during the mid-seventies it became immeasurably worse. Up until then, the posses had been made up of badly disciplined, disorganised men, with little real knowledge of weapons and how to use them. Suddenly, Jamaica was enmeshed in the global power struggle of the Cold War.

The ruling PNP under Manley was pro-Castro; the opposition JLP under Seaga was pro-US. So, with the Cuban DGI training the former and the CIA training the latter, the posses learned combat and espionage techniques that would prove to be very useful to them later in their purely criminal incarnation.

President Jimmy Carter's black ambassador to the UN at the time warned of a US plot to destabilise Jamaica. Violence peaked in the election year of 1980 with 1,100 killed, 125 in one month alone. Seaga, now in power, came under strong pressure from the international community to act. He responded by encouraging many of the rudies to go abroad, especially to the US. The first real wave of the rudie diaspora had begun.

Often travelling with easily obtainable false documents, the rudies headed for countries where there were already large established Jamaican and Afro-Caribbean communities. Once they arrived, they continued to do what they did best, namely murder and terrorise their own kind, all in pursuit of control of the country's drugs trade. They were extremely successful. Their advantage was an organisational genius developed by the DGI or CIA and a phenomenal capacity for unrestrained violence.

They would think nothing of slaughtering wholesale in public places, often in broad daylight. Soon there were former members of all the major Jamaican posses in many of the bigger American cities. That they often comprised a mixture of various posses and enjoyed a general autonomy from the parent Jamaican posse says as much for the fact that they could find all the drugs they needed within they US market as it does for their innate self-serving nature. Apart from their organisational ability, their particular edge vis-à-vis the local criminals was their capacity for violence. To put this into some kind of perspective, in Al Capone's worst years he managed only 76 murders in Chicago. In 1980, the rudies murdered three times that number in New York City alone.

By 1987, one federal agency estimated that there were approximately 70 posses in the US with a membership of between 20,000 and 40,000! In 1984, an ill-thought-out drugs policy actually redounded to their benefit. Ronald Reagan had put pressure on Seaga to do something about the vast amounts of ganja that were being smuggled into the US from Jamaica. Major crop-eradication programmes were introduced and ganja cultivation fell dramatically. The drugs bosses moved quickly, though, turning Jamaica into a major transhipment point for cocaine. At the same time, heroin also arrived from Nigeria.

This gave the rudies a new and increased lease of life. They quickly became a major supplier of cocaine to the US. Then came crack. With the advent of this phenomenally addictive and profitable form of cocaine, the US posses realised that they didn't have to be importers. They could afford to buy cocaine on the open market, 'rock' it up and distribute it at a massive profit. Their murderous methods ensured that they took over the local markets and soon they all but controlled the nation's crack trade.

Amazingly, the US law-enforcement agencies largely missed all of this. It was only the rudies' extreme violence that finally brought them to the attention of the authorities. Specialist squads and agencies were set up solely to deal with the rudies, and many posses were taken down. They are still a power to be reckoned with, but nothing like they were in their early days Also, a by-product of their power was the belief that, as the toughest crew in town, they didn't have to pay for anything. They became masters of the rip-off and didn't care whom they did it to.

One of the legacies of this was that the Colombians and other major wholesalers stopped dealing with them. There were also more direct repercussions. When it came to vengeful violence, the Colombians were second to none. Apart from any other considerations, if you are in the drugs business, you can't be seen to be ripped off. Otherwise, others will try it and you will be out of business.

This obviously didn't register with the rudies. In the early nineties, Willie Haggart's Black Roses Crew ripped off a large parcel of coke from the Colombians in the Bronx. The Colombians retaliated by killing Willie's sister locally, then followed the coffin back to Jamaica, where they killed his brother at the funeral. As the nineties progressed, the rudies came under extreme pressure in the US. It was time to move on to greener, less dangerous pastures.

There were long-established Jamaican communities in both Canada and the UK. With their chameleon-like abilities of assimilation, the rudies moved in among them. The Canadian authorities, though, were quicker to recognise the danger than their US counterparts. A steep rise in drug-related murders and violent bank robberies, including the killing of several police officers, alerted them to the presence of the posses. As early as 1984, they had set up the Black Organised Crime Squad, specifically to deal with the rudies.

As in the US, the crack explosion provided the rudies with an ideal milieu for their particular criminal abilities. Within a few short years, they single-handedly transformed what was previously a genuinely non-violent and well-ordered society. From their debut in the late eighties, the UK experience of the rudies was remarkably similar to that of the US and Canada. With the rapid growth of the domestic cocaine, and later the crack market, the rudies tried to take over within the Afro-Caribbean communities in places such as London, Bristol, Manchester, Birmingham, Leeds and Nottingham.

The largely unarmed British police found themselves facing a unique adversary who was both cunning and extremely dangerous. He was anonymous insofar as he travelled around on false papers and used various street aliases to do business. He was also extremely mobile. He could be in London today, New York tomorrow, Toronto the day after, briefly stopping off in Kingston before returning to London. Our rudie today could be yours tomorrow.

Further, unlike the native Jamaican posse, with its don and ranking gunmen, the 'overseas' posses had absolutely no hierarchical structure. Rudies from different posses would come together for a specific project, a drugs deal or an armed robbery, then go their separate ways when it was over. Also, a group of former Kingston Spanglers in London wouldn't necessarily be working for or on behalf of the native posse. Individual rudies might send some money back home against the day they might have to flee in a hurry, and there was the time-honoured tradition of sending for somebody when they were doing well and needed more manpower, but there the connection ended.

Taking all this into account, perhaps it isn't surprising that the rudies were hard for the police to identify as a significant threat. There was always their violent handiwork, but it was confined almost exclusively to within the black community, a community who didn't always cooperate with a British police they perceived to be racist and didn't trust.

Once the police realised the full extent of the danger, they formed specialised Yardie squads. Successful though they were, they eventually fell victim to political correctness. It was deemed to be too sensitive to have squads that focused exclusively on 'black' crime, and the rudies came to be dealt with within the wider framework of the anti-drugs task forces. However, the Operation Trident task force does focus exclusively on black-on-black murders, many of which are committed by the rudies.

The British police have never lost sight of the fact that the only way to understand the rudies, their outlook and criminal potential, is to take fully into account the wider context of the Kingston underworld. This is as relevant today as it was 20 years ago. It is an unfortunate fact that, when Jamaica became a major transhipment point for cocaine, it completely changed the power structure around the posses. With the economy in decline, the politicians had little to give the rudies in return for their services. In contrast, flush with money and guns from the coke trade, the posses started to run the ghettoes under their own banners, rather than that of the PNP or JLP. So the Frankenstein's monster that the politicians had empowered had escaped from their control to become a particularly vicious and uncontrollable form of narcoterrorism.

With the murder rate rapidly approaching a thousand a year, Jamaica found itself third in the world murder league, behind only Colombia and Chechnya, two countries ravaged by full-scale civil war. Small wonder that the embattled JCF found it ever harder to cope. Underequipped, often outnumbered and regularly outgunned, they increasingly had to call on the JDF for support.

On average, 12 JCF personnel are killed every year. When cornered or confronted, the rudies were quite fearless and often fought to the death. Many commentators saw their aggressiveness as something of a national trait. Lloyd Williams, a columnist for the *Gleaner*, Jamaica's largest and most prestigious newspaper, opined, 'Jamaicans tend to be aggressive.' Diana McCauley, a fellow columnist, went further, saying, 'We are a violent people and crime is rampant in our country because we believe in violence.'

If violence was indeed a national trait, it could only have been compounded by a further factor. As a by-product of Jamaica's being a major transhipment point for cocaine, domestic coke and 'crack' abuse became widespread. In 1992, the National Council for Drug Abuse estimated that there were 20,000 youths on coke or crack. The already suicidally violent rudies were now driven by coke-induced rage. Such was the effect of the terror this generated in the general population that the police could never find witnesses willing to come forward and testify against the rudies. The maxim of the ghetto was: 'See and blind, hear and deaf.'

Even when the police did manage to pull in one of the ghetto dons, they found themselves up against a combination of their political connections, the corrupting power of their wealth and the anger of their supporters. In September 1998, the police arrested Zeeks, a.k.a. Donald Phipps, allegedly a long-time top-ranking don of the Spanglers. A large crowd of his supporters immediately surrounded the police station. Things quickly got out of hand, with a soldier shot dead and several of the demonstrators fatally wounded. The police then asked Zeeks to help to control the situation. They took him to an upstairs balcony of the police station and handed him a loudhailer. Zeeks calmed the mob. They let him go without charge.

In the light of the general Jamaican crime situation, as unpalatable as it might be, the police have adopted extreme and radical measures. The

JCF shoot to death an average of 140 suspects each year. Many of the public support this policy, although to others the police have become nothing more than another posse, complete with their own ranking gunmen. The latter have become popularly known as 'supercops'.

Most famous of the supercops is Assistant Superintendent Keith Gardener, known throughout Jamaica as 'Trinity'. Formerly the personal bodyguard of Edgar Seaga, Trinity has, it has conservatively been estimated, shot and often killed dozens of violent suspects. In several instances, the government has had to pay out substantial damages to the victims or their surviving relatives. Assistant Superintendent Bigga Ford is another legendary supercop who is fast approaching Trinity's body count.

Nowhere has the collusion and corruption of Jamaica's body politic with and by the rudies been exposed more openly than at the funerals of certain leading dons. An absolutely classic example was the funeral of Jim Brown in February 1992. Brown, a.k.a. Lester Lloyd Coke, was a top-ranking don of the powerful Shower Posse.

Brown was in jail, awaiting extradition to the US on multiple drug-smuggling and murder charges. A US report had named him as responsible for 68 murders and the shooting of 13 police officers in Jamaica. He had been charged with 14 separate murders.

In circumstances that have never been fully explained, Brown was found burned to death in his cell. His funeral was a monumental affair, attended by more than 20,000 people, prominent among them being Edgar Seaga and other leading figures in the JLP. As Dawn Rich, a journalist, observed at the time, 'It shows quite clearly that the culture of the underworld is now the dominant one.'

Lest anyone think that this was unique, the funeral of Winston 'Burry Boy' Blake five years earlier proves otherwise. Blake, the leader of the Garrison Gang, was shot to death in a gunfight. His funeral was attended by Prime Minister Michael Manley and leading members of his government.

Armed with the above knowledge, I was in no doubt about what I was letting myself in for. I wouldn't be dealing with a bona fide guerrilla movement, complete with its own ideology and aims, who would be interested in remaining on good terms with the press. On the contrary, even at government level, there would be a vested interest in keeping the lid on things. At worst, some harm could come to me; or I could just be ignored. Clearly, I needed some sort of introduction, some 'edge'.

I first met Jay some 20 years earlier when I was just starting my life sentence. I was firmly in the 'mad-gunman' mould then, very violent and confrontational. In the prison world where negative is positive and vice versa, I was very much an elite criminal. I had become what I had aspired to be, a 'face'.

Jay was a couple of years younger than me and was doing five years for an armed robbery. In the criminal hierarchy, he was something of a nobody. He was also black, at a time when there were very few professional black criminals and even fewer who were accepted as equals by the dominant white criminal community.

Jay was a nice guy, though, and, much as I kept myself to myself at the time, occasionally we would speak. It was clear that he looked up to me and it was equally clear that he aspired to be a face.

One day he had a problem. A particularly racist white guy was having a go at him, insulting him and generally picking on him. Jay was courageous and brave enough and would have fought with the guy. However, this man was trying to make a race thing out of it and was involving other white guys. Black prisoners were very much in the minority in long-term jails at this time and were not a particularly powerful group. Jay couldn't look to them for support and, in truth, didn't want to involve them. He came to me and explained the situation.

Corrupt though the prison world is, decent men do aspire to act correctly and honourably. After all, what's right is right. Personally, I didn't like this particular white guy: he was loud and something of a bully. Also, it was clear that he was deliberately trying to involve other people in what was his own personal argument.

The upshot was that I talked to a couple of people and we all agreed that it should just be between Jay and this white guy, at which stage the latter rapidly backed off. But there had already been too much animosity and insults for Jay, a proud young man in his own right. He confronted the guy and, in the subsequent fight, soundly beat him.

Jay never forgot the favour I did him. We met several times over the years, me still doing my life sentence, and Jay, various short and not so short terms. I had heard in recent years that he had become a leading figure on the black crime scene. When I got out, many of my friends had heard of him. He had been a suspect in several murders and had the reputation of someone not to mess with. I thought it was time to renew my acquaintanceship with Jay.

He wasn't hard to find. A friend passed a message to a friend, Jay phoned me and we met in a quiet street of his choosing, one where we wouldn't be picked up by CCTV cameras.

Jay had put on a bit of weight, but the years had treated him well. He still had the mischievous sparkle in his eyes, although there was much that was serious about him now. He was so pleased to see me. He congratulated me on surviving so well and you could tell that he was measuring himself against the possibility that, one day, he might face an endless sentence. Then he asked me what he could do for me.

I knew that Jay was second-generation Jamaican. I guessed that he regularly went back. I told him about my Yardie piece for *Maxim* and asked him if he could get an interview with someone high up in one of the posses.

'What are you going to say, Norm?' he asked. 'I do go back regularly and, if you say something that upsets someone, it'll be on me next time I'm back. They don't like journalists.'

'Jay, you know me. I'd never compromise someone so they could get nicked and I'd never disrespect someone who was good enough to give me an interview. I just want someone to tell it as it is. If he wants to slag off the police, the government, that's OK. I'll let him say exactly what he wants.'

'You know you're the wrong colour for this, don't ya, mate,' said Jay, suddenly laughing.

'Maybe that'll work in my favour,' I replied. 'They might take it the wrong way if a black guy tried to do it.'

'The trouble is, I don't think there's any right way,' said Jay, serious again. 'I really can't promise anything, but I will ask for you.'

While I was waiting for him to get back to me, I went about setting up interviews with other people who would have a relevant view on the Jamaican crime scene. I went to the London offices of the *Gleaner* and got all the most recent issues. Crime featured strongly in all of them.

Amnesty International was a treasure trove of good leads. I spent an hour with the guy in charge of the Caribbean section and he gave me contact details of human-rights groups and people who worked among the poor in the ghettoes. I thanked him and asked if there was anything he would specifically like me to publicise. He answered immediately with one word: 'Braeton'.

Braeton is a poor area on the outskirts of Kingston. According to the recently formed Crime Management Unit (CMU), an elite rapid-response police unit, they cornered seven young male suspects in a shack there. The CMU claimed that the youths opened fire on them first and, in the ensuing gun battle, all seven were killed. The forensic evidence, though, showed that six of the youths had been shot in the head at close range and all in the same small bedroom. Local people say that the seven had all surrendered without firing a shot and were heard pleading for their lives.

Over the next few days I made several phone calls to Jamaica and set up interviews. Everyone seemed keen to speak to me, including a leading police officer. So, if all else failed, at least I would have something to make a story out of.

In the event, though, I need not have worried. Jay phoned to say that he had arranged for me to meet with Blackadouch, a friend of his who knew everyone on the Kingston crime scene. He had told him that I was a close friend and that I had once saved his life in jail, so he owed me. Jay gave me Blackadouch's mobile number and told me to call him when I reached Kingston. He would be expecting my call.

I communicated this latest piece of good news to the guy at *Maxim* and he seemed massively underwhelmed. I had thought that the chance of an interview with a top don was my ace in the hole. The response from the guy was to warn me that *Maxim* couldn't get involved in anything illegal. I couldn't for the life of me see the connection, but then it all fell into place. Many of the guys who worked for the lads' magazines felt under extreme pressure to be all things to all men and women: tough, sexy, stylish, streetwise and cool. In truth, most of them were quite nerdy. Whatever my other failings, I was extremely streetwise and had some excellent contacts – contacts that perhaps only I could have got.

This wasn't a particularly good start for me with *Maxim*. Whatever the standard of my work, writing was my art. It was essential to me that I retained editorial control. I had not encountered a problem about this at either *Front* or *Loaded*. They had been glad of my contacts and had admired me for them. I began to fear for the worst.

The second disappointment was that the guy refused my offer to provide my own photographer. I had worked with several good ones by now. The replacement, though, was far from a disappointment. He was a photographer who worked for the *Gleaner*, the best paper in town. Apart from his photographic expertise, he would be a fount of local knowledge.

As the ranking 'don' in my household, Marsha was also massively underwhelmed by the whole Jamaican assignment. She batted not one of her perfectly groomed eyelashes as I recounted murder rates and tales of homicidal gangsters. Her one moment of interest came when she asked me if I would be going near the beaches. When I reassured her that all the gangsters already had a tan, she forgot about the subject. I consoled myself with the thought that she must have an infinite faith in my ability to survive anywhere.

One immediate benefit of working for *Maxim* was that everything wasn't done on a shoestring. The flight was with a good airline and not a cheap economy one. That night I slept in a first-class hotel. If anything, it all put more pressure on me to come up with the goods. I just couldn't come back with a travel piece.

Bright and early the next morning, I presented myself at the *Gleaner* and asked for George, my photographer. George was a well-built handsome guy in his late thirties with a down-to-earth manner, a refreshing change from some of the dilettantes back home. He was intelligent, well informed and friendly. I was instantly at my ease with him.

In the car he asked me for my itinerary, where I wanted to go and who I wanted to see. Out to impress, I hit him with my ace in the hole. 'I'm a friend of a friend of Blackadouch, George. I've got his mobile number and he's expecting my call.'

For a couple of seconds, I couldn't make out the expression on George's face at all. I dismissed 'impressed' and, shortly afterwards, ruled out 'surprised'. It was the open mouth formed in a perfect 'O' that finally gave it to me.

Shocked, George reached behind him into the back seat. He searched through several old copies of the *Gleaner* until he came up with the copy he was looking for. 'Norman, you haven't read the papers, have you?' He handed me the paper.

The headline screamed that Willie Haggart, notorious don of the Black Roses Crew, had been murdered. According to the *Gleaner*'s account, there had been trouble at a recent dance featuring the Stone Love sound system. All the various posses went to these events and each had its particular corner. There was an unwritten truce that there should be no trouble there.

At this one, though, a glass of champagne had been thrown. The contents had splashed on to the shoes of Dudas, ranking don of the powerful Shower Posse from neighbouring Tivoli Gardens. Insignificant stuff among ordinary folk, but, in this context, a deadly insult showing lack of respect.

Angry words were exchanged between Willie Haggart and Dudas.

The incident can't be viewed in isolation. Nine years previously, one of Willie's crew had killed Dudas's brother, Jah T. Although a shaky truce has been in place, there is still a lot of bad feeling about it in the Shower Posse camp. The word on the street was that now Dudas had put out a contract on Willie.

Violent crime is already the hottest of topics and the politicians don't want any more bloodletting. A street battle between the Shower Posse and the Black Roses Crew, involving their many scores of members, would be like small-scale civil war. It was to be avoided at all costs. An emissary was sent to Willie to ask him to apologise to Dudas.

It's 3.30 in the afternoon in mid-April and Willie Haggart is sitting on the corner in Arnett Gardens, one of the most notorious suburbs of Kingston. But this is home turf to the Black Roses, so he and two of his crew are completely at their ease. So is the emissary who has been sent to counsel Willie.

As they talk, a car pulls up and four men dressed in the white shirts and dark trousers of Kingston's plainclothes detectives get out. At the last moment, it is clear that they are carrying assault rifles. They open up on Willie and his companions, killing him and one of his crew and seriously wounding the other. The emissary is also killed.

And the name of the emissary?

Blackadouch!

I was just about to bewail my awful bad luck when I thought of the fate of Blackadouch, who had obviously been killed by mistake. It was just as well that I had kept quiet, because George opined that it was clear that the killers weren't from Kingston, for Blackadouch was known and liked by everyone, and local gunmen would have spared him. I suppose that qualified as real bad luck.

George further opined that, following the murder of Willie, everybody was very nervous about repercussions and was keeping their head down. It would be very difficult to get anyone to talk, especially to an outsider. But I was way ahead of him here. I had already worked out that, with the death of my contact Blackadouch, I might as well forget about an interview with a top posse member. I had also realised that, with Kingston on the verge of small-scale civil war, the posse members would be keeping a low profile.

However, the rudies weren't the only ones with a relevant opinion on their activities. Fortunately, I had had the foresight to prepare the ground for interviews with people from other walks of life. I would just have to work through the list.

Yvonne Sobers must have been 80 if she was a day. Yet through the frailty shone a spirit that wouldn't have been out of place in a woman half her age. She was the chairperson of Families Against State Terrorism (FAST), a human-rights group that blames the upsurge in rudie violence firmly on the police.

We are sitting in the front room of her scrupulously neat little chalet in the suburbs of Kingston. Ms Sobers is a former teacher and photos of her with classes of children hang from the walls. It seems an incongruous setting to be discussing murder and mayhem, for the chalet wouldn't look out of place in England's suburbia.

'We can't claim to be a civilised society if our police pursue a policy of extrajudicial execution,' she avers. 'And it isn't as if it affects the big fish, the dons – they have an accommodation with the police. With many small-time ordinary criminals there is strong evidence that many suspects have been summarily executed.'

However, she concedes that many Jamaicans support the police's actions. A recent survey taken immediately after the Braeton incident showed that more than half of the people asked supported the police's actions, whatever the circumstances!

She fetches a big dossier from a nearby bookcase. Inside is case after case that FAST has compiled about police malpractice. Page after page of witness testimony describes how suspects were taken into custody fit and well, only to turn up later in the city morgue.

I ask her opinion on the recent murder of Willie Haggart. 'Hog Heart,' she replies almost immediately, and titters behind her hands like a schoolgirl. 'That's what some of us called him,' she continues. 'It might sound un-Christian to say it, but he got what he deserved.'

You could be forgiven for thinking that Monsignor Richard Albert was some Hollywood actor playing the role of a Roman Catholic priest. It's a combination of the strong American accent, the fat cigars he smokes, a bull neck on top of a powerful build and a manner that, if not actually aggressive, is certainly forceful. He speaks assertively and waves his hands about a lot. Clearly, he is a man who doesn't suffer fools gladly, quite unusual in a man of the cloth.

Monsignor Albert has worked in some of Jamaica's worst slums for over 25 years. He has built schools, skill-training centres and old people's homes in Riverton, Waterhouse and Olympic Gardens, where he is regarded with awe by the local people. This feeling isn't shared by the posse members, whom he ignores and refuses to have any dealings with. 'I tell all the people who work on my projects that, if I hear that they have allowed the dons to extort money from them, they will be sacked,' he says. 'I believe in empowering the people, so they will have their destiny in their own hands. Dependency is slavery.'

Noble sentiments indeed, but isn't such an attitude dangerous in posse-controlled areas? I ask.

'I suppose it can be dangerous at times,' he concedes, 'but many of the dons' children go to my schools. And, if somebody is wanted and decides to surrender to the police, I can arrange the surrender so that they are arrested rather than killed out of hand.'

As a result, the dons barely tolerate him. Brave and forceful he may be, but foolhardy he certainly isn't. He is more than aware of the tenuous nature of his existence within the local community. When I ask him about extrajudicial police killings, the Willie Haggart murder and the influence of the posses, he declines to offer an opinion. 'I try to treat everyone the same and keep my nose out of what doesn't concern me,' he states, drawing on his cigar and fixing his steely gaze firmly on mine, as if to say, You didn't really expect me to answer that, did you? Edward G Robinson couldn't have played the part better.

A man whose demeanour fits his role far more closely is Anthony Harriot, professor of criminal justice at the University of the West Indies. The calm studious manner befits the academic he so clearly is. We sit in his office in a block of the university, a rundown patchwork of a campus that resembles some South-London polytechnic. Like everything else in the public sector, education has been hit by the failing economy.

According to Professor Harriot, the failing economy has also been the root cause of the rise to power of the rudies. 'Sixty-two per cent of the national budget goes to service international debt,' he says. 'The economy is in decline and the politicians have no largesse to give out. The don, grown wealthy on drug dealing and extortion, has stepped into the breach. He provides what the state should provide and, therefore, has the support of the people. So now there is a situation where the don is pivotal to the political system.'

He goes on to say that the spectacle at Willie Haggart's funeral was clear evidence of this. Ironically, it was held on the very day I arrived. According to the media reports, though, it was another monumental affair. More than 5,000 mourners attended the service, which was held in Jamaica's National Arena. Prominent among them were Omar Davies,

Dr Peter Phillips and Dr Karl Blythe. They are, respectively, ministers for finance, transport and housing in the ruling PNP. In his funeral oration, Dr Davies said, 'I am here to pay my respects to a man who has assisted me in achieving some of my objectives in the community.'

I can't help but reflect on the impact this must have had on some of the parents of young Jamaicans whose lives have been devastated by the cocaine that Willie Haggart flooded the ghettos with. I try to imagine a parallel in England, but can't come up with one. The idea of Tony Blair and several of his cabinet attending the funeral of Reggie Kray is just too ridiculous to contemplate. It brings into perspective the level of corruption in Jamaican politics.

I don't know what I expected at my interview with the police. With local priests firmly in role as cigar-chomping American gangsters, perhaps pearl-handled pistols and a Stetson hat would be the chosen props of Deputy Superintendent James Forbes, of the Constabulary Communications Network. It was a refreshing surprise. Young, articulate, highly intelligent and soberly dressed in business suit and tie, he could have been a lawyer. Further, he came across as sincere about the work his force is doing in the ongoing war against the rudies.

'You only have to look at our annual murder rate to realise the extent to which the people live in fear,' says Forbes. 'We have a rampant gun culture here in Jamaica, with the criminals armed with machine guns, assault rifles and sometimes even rocket launchers. It costs the lives of, on average, 12 officers every year. The JCF feels that it is under siege.'

He acknowledges that the current state of the economy doesn't help. With some embarrassment he admits that the government has recently made a 50 per cent cut in fuel allocation for police vehicles.

I mention Braeton and the alleged extrajudicial-executions policy and he visibly cringes. To his credit, though, instead of blatantly denying such allegations, as many police officers would in many other countries, he tacitly admits some culpability. 'Look, of course there are officers we would like to get rid of, but it's not always that easy. Already this year we have a record number sacked and on suspension. I'm not defending their type of behaviour, but, when no one from the ghetto will come forward to give evidence against these criminals, the police see guilty men go free time after time.'

'See and blind, hear and deaf,' I chime in, repeating the mantra of the ghetto.

'Exactly,' says Forbes, and smiles as if to acknowledge my awareness. 'Add that to the fact that some of the people we go up against are better armed and equipped than we are, then you begin to see the extent of the problem.'

He had earlier promised to show us some of the weapons his men have captured in the last three months and allow us to photograph them. At this stage he leads us into another part of the building and into a room where two uniformed policemen stand next to a very large table covered in scores of every conceivable type of weapon, from tiny handguns, through assault rifles and machine guns, to even a couple of rocket launchers.

'This is what we have confiscated in only the last three months. The previous three months we confiscated the same and, no doubt, we will find the same in the next three months. My men don't have access to many of these weapons, and, even if they did, they wouldn't be allowed to use them on the street, because they are too indiscriminate. Innocent people would be hit also. The criminals have no such inhibitions.'

Having heard so much about Braeton, the burning criminal issue of the moment in Jamaica, I decide it would be a good idea to visit the scene of the alleged crime. A half-hour drive sees us in semi-rural area, with one-storey, tumbledown, prefabricated dwellings dotted about in the ever-encroaching undergrowth of rampant vegetation. The people here are obviously very poor.

The 'house' is really little more than a wooden shack. Inside, the rooms are all small and dingy, the window shutters all riddled with multiple bullet holes. I'm no forensic expert, but I've read enough to look for certain things. With a pencil I probe the bullet holes. The vast majority are incoming: small hole on the outside, larger hole on the inside. If there was a gun battle here, it must have been very one-sided, with virtually all of the shooting coming from the police on the outside.

The tiny back bedroom was where the seven bodies were found. There are still two heavily bloodstained mattresses lying on the floor. I go to the one very small window in the far wall and open it to look out. To my surprise I am looking into an enclosed shed, attached to the building. There's no access to the shed from the tiny bedroom, but, far more importantly, no view of the outside. If this is the room the seven youths chose to make their last stand, then it is singularly unsuitable. They would be able to see neither who to shoot at nor who was shooting at them. Further, there was no way to escape.

It is all too obvious. This is where the police would have dragged the youths, to shoot them, out of sight of the prying eyes of neighbours. I recall what the Amnesty guy told me about six of the youths being shot in the head at close range. I try to imagine the terror of the last youth as he is dragged, screaming and struggling, into the room where the bloodied corpses of his companions lie.

Outside, the bright sunlight purges the vision from my mind. Horror's place is in the night. A small group of local residents have gathered a short distance away. They look at us curiously, warily. When they see that we are not dressed like police and that I, quite obviously, am a foreigner, a few of them approach.

They make no outright allegations of murder – from their manner you can tell that they are still very wary. No one will admit to actually seeing or hearing anything. However, the general view is that an inquiry should be held into what happened here.

Although I feel I have got some good stuff, some strong interviews to support my article, I am very much aware that, in many ways, the star of the show is missing. I haven't so much as seen, let alone spoken to, one rudie. And I realise that I am not going to, because now really isn't the time.

With George's assistance, I visit the photo archives of the *Gleaner*. There is one particular photo I am looking for. Although it was over a decade ago, the funeral of Jim Brown is still very much in the national memory. I leaf through sheaves of photos of the cortège, the ceremony, until finally I find the one I am looking for.

Even in death Jim Brown looks ominous. Only the face is visible as he lies in his casket, no doubt the rest of him too damaged by the fire to be put on display. Black sunglasses cover his eyes and a black beret-type cap covers his head. Immediately in front of the casket are two weeping women, one holding a baby. But, there in the background, is the face I am looking for. Like the moon looming on a starless night, the pale face, wearing dark shades, looms above and behind the other mourners. Suitably sombre, Edward Seaga, Prime Minister of Jamaica, is paying his last respects to notorious gangster Jim Brown.

On my penultimate day, we drive down to Montego Bay. This is the Jamaica the tourists see, clean, opulent, well ordered, safe. The first thing that stands out is the tourist police in their garish uniforms. They are stationed, literally, one every 20 yards along the pavement. This might as well be another country for all the resemblance it has to the rest of Jamaica.

On my last day, not having actually seen any rudies, I ask George if we could at least cruise some of the areas where they hold sway. George doesn't look enthusiastic, but you can see that he doesn't want to let me down in any way. With a look that says that this is very much against his better judgement, we set off.

Kingston reveals itself to be a hot, dusty, decaying city, surrounded by sprawling slums. Trenchtown, Jones Town, Spanish Town – we know of the names from the songs about them by some of their famous sons. But it doesn't prepare us for the utter poverty. There are but a handful of European faces in central Kingston, none at all in the ghettos. I stand out like the proverbial sore thumb.

As we cruise around, it quickly becomes apparent that whole areas of the city are no-go areas for the police and anyone else the local posse doesn't approve of. Mathews Lane, home turf to the Spanglers, lies to the rear of Kingston Public Hospital. Both ends of the street are blocked off by a makeshift barrier of old fridges, concrete blocks and wrecked cars. In the gaps are posse members, the last word on admission or refusal to the area.

Cruising into Tivoli Gardens, home to the Shower Posse, we find ourselves in a circular area surrounded by buildings. On the right is Tivoli Gardens Community Centre and, directly opposite, the office of Dudas, the all-powerful local don. Further progress is blocked by a burned-out car across the road.

Our car is unknown in the area. What's more, it has tinted windows like the car of the gunmen who killed Willie. Furtive looks are cast in our direction. Suddenly, as if out of nowhere, a guy on a powerful motorbike speeds up besides us. He raps sharply on the window.

Though usually laidback, George reacts like lightning. We jolt up through the gears as he heads towards the fortified police station barely 200 yards away at breakneck speed. He is about to pull in when the motorbike veers away. We idle by the entrance for several minutes until we are sure the danger has passed.

After this latest close shave, we should really be heading back to the hotel, but there is one final item on my itinerary. I want to visit the scene of Willie's murder in Arnett Gardens. It's growing dark as we drive along Lincoln Crescent, our tinted windows again getting us suspicious looks from passers-by. As we round a bend, there, right in front of us, is a larger-than-life-sized mural of Willie Haggart.

'Can we get a photo of that?' I ask George.

We cruise to a halt and he gives me what my mother used to call an 'old-fashioned look'. It is questioning, sarcastic and humorous all at the same time. Without a word of protest, though, George collects his camera from the back seat and climbs out of the car. As he gets ready to set up the shot, I climb into the driver's seat just in case we have to make a speedy departure.

Suddenly, out of nowhere, a very angry rudie is confronting George. 'Wha doin?' he demands, his finger inches from George's face.

Suitably intimidated, George backs away, waving his arms in a calming placatory manner. He, better than anyone, knows that he is in imminent danger of being shot. 'Willie was a friend of mine,' he manages to stutter.

'Wha's all this Willie ting?' snarls Mr Angry. 'Willie goan, new man in charge now.'

Still backing away towards the car, George nods maniacally. I slide over to my side as he gets in. He pulls away quickly without a backward look at the rudie. For a couple of minutes, we drive in silence. 'I got the photo, by the way,' says George suddenly. It is enough to break the tension. I can't help but burst out laughing. George joins in. But it's nervous laughter rather than the humorous type. This time we head directly back to the hotel.

From my writer's perspective, the return to England was a definite anti-climax. Even though I didn't manage to get an interview with a don, I felt I had enough to make the story interesting. However, I am concerned about the *Maxim* factor: what will this 'editor' do to my piece? Even though he might chop it to pieces, it will still be going out under my name. For anyone with any pride in their work, this was anathema.

The article duly came out in the November issue and all my fears were realised. I knew there would be very little scope for gonzoism; what I didn't realise was that they would virtually write me out of the story altogether. The only mention of me was right at the start, immediately under the story headline. 'Words by Norman Parker' read the legend. I mused that, should this guy ever write about a symphony or a great building, he would put, 'notes by Beethoven' or 'bricks by the architect'.

Everything was written as '*Maxim* does this' or '*Maxim* goes there' as if some animated magazine were doing the work. The whole episode of my getting the introduction to Blackadouch and his being murdered before I could meet him was missing. What greater testimony could there be to the violent nature of Jamaican society than that my contact had been murdered even before I could speak to him?

From a structural perspective, it was a completely different article. My beginning had completely disappeared and my end was somewhere in the middle. Needless to say, as an article, the piece just did not hold together.

In the heat of the moment, I resolved never to write for *Maxim* again. However, the reality was that this was the nature of the industry. When you weren't a famous author, you had little editorial control over your work.

I was thankful that I hadn't managed to get an interview with a don and guaranteed him the integrity of my copy. No doubt by now there would be a contract out on me all over Jamaica. I did resolve never to write for them when I had a hot source who would expect me to keep my word about what would appear in the article. So, in this way, *Maxim*'s editorial policy works directly against them.

One person who wasn't at all surprised by the treatment I got at the hands of *Maxim* was Marsha, of course. And, had I been looking for sympathy, there would have been none from that quarter. 'That's what you get when you write for porn magazines,' she declared.

CHAPTER ELEVEN
THE DAY THE MUSIC DIED

Now I had witnessed at first hand the dynamic that often drove the infernal machine of black-on-black shootings in England, I felt that I was well placed to write a piece on it. I knew at least two black guys who were shooters who were willing to talk to me so long as I didn't identify them in the piece. But I couldn't write the article purely from their perspective. For a balanced view, I would have to include the opinion of 'straight' people too.

I quickly identified a prominent member of the black community who would have a very relevant viewpoint, as well as the mother of a victim. However, whatever way I looked at the subject, it seemed unavoidable that I would have to include the work and views of staff from Operation Trident, the specialist police unit that dealt with black-on-black shootings.

And therein lay the problem. It would be naive in the extreme for me to think that, once I made an application to interview a member of the Trident team, they wouldn't figure out who I was. A quick check on the police computer would reveal that I had committed a couple of shootings myself and had just finished serving a life sentence for one of them. In those circumstances, would they even speak to me? The only thing for it was to take the bull by the horns. With the support of the editor of *Front*, I wrote to them.

My name is Norman Parker and I am a freelance journalist (NUJ No. 009558) working for the men's magazines Maxim, Loaded *and* Front. *I have been commissioned by the editor of* Front *to do a piece on the work of 'Operation Trident'.*

Front *sells approximately 175,000 copies per month, which means that it has a readership of about 350,000. These are mainly impressionable young men between the ages of 15 and 23, precisely the sort of people to whom 'Trident' should be getting its message across.*

Neither the editor nor myself want a piece glamorising crime and violence. On the contrary, we feel that reports of shootings and murders get far more publicity than the conviction of perpetrators, often giving the impression that few are brought to justice for these crimes. We know this isn't correct and that 'Trident' has an exceptionally high clear-up rate. This is the message we wish to get across in the piece.

The help I would like from yourselves is as follows:

- *A dramatic scene-of-crime photo (to grab the reader's attention).*
- *Quite detailed statistics of offences and clear-up rates.*
- *An interview with an active member of the squad, including a 'mission statement' as well as anything else he/she would like to get across.*
- *An interview with one of the Jamaican liaison officers (the Jamaican connection).*
- *An interview with the relative of a victim.*

Now I know the next thing that I ask is controversial, but we feel it is very important. I would like as many photos (just head shots) as you can provide of convicted perpetrators. Front *is a very visual magazine. We would cover a complete page with the 'mug-shots' of all these young men who are now doing very long sentences for 'Trident' crimes. It would stick in people's minds and get the message across that 'people are getting nicked'.*

Bernie Ford gave me the number of Lee Jasper of the Police Advisory Body and I intend to get an interview from him. We would be very grateful for any suggestions the 'Trident' team might have on other suitable people to interview.

I sent the letter off and had a reply within a week. Trident would give me my interview. To give credit where it is due, they were very helpful and cooperative. I would be writing for *Front* again, so I was confident that they would print my 'copy' virtually verbatim. The following is the piece they printed.

THE DAY THE MUSIC DIED
The day the music died came early this year. In the early hours of New Year's Day an illegal pay-party was winding down at 18 Shore Road, Hackney, next to the Business Centre. More than 40 people, mostly black and of varying ages, had been partying to the sounds of DJ Creation a.k.a. Ashley Kenton.

At some stage, in the crush of a large party in such a small flat, someone trod on someone else's foot. Apologies were demanded, but were refused. Trivial stuff to most people, but among some young black men involved in drugs and street life it was the ultimate crime. Disrespect.

Suddenly, shots rang out. One bullet hit Ashley Kenton, 22, in the neck. Another passed through a partition wall and hit Wayne Mowatt, 29, in the head. The police were called and both men were taken to local hospitals where they were pronounced dead. To the officers of 'Operation Trident' it was a particularly bad black-on-black shooting to start the New Year with.

I am sitting deep within New Scotland Yard in the presence of Detective Chief Superintendent Andy Sellers, one of the top officers of 'Operation Trident'. '"Trident" started about four years ago purely as an intelligence gathering operation,' says Sellers. 'I was serving in Lambeth then and there was a perception that there had been a marked increase in black-on-black violence. We didn't have particularly good links with the black community then. They didn't trust us and we got little information from them. But the results surprised even us. Our intelligence showed that there had been a very serious increase in extreme violence, often involving guns, between black males. We further found that, in many cases, Jamaican gangsters, often known as Yardies, were playing a leading role.'

The shootings grew, both in frequency and boldness. Often victims were gunned down in broad daylight. Sometimes there were car chases with gunmen spraying bullets at each other from machine guns. Common stuff on the mean streets of Kingston, but unusual in the extreme for London.

As the problem grew, so 'Trident' evolved from an intelligence gathering operational unit into a permanent, structured 'command unit', similar to other 'command units' like the Anti-Terrorist Squad. It targeted crimes where there was a black victim and a black suspect, often with the involvement of drugs and guns. It had both a reactive role, responding to specific crimes and investigating them, and a proactive role, acting on intelligence to go after top players.

'Quite often we got to know who did a particular shooting, but couldn't prove it,' continues Sellers. '40% of victims who survive won't speak. Often there are no victims, just pools of blood and bullet holes in cars. The black community didn't trust us and the gunmen generated such fear and intimidation that witnesses were afraid to come forward. So we would put top suspects under surveillance, hoping, either to discover evidence to link them with a past crime, or catching them in the act of committing their next one.'

Despite 'Trident's' efforts the problem has continued to get worse. The year 2001 saw a 96% increase in black-on-black shootings over 2000 and in the first eight months of 2002 there has been a 46% increase over the previous year. In the same period though, 'Trident' has grown in power and influence. It now has 250 full-time officers, increasing to 265 next year. It also has a witness protection programme. But probably its greatest achievement is its improved links with the black community.

'Trident' now works in conjunction with the Independent Advisory Group, members of the black community concerned at the way the violence is affecting their communities. With the clarion call of 'Take responsibility for your children', it has exhorted other black citizens to do something about the crimes that are killing their children and terrorizing their community. 'Trident' also has a well-resourced advertising campaign. Its logo, a T in a circle, is well known, as is its advice to 'turn your back on guns and drugs'.

Lee Jasper is a leading member of the Independent Advisory Group and has worked with DCS Sellers since the early days of its creation in Lambeth. He is now Senior Policy Adviser on Policing to the Metropolitan Police and has an office in Ken Livingstone's City Hall overlooking the Thames. 'A major problem when "Trident" started was the police's use of informers,' says Jasper. 'They were dealing with some of the most dangerous criminals in *the black community. For ordinary, law-abiding members of our community, who were already intimidated by these people, it totally undermined their confidence in the police. They saw these violent criminals acting with impunity, without being arrested. The latter would even boast that their contacts in the police would tell them if anyone informed on them. Any chance there ever was of the black community cooperating with the police was lost.'*

Sellers acknowledges this, but argues that, at that time, 'Trident' was in a Catch 22 situation. Because they had such a poor relationship with the black community they didn't really know the true nature of the informers they were dealing with, but they were the only informers they had. However, things are much improved since then and they have a very good level of intelligence now on 'black' crime.

Even so, Mrs Patricia McClarty for one doesn't agree with DCS Sellers' optimistic take on 'Trident's' newfound cooperation from the black community. I am sitting in on a press conference at Tottenham police station called by 'Trident' to mark the first anniversary of the murder of Tyrone Rowe, Mrs McClarty's son. DCI Julian Headon tells how 18-year-old Tyrone was sitting in a car with three friends when six young black men approached. Two pulled out guns and fired 11 shots into the car, killing Tyrone and wounding one of his friends. Despite the fact that it was 1.30 a.m. there were scores of people about. Yet no one has come forward to identify the assailants.

'I am angry with the community for not giving enough support,' says Mrs McClarty. 'Tyrone was a good boy, not involved in drugs and crime. It has devastated my life and I can't move on. I am making a stand by being here today asking for information. I need others to stand up too.'

So is 'Trident's' message really getting through to the Yardies? With the murder rate in Jamaica running at a record high of 1,100 dead for the year and four police officers killed in one week, what could possibly deter such people?

'They're afraid of us,' says Sellers, 'especially our armed response units. But now we have another problem. Two to three years ago the proportion was 80% Jamaican gunmen to about 20% black British. Now it's more like 60% Jamaican to 30% black British, with a further 10% Africans involved in the growing heroin trade. Whether the Jamaicans have just set a bad example *or if the other gangs have had to become more violent just to compete, we don't know.'*

Historically, cocaine, especially 'crack', has been the engine that has driven the violence. Jamaica is a major trans-shipment point for Colombian cocaine, a kilo of which can be bought for £2,000 to £3,000 on the streets of Jamaica. The same kilo can fetch £30,000 as powder in London, or more than twice that as 'crack'. It is the 'crack' market, with its emphasis on street sales and therefore market share, that has generated the violence.

So do the homicidally violent drugs gangs or posses of Kingston now call the shots on the streets of our major cities? DCS Sellers doesn't think so. 'The smuggling can be quite organised. However, many people try to "body-pack" cocaine into this country on international flights. On one Air Jamaica flight recently as many as ten per cent of the passengers were carrying drugs. But the Jamaican gang structure over here is quite chaotic. They tend to form loose groups that change members between them, but there is linkage. Often a shooting in London can have violent repercussions in Kingston within hours.'

A frightening development is that not all of the violence is drug-related now. A distinct culture of violence has grown among some young, black youths. In some cases guns equal credibility equal respect. Consequently there has been an upsurge of 'disrespect' violence, where one person is thought to have been rude or disrespectful to another. A recent survey among 10- to 11-year-old black children in Lambeth reported that, among all the things that worried them in their environment, the fear of being murdered was the worst.

'I suppose it's a sign of the times,' says Sellers. 'Whereas violent white criminals would immediately dispose of a gun after use, this new crew values it the more. We've heard of instances where a gun that has been used to murder so-and-so has been sold on at an increased price, precisely because of that fact.'

The last word belongs to 'Ricky', a seventeen-year-old, mixed-race youth who lives in Harlesden, an area of London plagued by black-on-black shootings. He is intelligent, articulate and very wary of incriminating himself. His name has been given me by someone who has been involved in extreme violence in the past.

'I'm not saying this is me,' says Ricky. 'I'm not saying I've actually done anything, but this is how I see it works. There are *places in London, and Harlesden's one of them, where there's lots of street crime. Burglaries, muggings, assault, harassment and bullying. The police don't seem to be able to control it. Maybe they don't care about controlling it because we're only poor people. To us it looks like society has broken down. So you have to take care of your own. Stand up for yourself, your family and friends. If someone comes to fuck with you, you have to deal with it yourself. And there's only one way to do that, violence. If a man comes with a knife, then you will have to have a knife. If he comes with a gun, then you'd better have a gun yourself. Whatever it takes to protect yourself.'*

I ask about the influence of 'gangsta rap' music and its violent themes, not because I actually believe it has influence, but because it has been mentioned as a contributory factor by some people. Ricky agrees with me. 'People make music about all kinds of things, good and bad, happy and sad, ugly and beautiful. The things we see around us. So-called "gangsta rap" just reflects one aspect of life in the ghetto. The violence is already there. No one goes and shoots someone just because they heard someone singing about that on a record. But if someone gets in your face where you live, then the only practical solution is to blow him right out of your face.'

CHAPTER TWELVE
THE HIT MAN

A recurring request from many of the magazines and from some newspapers was for me to do a piece on hit men, so-called professional killers. If I had put my mind to it, no doubt I could have turned out a piece that was extremely well informed. I regularly met with friends who were still involved in the crime scene. I suppose we were much like stockbrokers in this respect. Whereas whenever stockbrokers meet the talk invariably turns to the current state of the stock market, with us the talk invariably turned to crime.

In many ways, criminal life was like an ongoing mystery story. Someone would be shot and next time we met we would discuss what was behind it and who actually did it. Occasionally, we were very accurate. But could I write an article about that?

First, I might give information that the police didn't have, which could lead to somebody's being arrested. After this, who in their right mind would speak to me about anything in confidence? All my sources of information, my contacts, would dry up.

Second, if I hinted in general terms about specific crimes, the police could well bring me in for questioning and even subpoena me to give evidence. Last, and certainly not the least, the gunman involved would not take kindly to my compromising him. Of all the denizens of the underworld, these are the ones it's best not to offend.

However, that didn't mean that I couldn't do an ironic piece, something of a send-up of the whole genre of murder for hire. Quentin

Tarantino had been doing it for years. He had been a movie buff, not someone involved in crime, yet he had chosen to portray violent killers for hire in his movies. And, rather than do a written piece, I would do it in the medium that Tarantino himself had used – film.

During the several months since I had done the Colombian cocaine-kitchen story, four different TV-production companies had expressed an interest in working with me. I found that TV was a medium I could work quite well with and, if the main aim of my writing for magazines was to raise my writer's profile, then TV was as good a way to achieve this as any. The setting for the piece was a suitably dark and sinister location in the basement of a club. The script I wrote and 'read' was suitably sinister, too, even if it did have a leavening of humour to it. This is the piece.

> I'm Norman Parker, journalist and author of four true crime books. I also served 24 years for what the police described as a 'gangland murder'. On my travels through the top-security jails I met quite a few professional hit men, people who would kill for a price.
>
> Now according to the gospels of Tarantino and Lockstock, crime is ubiquitous and sexy, with the hit man as the star player. And, in this respect, nature has a funny way of imitating art. Go into almost any pub nowadays and you're almost sure to find someone who says he knows how to locate a hit man. Don't necessarily believe it. It's probably all part and parcel of popular 'gangster chic'.
>
> Your wife of ten years been cheating on you with your best friend for nine of them? Your business partner conned you out of your life savings? Your neighbour from Hell finally pushed you over the limit? You need a hit man. So how are you going to go about finding one?
>
> Your first problem is that you are almost certainly a 'straight-goer', that is, not a professional criminal. Your hitter, if he's any good, will be a consummate professional. There's no way he'll deal with you. 'Straight-goers' crack under police interrogation. What's more, they have something called a 'conscience'. This often causes them to confess. And when they do they're quite magnanimous about it, they confess for everyone involved.
>
> You'll have to deal through a middleman anyway, who will find out exactly what you want done, pass on photos, addresses, times,

et cetera. But Catch 22 kicks in again here. The middleman will also be a professional, so he won't deal with you either.

So you make an offer of well above the market price, say thirty to fifty grand, just to get his attention. You want the security of knowing that not only will he get the job done, but that, should the hitter get caught, the buck stops with him. This is the main selling point of the professional hit.

And forget about making some kind of statement. For example, your wife's lover decapitated with a Samurai sword at midnight on the 13th of the month. The hitter will want to keep it simple to give himself the maximum chance of getting away with it.

The odds are that you'll still be out of luck. Professional hit men work almost exclusively within the 'underworld', mostly for drugs gangs. You could say they're the judicial arm of organised crime. Times are hard on the street, but a bit of 'private work' for a 'straight-goer' who just might be undercover 'Old Bill'? Not really!

So you're going to have to lower your sights a bit and find some enthusiastic amateur. Thanks to the ever-burgeoning drugs trade, this shouldn't be too difficult. This is where the somebody-who-knows-somebody factor comes in. Somebody knows a gram dealer, who knows an ounce dealer, who knows someone who deals kilos. Somewhere along the way someone will know of the guy you're looking for.

There's a surfeit of 'crack-head', 'smack-head', Tarantino-esque wannabes just looking to make a name for themselves, and more money than they can get from a dozen minor drugs deals. They'll kill your mark for around ten grand. However, there may well be a number of problems.

If you pay a deposit in advance, you'll probably never see him again. He'll be, 'dead', 'nicked', 'on the run'. What're you gonna do, sue? Then if he's too 'smacked' or 'cracked' up at the time of the hit, anything could happen. He could kill the wrong person entirely. Or you by mistake if you're standing nearby.

Then, after it's all over, it may never be over. He'll blackmail you for the rest of your life. You'll need another hit man just to get rid of him.

Lastly, when he finally messes up on some later hit and finds himself in a cell facing forever without whatever drugs he needs, he just might do a deal and confess to everything he's ever done. You're nicked!

CHAPTER THIRTEEN
DAVE THE RAVE

Although I had taken a whole series of wicked oaths that I wouldn't write a serious article for *Maxim* again, the reality of the situation was that I needed them a whole lot more than they needed me. It broadened my profile to write for a number of magazines and it also prevented *Front* from getting too complacent about my always writing exclusively for them.

In many ways the subject matter of the article was dear to me in that it was a tragic tale of someone who had once been a friend. I didn't doubt that *Maxim* would place the emphasis in all the wrong places and I wasn't to be disappointed. Their emphasis was on the 'cross-dressing bank robber dressed in a tight black leather miniskirt'. To those of us who knew him well, Dave Martin was a whole lot more than that. For us, the emphasis was on a system that could turn a gentle, genuinely non-violent guy into something that was a parody of his former self. That it ended in tragedy was all too predictable. This, then, is the story of the life and tragic death of 'Dave the Rave'. But a short glossary is required before I go on.

GLOSSARY

'A'-man: A prisoner in the highest-security category.

Chaps: An almost mythical grouping of criminals whose ethos includes professionalism in the pursuit of crime; loyalty to others of their kind; hatred of and non-cooperation with authority; and courage (many aspire to membership, few qualify).

Chief: Chief officer, the most senior uniformed officer in the jail.

Con: Convict or prisoner.

Face: Person well known among criminals, one of the 'chaps' (q.v.).

Firm: Group of criminals joined together for a criminal project.

Fours: Fourth landing in a jail.

Met: Metropolitan Police.

Ones: Ground-floor landing in a jail.

PO: Principal officer.

Raver: Prison homosexual.

Slop out: Empty the contents of one's chamber pot in the recess.

Staunch: Loyal and trustworthy.

Around every prison there are always flocks of scruffy moth-eaten pigeons, and Parkhurst was no exception to this rule. There was a constant scrum of them out in the yard, fighting over a crust or some other scrap of discarded food.

Suddenly, a seagull would land among the throng, its pristine white feathers and clean lines making it stand out as a thing of beauty compared with its fellows. By comparison, it seemed a queen among birds.

Dave Martin's arrival at Parkhurst had all the imagery of a seagull landing among pigeons. Parkhurst was an old down-at-heel prison, with the average age of the cons much higher than at most prisons. The weather hardly encouraged stylish dress, either. On the other side of the hill to Albany Prison, Parkhurst took the brunt of the cold winds. The all-pervasive stench from the nearby sewage farm added to a general atmosphere of decay.

Consequently, the cons dressed for comfort rather than appearance. Long grey overcoats and shapeless khaki raincoats were the order of the day. Old blue berets were pulled down tightly around the ears to keep out the chill. On the wings, people lounged around in untidy grey jumpers or discoloured granddad vests. Had there been an award for

Britain's best-dressed con, it would never have been won by an inmate of Parkhurst. You could imagine the entire population being transferred to some Russian gulag and no one looking a bit out of place.

One day, into this sartorial wasteland, came Dave Martin. I was lounging in the cell doorway of Dave Bailey, a close friend, when I saw two warders coming along the 'ones' landing escorting a con I had never seen before.

He was quite tall, but walked with his head bowed, giving him a stooping look. The most striking feature was his hair. It was a cascade of auburn that fell around his shoulders, bouncing and glistening with a sheen that the Silverkrin girl would have been proud of. It framed a long angular face with a large hawklike nose. The nose was a decidedly ugly feature, but such was the softening effect of the hair that the overall impression was one of some beauty.

His neck was long and thin, with a prominent Adam's apple. Fastened around the midpoint was a silver necklace of interlinked shields, each about an inch square, making it look like a silver band around his neck.

Narrow shoulders gave way to a chest bordering on the emaciated. This was flanked by two painfully thin arms. Draped around his upper body was what could only be described as a blouse. It was of a black silky material, with an exaggerated collar and long sleeves that ended in butterfly cuffs. From one wrist dangled a gold bracelet.

The next striking feature was his trousers. The length and slenderness of his legs was highlighted by a pair of blue jeans with a bright yellow stripe of a different material down each outside seam. The stripes meant that he was an E-man, someone who had tried to escape and was now on the 'watch' list.

Such watch-list clothing was generally referred to as patches. These usually consisted of a shapeless pair of prison overalls with a piece of yellow material sewn down each side. This guy's patches, though, were a pair of faded denims, skin-tight at the waist, hips and thighs, but flaring out downwards from the knees. The wide, bright-yellow stripe either side was an integral part of the jeans. They had clearly been tailored with some skill. On his feet was a pair of brownish moccasins. The lack of any rigid sole made him drag his feet to cushion the impact as he 'skated' along.

This was a startling apparition by any standards. On the 'ones' in Parkhurst, at 8.30 in the morning, it was incongruous in the extreme.

''Ere, Dave. Have a look at this guy,' I managed to blurt out as he passed by on the other side of the landing.

Dave came and joined me in the doorway. By this time the figure was just disappearing through the door into 'D' wing, the wing where I lived. 'Oh, that's Dave Martin,' said Dave with a smile on his face. 'They call him "Dave the Rave" because he's a raving poof. He's all right, though. Very staunch, with plenty of guts. He's a bit warm at escaping, too. He was in the escape at Brixton and his gameness put a few of the so-called chaps to shame. To be arriving at this time he must have just been slung out of Albany.'

As I took all this information in, I realised that, as he was going to be on the same wing as I was, Dave Martin and I would probably come in contact with each other quite a bit. Now there was a rather ambivalent attitude to gays in most prisons, and Parkhurst was no exception. Generally speaking, they were beyond the pale. There was all the usual hypocrisy. Although quite a few of the chaps would have a dabble at different times and in different places, blatant effeminate gays were not accepted in the company.

It was nothing to do with their being weak or not staunch, because some gays were very violent indeed and would never grass, no matter what. Many of us were just locked into the code of the chaps, where gay behaviour was publicly condemned. Quite simply, it was blind hypocritical prejudice and I was as guilty of it as anyone else.

When I returned to my wing a little later I saw the newcomer talking to Jeff, who lived in the next cell to me. Jeff was gay too. At just five foot three tall, with dark Italian looks and flowing black hair, Jeff had been a sometime companion of several of the chaps in other jails. Although he was generally accepted and everyone talked to him, the chaps wouldn't have him permanently in their company as a friend either.

I knew him from the trouble at Albany a couple of years previously. He had acquitted himself well in the riot, as well as the subsequent hunger strike in the punishment block. He was the first person to welcome me when I arrived at Parkhurst. We weren't close friends by any means. In truth, his homosexuality embarrassed me. However, it normally went unmentioned, unless he made a joke at his own expense. We often spoke and got on quite well.

I suppose I could have guessed that he would link up with Dave. It transpired that they new each other from Albany. As I approached, Jeff did the introductions. I was immediately struck by Dave's soft-spoken, intelligent, cultured manner. His large bony hand shook mine with no trace of effeminacy. I was relieved that, like Jeff, Dave wasn't exaggeratedly camp. In fact, neither was camp at all.

As part of the introductions, Jeff mentioned that Dave was a clever and resourceful escape artist. That immediately pulled me up short. Jeff had obviously told Dave who the most resourceful escapers on the wing were and was trying to link him up with me in this respect.

The hope of escaping was one of the things that kept me going. Further, my close friends were similarly engaged in trying to escape and we currently had quite a viable plan going. Secrecy was paramount. This, coupled with my prejudice against gays, meant that there was no way that Dave could be in on the plot, whatever his skills.

There were four of us involved in the plan, Stewart, John, Mick and I. We were part of a much bigger group of Londoners, many of whom suspected that we were plotting an escape but weren't party to the details. That didn't mean that collectively and individually they wouldn't help us in any way they could. This 'network' was the one thing that Dave Martin didn't, and probably couldn't, have.

Mick had been at Parkhurst for several months and had managed to make some useful contacts. The most important of these was his relationship with a civilian tradesman in the Works Department. To all intents and purposes these were ordinary plumbers, bricklayers, carpenters etc., who worked for the prison. While it was much frowned upon to get close to the warders, it was accepted that a 'Works' tradesman who treated the prisoners decently could be similarly treated in turn.

In truth, the relationship was basically a financial one. Mick paid the civilian to bring in various articles such as drink and tobacco. The problem, from my point of view, was that Mick liked to plan almost as an intellectual exercise. Very little actually got done. I prevailed on him, though, and he got the civilian to bring in two pairs of bolt croppers. These were to cut the wire of the perimeter fencing.

I had been thinking of the small single-handed variety and had even provided Mick with a British Standard reference number taken from a catalogue in one of the prison workshops. Mick said that he didn't need it and insisted that he knew what he was doing. In the event, the civilian brought in two pairs of double-handed bolt croppers, each about two foot long. As far as effectiveness went, they were ideal, but for secrecy and ease of concealment they were much too big.

To make matters worse, they were handed over to us in the compound at exercise time. We had the cover of a couple of hundred cons milling about, but very little else. The bolt croppers were much too big to hide down our trousers, but luckily one guy was bringing in a pillowcase full of laundry. He took both pairs off us, stuffed them inside the pillowcase, draped a towel over the handles that protruded and blatantly walked into the wing past dozens of warders.

This was typical of the solidarity that existed among many cons at Parkhurst. Had the guy been caught, he would have lost six months' remission, spent two months in solitary confinement, probably including 15 days of bread-and-water diet, and then been transferred out to another jail. Ironically, the guy wasn't even a close friend, just someone who believed in the code of the 'chaps'.

Once inside the wing, we now had the problem of hiding them until they were needed. One pair we hid inside a partition wall up on the 'fours'; the other was buried out on the sports field by one of the gym orderlies as he marked the football pitch for the weekly game. Again, this orderly wasn't a close friend, just a loyal honourable guy.

The civilian workers, just like the regular warders, had a bunch of keys that let them through strategic doors and gates. Now I asked Mick to get his man to give us an impression of the key that opened all the barred gates in the jail. We told him how to do it and he brought in a piece of cuttlefish inside a matchbox, with a perfectly pressed impression of the key we needed.

The next stage of the plan was to put the matchbox containing the impression inside a large soft toy which someone had made on a hobbies class and hand it out on a visit. It had to be handed out by someone who had children, which excluded the four of us. However, there was no shortage of volunteers. The only misgivings the guy who handed it out had was that his wife might have trouble getting the toy off his child in the car park, where it was due to be handed over to someone else.

The impression was to go to 'John the Bosch', a well-known and very experienced 'key man' in London. It was no mean feat to make a copy of a Chubb key, yet 'the Bosch' had managed to do so on several of his prison sentences with a minimum of tools. Outside, with a workshop at his disposal, it should be comparatively easy for him. However, as the visit was still over two weeks away, we had to keep the impression hidden in the meantime.

Over the next few days I caught glimpses of Dave Martin about the wing. He rarely seemed to wear the same thing twice. There was a stylishly tailored denim jacket made out of an overall jacket and a little thing in purple that could have been a tie-dyed gym vest. Two more coloured blouses and a cut-down grey overcoat added further depth to his wardrobe.

The effect on the warders was quite amusing. They obviously knew he was a skilled escaper, but other than that they just didn't know what to make of him. His camp appearance, if not manner, embarrassed them. They were as much locked into their chauvinistic codes as we were.

As an E-man he had to have regular security searches. Any warders detailed to carry out these searches came in for a ribbing from the others. Dave took full advantage of this. As slight as he was, and there were some burly brutal warders at Parkhurst, he wasn't at all intimidated by them. If, for example, one of the warders insisted he strip right off, Dave would say something like, 'Oh, if it's just my arse you want to see ...' and proceed to pull his trousers down, revealing coloured frilly knickers. At this stage the warder would rapidly back off.

This was quite a clever strategy by Dave, because one of his favourite hiding places for contraband items was behind his balls. After all, what warder is going to run his hands over a notorious gay's private parts in full view of other warders? The outcome was that Dave hardly ever got a thorough search.

Most evenings, when allowed out for 'association', I would hang about the wing with Stewart and another friend of ours called Barry. They would smoke what they called 'laughing baccy' and the warders called cannabis. I thought 'laughing baccy' more appropriate, because when they were on it they spent most of the time laughing and fooling about. Both had a well-developed sense of humour and both were quite mischievous with it.

Sometimes when they were 'off their faces', they would suggest that we should pay a visit to 'poof's parlour'. This was a reference to Jeff's cell, where he would regularly sit with Dave. There was nothing remotely sexual in our visits. Barry and Stewart were notorious mickey takers. They were obviously intrigued by the fact that two effeminate, 'bitch' poofs were together. A favourite joke was: 'Whose turn is it to wear the trousers this week?' It was just fun, with no vindictiveness. Everyone would laugh and enjoy themselves.

It was during these sessions that I got to see more of Dave's character. In public, about the prison, he seemed quite shy and timid. There was no surprise about this. Parkhurst was an extremely violent prison. Many of the cons had been thrown out of other jails for their violent conduct. In many ways, Parkhurst was the Home Office's 'end of the line' for recalcitrant prisoners whom they had given up on reforming.

Although he was no coward, Dave was no warrior, either. He had never done martial arts and had no boxing skills, so his slender frame didn't lend itself well to physical combat. Nor did he have the crazy viciousness that would drive him to use a knife or iron bar. So, in a prison where there were many predatory, violent cons, he was at a considerable disadvantage.

Even for those of us who were quite capable of extreme violence, some of these 'nutters' could be a problem. But then the support of the chaps would swing into operation. It would be treated as a 'bit of work'. Plans would be made and weapons readied. The attack, when it came, would be unsuspected, short and extremely brutal. The offender would be cornered in his cell, the recess or somewhere else out of sight of the warders. He would be coshed, stabbed and left severely injured. The weapons would be disposed of and clothes would be changed. Other cons would be ready to say that the perpetrators had been with them, well out of the way, at the time of the attack.

With this kind of network of support, even someone like Mike Tyson wouldn't be too much of a problem. We prided ourselves, though, on the fact that we weren't liberty takers and bullies. Anyone who got this treatment had made a move against us first. And it was the only way to survive in the violent world that was Parkhurst.

Dave didn't have this kind of support. He would, quite literally, be at the mercy of some predatory bully who decided to have a go at him. This must have been all very unnerving for him.

Even though he never spoke about his previous crimes, bit by bit, from various people, details did emerge. We knew he hadn't been an armed robber or notoriously violent criminal, because none of us had 'worked' with him, heard of him or knew others who had. So, if 'professionalism in the pursuit of crime' is a prerequisite for membership of the chaps, then Dave surely didn't qualify. He would have been more aware of this than anyone.

Dave grew up on a rundown sink estate in Highbury, the only child of honest, hardworking, if poor, parents. This was no disbarment from anything, as the majority of us working-class criminals had similar backgrounds. Unlike the case with us, though, there was no 'borstal' or 'approved' school to curb his teenage criminality, because he had worked as a racing-car mechanic until his early twenties.

Dave's pride and joy was his Lotus-Carlton, on which he lavished hours of his spare time and hundreds of pounds of his wages. Its subsequent theft devastated him. I met his father, Ralph, many years later, still living in the dingy flat on the rundown estate, and he was adamant that this event had turned his formerly hardworking son to crime. Soon, Dave was stealing cars himself and, in 1970, was sentenced to three years for car theft.

He served part of this sentence in Maidstone Prison and, despite serving time alongside him, fellow prisoners could hardly remember him. He was that quiet and unremarkable. Whatever other effects it had on him, Dave came out bisexual. A high degree of coercion and intimidation is used for sexual ends in jail and no one knows whether this change was brought about willingly.

The lust for revenge he emerged with was entirely of his own volition. That it was directed at the chief superintendent who had supervised his arrest says as much about his lack of professionalism as it does about his rebellious spirit. To the professional criminal, the police are an occupational hazard. They are hated as a species rather than as individuals. No professional criminal goes out of his way to antagonise them unnecessarily. Not Dave, though. That the chief super was stationed at his local police station made his conduct all the more reckless.

Like Dave, the super was a racing-car enthusiast. His pride and joy was the classic Jaguar XK120 that he parked in the secure yard at the back of the police station. With car theft rapidly approaching epidemic proportions in London, it was safe here. Or, rather, it was safe from anyone but a person with the skills, determination and sheer cheek of Dave Martin!

One moonless night in 1972, Dave, dressed in black camouflage clothing, climbed into the yard at the back of the police station. Lighted windows overlooked the yard and officers could be seen working at their desks. Occasionally, other officers parked or retrieved their cars from the yard. Quite unperturbed, Dave worked away quietly.

He cut the padlock on the yard gate, then broke into the XK120. After releasing the handbrake, he pushed the car through the now open gate and into the street. Here he started it up and drove away at speed.

One can only imagine the super's embarrassment. Within hours, the theft was the talk of the station. He was a man not known for his good humour either. His passion for the car was well known. Station staff walked on eggshells lest they do something to incur his wrath.

Late the following afternoon, Dave phoned the station. The officer who answered asked the nature of his enquiry. Dave said that he wanted to speak to the super. When the officer prevaricated, saying that the super was a busy man and couldn't come to the phone for anyone, Dave interjected. 'Tell him to come to the phone, otherwise I'll set light to his fucking car,' he thundered.

The super was rage personified. 'Who the hell are you and what do you know about my car?' he roared into the phone. Every head in the large office turned.

'You listen to me very carefully,' said Dave evenly, he was enjoying himself now. 'I've got your car and if you don't do exactly as I tell you I'm going to set it alight.'

In the face of this threat, all of the bluster went out of the super's tone. Noticeably lowering his voice, he asked what Dave wanted.

'I want you to repeat after me: "Please can I have my nice car back?"' instructed Dave. 'Do it, or I'll definitely burn the car.'

The super hesitated, then glanced surreptitiously around the office. Every eye was on him, but quickly turned away. Lowering his voice even more, the super pleaded, 'Please can I have my car back?'

'No, that's not what I asked,' said Dave, as if reasoning with a child. 'You forgot to say "nice". It's "Please can I have my *nice* car back?"'

Closing his eyes and screwing up his face, the super said, in a voice that was little more than a throaty whisper, 'Please can I have my nice car back?'

'Of course you can, super, of course you can.' Dave's tone was conciliatory now. 'It's at the airport.'

'Which one?' asked the super eagerly.

'Orly, you cunt,' said Dave as he put the phone down.

Now this was all very funny stuff, but, from a professional criminal's point of view, it was sheer stupidity. The outcome was that the super and the local police concentrated all their attention on catching Dave. That he was wanted only for car theft, burglary and fraud didn't at all merit the resources they poured into the hunt.

Soon there was a high-speed car chase, ending in a crash. Now it was time for the super to have his laugh. Dave found himself in Brixton Prison charged with car theft and attempted murder as a result of the car chase. Further, his police report was so damning that he was placed on the escape list by the prison authorities and had to wear 'patches'.

For most people, this would have been the end of the story, but not for Dave. His first priority was to escape. This was easier said than done, because, as an E-man, he was located in 'A' wing.

'A' wing was home to top-security prisoners, mainly armed robbers, facing very long sentences. Needless to say, everyone was under a lot of stress. Many had been put away by informers, so were virulently intolerant of anyone they didn't know or trust. The effeminate Dave was still very much an unknown quantity. Once again, he was regarded as being 'only a poof'. The vast majority ignored him.

On the wing, waiting to go to trial, were the notorious and prolific 'Wembley Mob'. These were exclusively Premier Division 'chaps', who, as well as a string of major bank robberies, had robbed one bank of over £250,000. They were innovative and had a certain organisational flair. Some were natural leaders. Soon they had a viable escape plot going.

There were several linked elements to the plan and, for it to work, each had to be carried out smoothly. The most audacious element was to overpower all the warders and take control of the wing. Then, using a key taken from a warder, they would let themselves out into a side yard, where dustmen were emptying bins into their dustcart. The exit from this particular yard was through double wooden gates. The dustcart would be driven at and through these. Once into the street outside, some would get away in waiting cars; others would take their chances on foot.

The essence of this plan was timing. Once the warders were overpowered, there would be only a short time before the general alarm was raised and police rushed to block off roads surrounding the jail. Further, the dustcart was in the yard for only a short time.

Breaking the various elements down further, the plotters were confident they had everything covered. There were certainly enough 'heavies' to overpower the warders and the Wembley Mob's driver, Dan, was one of the best wheelmen in the business. He was confident he could drive the dustcart through the wooden gates. However, opening the wing gate to the yard with the captured keys was problematic. There were quite a few keys on the warders' key rings. It could take some time to find the right one to open the yard gate. Precious seconds could be lost and these precious seconds could mean the failure of the plot. The ultimate nightmare would be for the wrong key to jam in the lock.

By coincidence, there were a couple of chaps on 'A' wing who knew of Dave's abilities with keys and locks. Had he made the approach himself he would have been rejected out of hand. With their recommendation, though, he was in on the plot.

It was May of 1973 that the plan was put into action. By now, 30 or so people were involved and everyone took their position. The first move was to be made by a leading member of the Wembley Mob. Henry was to jump on the wing's principal officer in his office and take his keys. That would be the signal for everybody else to overpower the rest of the warders.

There had been no doubt that Henry was equal to the task. At six foot tall and 15 stones, he was facing a 20-year sentence. Henry hovered near the doorway to the PO's office. Then he hovered some more. Other people standing about started to get uneasy. They couldn't understand why Henry hadn't jumped on the PO.

To Dave, standing very close to Henry, it was all too clear. The pasty white face spoke volumes. Taking the initiative, Dave threw himself at the PO. Both fell to the floor of the office with a resounding crash. Other inmates piled in and helped him subdue the PO. Elsewhere on the wing, desperate inmates threw themselves upon the nearest warder.

With the PO's keys now in his hand, Dave led the charge down to the yard gate. He had already identified the key he would need. He thrust it into the lock and swung the gate open, all in one smooth movement. The mob behind him brushed him aside as it thundered into the yard where battle immediately commenced.

This was all too much for the dustmen. Terrified, they fled to the far corners of the yard. The two warders guarding them fought back, though, as more warders poured through the gate behind the escaping mob. With the inmates armed with the dustmen's brooms and shovels and the warders with their riot sticks, the battle raged around the dustcart.

Dan, the Wembley Mob's wheelman, had jumped behind the wheel of the dustcart. Dave had jumped in beside him. Dan froze, puzzled by the unfamiliar controls. The lifting arm of the dustcart was up, holding an unemptied bin. It would have to be lowered to pass under the brick arch over the wooden gates. He tugged at various controls with no effect.

Suddenly, Dave pushed him aside. Taking the wheel, he started the cart and drove it straight at the wooden gates. The gates shattered as the front of the cab smashed through, but the upraised lifting arm and dustbin collided with the brick arch and the cart came to an abrupt stop. There was a path to freedom via either side of the cart, though. Battling inmates broke free to run past the cart and into the street.

The Wembley Mob had arranged for a large van to be left in the street. Now they fought their way towards it. This was to be their mistake, for, by now, more and more warders were arriving on the scene. With the windscreen smashed and a warder lying across the wheel, the van was going nowhere. Then the police cars started to arrive. Soon the escapers were lying battered and bloody in the road.

But not Dave. He had taken one look at the situation with the van and decided that it was a poor prospect. With another escaper following, he ran through the door of one house, into a back garden, through another house and into another street. They repeated this process several times. Within minutes they were a quarter of a mile away. Dave hailed a passing taxi and they piled in.

This was his fatal mistake. Black taxis are part of the police radio net. The driver heard news about the escape on his radio. Surreptitiously, he called the police and said that he thought he had two of the escapers on board. Police cars quickly surrounded the taxi and Dave and the other escaper were both arrested. By some considerable irony, the other, nearly successful, escaper was also openly gay.

Dave was returned to Brixton and placed in solitary. A further charge of escaping was added to the other charges he was already facing.

At his trial, Dave refused to recognise the court. Again, from a professional criminal's point of view, this was sheer stupidity. The chaps were well aware that the legal process was something like a game. Both sides made various manoeuvres to try to influence the jury one way or another. One well-known chap had a ploy of bursting into tears at a crucial point in his trials. It had won him several unwarranted acquittals and no one condemned him for it. It was all part of the 'game'.

Only political prisoners, such as the IRA, ever refused to recognise courts. By doing so, Dave could only have antagonised the judge. As a result, he was sentenced to ten and a half years, probably double what he would have got if he had behaved sensibly.

I had learned none of the above from Dave personally. A likable aspect of his personality was that he never bragged about his achievements. This impressed me all the more.

However, if Dave had thought that his latest gutsy exploits would lead to his being fully accepted, he would have been disappointed. Unfortunately for him, the category 'poof' cancelled out all the other factors in many people's eyes. This was further compounded by the fact that Dave couldn't have a fight to save his life. If he had been violent, his gayness could well have been ignored. Ronnie Kray was gay and no one ever called him a poof.

Even though I was now aware of Dave's abilities, I had no intention of asking him to join in our escape plan. We didn't need him, or anyone else for that matter. Quite obviously, the more people involved, the greater the difficulty in getting away unseen or, at least, with a decent start. And, if we were going to include someone quite gratuitously, then we would have chosen them from our immediate circle of friends.

But Jeff had heard about the forced delay in handing out the impression of the key. Normally, our security was tight, but another failing of Mick's, apart from his dithering, was that he told too many people about his business. We guessed that Mick must have told him, because Jeff pulled me to one side and asked if, in view of the delay, Dave could have a go at making a key from the impression.

I, personally, was against the idea. Although I quite liked Dave as an individual, I still wasn't over-impressed by his professionalism. My fear was that he would damage the impression or, worse, lose it. Then we would be back to square one again.

John, Stewart and Mick, though, were of the opinion that it was worth a chance. Dave assured us that he knew what he was doing and that he would not only make a working key but would also hand the impression back completely undamaged. I duly handed the impression over, saying that I wanted it back as soon as possible.

To my great surprise, Dave gave it back to me the following day. At the same time, he showed me the key he had made. I was immediately impressed. It actually looked like a proper key, the shiny metal silver-soldered together, but with the rectangular 'flag' blank and blackened with candle soot.

He had a further request of me. As he was in 'patches' and worked in the top-security mailbag shop, Dave would never get the opportunity to try the key out in a gate. He knew that I worked in the tin shop, which had several sets of gates in obscure corners. He asked me to take the key into the shop and try it out.

I was committed to help him now, although, secretly, I still doubted that he would be able to make a key that worked. Once again, it was down to his 'image'. He was so far from what I considered a capable professional criminal to be.

There was a room called the spray shop that was attached to the tin shop. It was separated from the tin shop by double unlocked doors. Two cons worked in there on their own, although all workers in the tin shop had easy access to it. A civilian instructor would go in occasionally, but the warders, sitting in set posts in the main shop, never did.

I didn't know either of the two cons personally, but once again the

'Parkhurst solidarity' factor kicked in. I entered the spray shop and approached both of them. 'Do either of you two fellas mind if I try a key out in that gate in the corner?' I asked.

One immediately jumped up from where he had been sitting and replied, 'You go right ahead, mate. I'll watch the door for you.'

I turned the key in the lock and, being a 'blank' of course, it struck against something inside and wouldn't open the gate. But, where it had struck the lock's levers, there were now scratches and scuff marks on the blackened 'flag'. I took the key back to Dave.

He worked on it over the lunchtime lockup period and handed it back to me as we unlocked. The flag was completely blackened again, but he had cut shallow notches along one edge. I took it into the shop and tried it in the lock again. Once again it didn't turn the lock, but there was now another set of scratch marks on the 'flag'.

Over the next several days, deeper notches were cut. Each time I would try it in the spray-shop gate. Each time it wouldn't turn the lock. I was now rapidly running out of patience. Trying the key out each time wasn't without risk, for both me and the two fellas who were looking out for me. Further, I was on the top-security, Category 'A' list myself. Should I be singled out for one of the special searches that 'A' men regularly had, the key would be found. That would be the end of me and this particular plot.

Nine times I tried the key and nine times it wouldn't open the gate. On the tenth time, I had resolved to tell Dave that was enough. To my great surprise, on the tenth try, the key turned smoothly in the lock and the gate opened. Just to make sure, I repeated the process several times. I hurried back from work that teatime to tell the others in the escape that we didn't have to send the impression out now. We had our key.

This immediately put us on an action footing. It meant that we could have a go within a couple of weeks. However, we would have to decide where we would go from. I was the only one of the group who worked in the tin shop, so that wasn't an option. We still had a lot of planning to do.

We now had a gate key that would let us out of the wing and bolt croppers to cut the perimeter fences. But the main problem was getting to the perimeter fences unseen, because, if the alarm went up before we got there, the police would have the jail surrounded before we could cut through the fences.

Then there was the problem of getting away. We had some outside help, but you couldn't ask them to come over to the island, because when the alarm went up the island would be sealed off and our help sealed in with us. We would have to make our own way off the island and link up with our help on the mainland.

Dave, with his newly enhanced credibility, now sat in with John, Stewart and me when we discussed the escape. Quite strangely, Mick was suddenly decidedly unenthusiastic about the whole project. I quickly came to the conclusion that he didn't want to go. He had been involved in the Brixton escape and all the trauma that a failed escape entailed. An escape attempt was one of the most serious of prison offences. The penalty was normally two to six months in solitary in the punishment block, including 15 days on a bread-and-water diet. For those with a fixed sentence, there would be anything from two to six months' loss of remission. Then the offender would be placed in 'patches' and probably spend several months in the punishment block of a local prison, where conditions were always Spartan and brutal.

Mick had settled into his sentence at Parkhurst and had even got himself a budgie, a sure sign of settling down. In addition, his appeal against sentence was due to be heard shortly and he was hoping to get some time taken off. We decided to press on without him.

The ideal escape scenario was for us to get out of our cells at night, tie the couple of old watchmen up, let out scores of people, get out of the wing and storm the fences. For this plan, though, we would need several more things, the first of which was a cell-door key. Even with that, though, someone would still have to get out of his cell first, to be able to unlock others.

Dave said that he could make a cell-door key easily, and after what we had already seen no one doubted him on this. He went on to say that he could take his cell door off from the inside by sawing through the hinges with a hacksaw blade that he had. Then he could let others out with the cell-door key. The final obstacle would be a double-locked wing gate that the 'singles' key wouldn't unlock.

Much of this made for an attractive plan. A mass breakout in the middle of the night would mean that quite a few of us would stand a good chance of getting away. The final double-locked gate wasn't an impassable barrier, either. With the night-watchmen tied up we could afford to break it down, then storm the fences with the bolt croppers.

The hardest part, in my opinion, would be for Dave to take his door off from the inside. I had never heard of its being done before. With the greatest skill and patience, he would have to cut silently through the two big hinges, which were partly concealed by the locked door. Then he would have to lift at least 200 pounds of steel and wooden door out of its frame while the lock and bolt were still shot into the jamb. And, as this would be in the quiet of the night, he would have to do it all without making a sound.

It would be a feat that would need incredible patience, skill and strength. I thought it couldn't be done without making enough noise to alert the night-watchmen. And, even if it was possible to do such a thing, it wasn't possible for Dave to do it, he of the 32-inch chest and skinny arms. I vetoed the idea, much to Dave's annoyance.

Suddenly, though, everything had to be put on hold. We were told on good authority that, after lockup one night, a dozen warders had stayed behind with the night-watchmen. They had stayed out of sight in the night-watchmen's office. Quite clearly, something had been said. Even Parkhurst wasn't without informers.

None of our immediate group was suspect, but Mick was still being informed about our progress, more out of courtesy than anything else. However, although he would never inform on anyone, he was often quite lax about who he discussed things with. Our guess was that he had said something to the wrong person.

As it was, Mick took the opportunity to declare that, in the circumstances, he wasn't going to do anything for a couple of months. Reluctantly, we had to concede that we would lie low for a couple of weeks at least.

Dave wanted to keep working on ideas, though. He lived on such a high state of alert that all the new heat made little difference to him. Our feelings were that, if he wanted to carry on, that was up to him. We could hardly stop him, anyway.

As the days passed, Dave would occasionally pop into my cell and bring me up to date with the ideas he had and the progress he was making. Since we couldn't make our move at the moment, it was all largely academic to me and, in truth, I gave him only part of my attention. I continued to underestimate him and he continued to surprise me.

One day, Dave said that he thought he could make a 'doubles' key. Now no one had made a 'doubles' key before, in any jail or at any time. Some of the old great 'key men' had made 'singles' keys that worked, as had Dave so very recently, but none of them had even tried to make a 'doubles' key.

For a start, no one had ever had so much as a glimpse of one. Out of all the warders in the jail, only the security PO had one. He would go around, on his own, 'double-locking' strategic gates and doors late in the evening, and unlocking them early the next morning. Once they had been locked on the 'double', they couldn't be unlocked with an ordinary 'singles' key.

From looking at any jail-gate lock, it could be seen that the 'doubles' keyhole was set up and out to one side of the 'singles' keyhole. Further, legend had it that the 'flag' on the 'doubles' key wasn't fixed to the 'shank' at an angle of 90 degrees as it was on 'singles' keys. But, since no one had ever managed to bribe a security PO, no one had ever seen one, so everything was just supposition.

Dave suddenly came up with an idea that was a quantum leap in key-making logic. He suggested that, if he put the 'singles' key that he had made into the 'singles' keyhole and turned it, at the same time as he put a straight 'shank' of a key with a prong sticking out at an angle into the 'doubles' keyhole and turned that, then the double-locked gate would open.

If he was expecting my opinion, he would have been disappointed. While he might be a mechanical genius, everything that went on in the obscurity of a lock was a total mystery to me. I couldn't appreciate the problems, so I couldn't offer any suggestions. It was all way beyond me, and everybody else for that matter. But, as he didn't actually require me to do anything to help, and as I still didn't take him completely seriously, I just told him to carry on.

Just above the 'fours' landing was a raised 'catwalk' that led to a gate that opened into the roof space. This was a crucial line of defence for the prison. Anyone who got into the roof space could easily remove several tiles, climb on to the roof itself and then lower themselves to the ground with a rope. As only the Works Department ever went into the roof space, and then very rarely, this gate was always locked on the 'double'.

This gate would be very difficult to get to without being seen. Any warder walking the length or breadth of the lower landings couldn't fail but to see someone going across the exposed 'catwalk'. And, once across the 'catwalk', Dave would have to stand at the gate, right out in the open, to tamper with the lock. Taking all the circumstances into account, I would have said that it was logistically impossible. For everybody else it probably was, but not for Dave.

He had noticed that, during the lunch hour when everybody was locked up, the few warders on duty stayed in the wing office. No one patrolled the landings. The only inmates allowed out were the two 'hotplate' orderlies, one of whom was his friend/lover, Jeff.

Dave first made a cell-door key, which he gave to Jeff. Waiting until the warders were in the office having their lunch, Jeff crept along the landing and unlocked Dave's door. Dave went straight up to the 'fours', crawled across the 'catwalk' and went to work on the lock. He inserted his 'singles' key into the 'singles' keyhole, inserted the 'shank' with the prong into the 'doubles' keyhole, and turned both. The gate sprang open!

Working quickly, he removed the whole lock assembly with a screwdriver and hurried back to his cell. Once inside, he took it to pieces, measured all the levers and other parts with a small metric ruler and reassembled it. Then he hurried back up to the 'fours', replaced it and 'double-locked' the gate, before returning to his cell and locking himself up. The whole operation had taken less than 20 minutes. You couldn't fault Dave for his nerve, and his genius was breathtaking. It was something straight out of James Bond. Bond, though, didn't have an image problem because he was gay.

The following day, Dave came into my cell and told me what he had done. We now had a 'doubles' key at our disposal, which added a whole new dimension to our escape plans. It meant that there wasn't a gate or a door that we couldn't go through, at any hour, day or night. In fact, we could go through doors that none of the warders, except the security PO, could go through.

It raised some interesting possibilities. At various points in the inner perimeter fence were set massive double gates. They stood 18 foot high, the same as the fence, and were made of the same thick wire mesh mounted on a steel tubular frame. Once you were through these gates, there was only the second perimeter fence, which adjoined a 16-foot-high wall. You could make a choice: either cut the fence or rope and hook the wall.

Normally, would-be escapers didn't consider these double gates to be a weakness, because they were always locked on the 'double'. For all intents and purposes they were part of the main fence. With our 'doubles' key, though, now we could stage a mass escape from the main prison yard.

Such an event would undoubtedly have been the most spectacular escape in penal history. Parkhurst housed some of the country's most dangerous inmates, including a dozen or so IRA men doing very long sentences. This was a classic example of why Dave came to be viewed with such seriousness by the prison authorities, if not by his fellow cons. The former weren't concerned so much about his escaping on his own. The hue and cry would be minimal, as he was doing only ten and a half years for largely non-violent offences. What really concerned them was all the violent and dangerous men he could take with him.

However, it was still only a few days since there had been the alert over the warders staying behind at night. John and Stewart both thought we ought to lie low for a bit longer. In truth, Dave was still suffering from his credibility problem. If one of the chaps had achieved what Dave had achieved, then his opinion would have carried much more weight.

This time, we resolved to keep the secret among Dave, John, Stewart, Jeff and me. Jeff had decided that he now wanted to escape too. As Dave had made so much progress on his own, we could hardly say that he couldn't include his mate. But we did stipulate that we would tell others who might want to be involved only at the last moment. This was a sensible security measure.

At this stage, I was still making most of the decisions. With Mick out of the running, strictly speaking, the 'singles' key was mine. Even though Dave had made it, he had done so with my impression. However, he had gone on to make a cell-door key and a 'doubles' key, so the situation regarding 'ownership' of keys and when they should be used was now quite ambiguous. But, as Dave was being perfectly open with me, this wasn't a problem.

Dave then decided that we now had everything we needed for the escape and to wait could only jeopardise our chances. The situation was always fluid in top-security jails and anything could happen. Apart from anything else, a chance and thorough search could reveal the keys. Dave wanted to press on.

He now knew that, during the mealtime lockups for breakfast, lunch and tea, there were very few warders on duty. Further, his mate, Jeff, would be out at these times, in his role as an orderly. He had already demonstrated that Jeff could unlock someone's cell and let them out. He then came up with a brilliant and audacious plan.

As part of his orderly's duties, Jeff was always in and out of the wing office, cleaning and fetching cups of tea for the warders. He had noticed that there was a locker in one corner of the office that served as a cloakroom. Here the warders hung their overcoats and other parts of their uniform that they weren't going to wear immediately. Over time, bits and pieces of spare uniforms had collected in this cupboard, together with hats, ties and boots.

Dave got Jeff to steal parts for two complete uniforms, together with two spare hats. Apart from all his other talents, he was something of a skilled tailor. In his cell, he altered the uniforms and hats so that they fitted Jeff and himself perfectly. This was especially difficult, as he was much too thin to be a warder and, at only five foot three tall, Jeff was much too short. When he finished, he got Jeff to replace them in the office cupboard.

Then Dave came to me and explained his plan. One breakfast time when the wing was locked up, Jeff would unlock Dave's cell. He would go in and both would change into the two altered uniforms. Then they would unlock me.

Dave would then let the three of us out of the wing and into a short corridor. At the end of the corridor was a gate that led outside. Once outside, Dave and Jeff would make out that they were two warders escorting me somewhere. They would escort me down a hill towards the punishment block.

The pretence was necessary because, although it was very unlikely that they would bump into any warders at this time of day, the path down the hill was covered by a CCTV camera on the nearby security wing that was monitored in the control room.

A short distance past the camera was the gate to the exercise compound. As all the cons were locked up, this would be deserted and unpatrolled. However, just inside the gate was another CCTV camera that would see anyone entering the compound. Here again, the warders' uniforms would play a vital part.

At the far end of the compound was a double gate. Dave would unlock these gates with his 'doubles' key and then we would be between the fences. It would be a simple matter to cut the outside fence with the bolt croppers that were buried out in the compound anyway.

It was another brilliant plan, but my first emotion was anger. Although Dave had made provision for me, there was no provision for John and Stewart. Further, there was no realistic possibility of their being involved. Two warders couldn't escort three cons: that would immediately raise suspicion. To alter more uniforms would take more time and the bigger the group of people moving outside the wings at this time the more it was likely to raise suspicion.

When I explained all this to John and Stewart, they said that it was best that just the three of us go – Dave, Jeff and I. I was nothing if not loyal, though. Even with their blessing, it might still look like a slippery move. There was also a second problem. The unwritten, largely unspoken chaps' code was all-powerful in Parkhurst, and 'gayness' was a major barrier to acceptance in polite society. I was in the code's grip as much as anyone.

As Dave and Jeff's homosexuality was a major facet of their characters, it would certainly be mentioned in their records. In the event that all three of us escaped together, the press could well pick up on this fact. I could imagine banner headlines about 'gay escapers'. Silly as it may sound, this was a major deterrent to me.

Last but not least, the authorities had me down as one of their most violent and dangerous prisoners. Because I was an 'A-man', my photo would be permanently on display in the gatehouse, where warders would see it every time they came and went to and from work. Therefore, I had a highly recognisable face. Should the warders in the control room pick me out on one of the CCTV cameras, they would surely wonder where the two 'warders' were taking me at this time of the morning.

I told Dave that I couldn't go with them and was on the verge of telling him that he had taken a liberty to go so far without us. As far as John, Stewart and I were concerned, that was the end of any escape plans for us. We would have to start all over again. After Dave and Jeff had made their attempt, at the very least, all the locks would be changed and, no doubt, other security measures would be put in place.

I could have got heavy with them and threatened them, but that itself would have been 'out or order'. The rights and wrongs of the situation had become confused. I had provided the impression, but Dave had gone on to do so much more by himself.

By now, they both were sitting there, quite shamefacedly. I couldn't help but feel sorry for them. They were both nice guys and it wasn't easy for them in prison. 'And I suppose you want a pair of our fucking bolt croppers to do the perimeter fence with too, don't you?' I asked in a tone that sounded angry but was meant to be ironic.

Dave nodded his head sheepishly. I told them exactly where a pair were hidden, in a partition wall up on the 'fours'.

Once evening association had started, just after 6 p.m., there would be no more spot searches for the day, unless there were very unusual circumstances. By late afternoon, Jeff had collected both the bolt croppers and the two altered uniforms, caps and so forth, and taken them to his cell. Now they were ready for the following morning.

I saw Jeff at breakfast the next day, but we didn't speak. There was no sign of Dave, but that wasn't unusual, since he never got up for breakfast. The meal served, the warders went around and locked everyone up, except for Jeff and the other orderly.

This other orderly was something of a strange guy. A violent and well-known 'face' from South London, Terry was doing 15 years for a string of highly professional armed robberies. However, he had made himself unpopular with the chaps at Parkhurst by becoming too close with the warders. Not only did he make tea for them, he also socialised with them about the wing. This didn't mean that he wasn't staunch, though. He knew about the escape plot and distracted the warders when Jeff wanted to do something.

Recently, he had begun leaving his radio on the hotplate, playing loudly. This would serve to drown out any noise Dave and Jeff might make on their way out of the wing.

Terry made tea and sandwiches for the two warders left on duty in the office and stood in the doorway, laughing and joking with them. Outside, his radio was playing loudly.

Jeff immediately hurried along the landing and quietly let himself into Dave's cell with the cell-door key. They quickly put on the close-fitting uniforms and boots, tucking their long flowing hair up inside the caps. The blue shirts and ties added the finishing touches.

They were now wearing what every warder in Parkhurst was wearing, but there the similarity ended. For they were two of the most unlikely-looking warders you would ever see in your life. The tall gangly one was undoubtedly the skinniest warder in the prison service. The short one was equally skinny, but the striking feature was his height. He failed the minimum requirements by at least three inches. Individually, they looked distinctly odd. Walking along together, they looked extraordinarily comical.

They left Dave's cell carrying the bolt croppers concealed in a pillowcase. There was nothing out of the ordinary in this: warders were forever walking about with inmates' possessions in pillow cases. Then they crept across to the wing gate. This was a tricky bit, because Dave would have to unlock the gate and lock it again, all without making enough noise to alert the warders in the office barely 20 feet away. The heavy gate always made a high-pitched squeal as it swung open. The warders knew this sound well and listened out for it. It could herald a PO or chief on his rounds.

This morning, though, the squeal was drowned out by Terry's radio. After locking the gate behind them, Dave hurried along the short corridor to the gate that led outside the wings. Within seconds, Dave and Jeff were outside. They had overcome the first hurdle, but the second one beckoned.

Walking as upright as possible, with their caps tilted down slightly over their faces, they strolled down the hill towards the CCTV camera. They would find out soon enough if those presumably watching in the control room noticed anything untoward. The camera stayed pointing up the hill and didn't swivel to follow their progress. They were past the second hurdle.

They approached the gate of the compound and, perhaps, the most difficult hurdle. Here the camera was barely yards away and focused on the gate. Dave unlocked the gate and they both passed through. The camera stayed pointing at the gate. The most difficult part was behind them.

They walked quickly to the far end of the deserted compound and up to the massive double gate. Using his 'doubles' key, Dave unlocked the gates, pulled down on the long lever that disengaged the gate's bolts and swung it open. They passed through and Dave locked it behind them. No one but the security PO could follow them now. There was only the perimeter fence that stood between them and freedom.

Taking the bolt croppers from the pillowcase, Dave went to the section of the fence that adjoined the wall. Here he would be partly shielded from outside view by the wall. The first snips were awkward, but once the blades of the cutters were through the mesh he made a yard-long horizontal cut at knee height. Turning the cutters upwards, Dave now made a vertical cut. Jeff had put on a pair of heavy canvas gloves taken from one of the workshops. As Dave levered the section inwards, Jeff gripped the edge and pulled.

Until this point, everything had gone according to plan. But, as with most plans, there is always an element of luck. Their luck now ran out.

It was a fact that the compound and the compound fence weren't patrolled at that time of day. However, Parkhurst wasn't the only prison on the island. Camp Hill, a lower-security prison was just a few hundred yards further up the road. One of their dog handlers had gone home for breakfast, taking his dog with him. Returning the way he had come, he walked along the outside wall of Parkhurst. As he reached the point where the wall ended and the fence began, he suddenly came upon Dave and Jeff. Both parties were taken completely by surprise.

By now, Jeff had managed to pull the cut section of the fence inwards, exposing a triangular hole. Dave made a dive for it, thrusting his head and shoulders through. The dog barked furiously and went to bite him. At the same time, the warder pulled out his stick and started to beat Dave about the head and shoulders.

Realising that he stood no chance against this determined assault, Dave pulled himself back inside. To crawl through the hole unhindered would have been difficult, the efforts of the warder and his dog made it impossible. The two of them had to watch helplessly as the warder took his radio from his belt and put in an emergency call.

Dave quickly stepped behind the wall, out of sight of the warder. Within minutes other warders would be everywhere. He didn't want them to find his keys.

Barely two minutes passed and a large group of warders came running into the compound. Dozens more appeared outside the fence. Temporarily though, Dave and Jeff were still safe. No one had a 'doubles' key to get them through the big gates.

Another few minutes passed and the security PO duly appeared. He unlocked the double gate and the warders poured through. They grabbed Dave and Jeff roughly and marched them back the way they had come. The gates of the punishment block were already open as the posse of warders propelled Dave and Jeff inside. They were pushed into separate cells and made to take everything off. Completely naked now, they were turned around and doubled over so that the warders could see between the cheeks of their arses. But it was all too late.

Satisfied that nothing remained hidden, they threw the pair a boiler suit each and retreated with all their clothes. As the doors banged shut, Dave and Jeff contemplated a thoroughly depressing future. There would be the solitary confinement and the loss of remission, of course, but they would also be separated and sent to different jails.

By lunchtime the escape was the talk of the jail. There were several different versions circulating, but all of them told of their being nearly through the perimeter fence. There were also a variety of reactions. Some thought it hilarious that a pair of 'poofs' had nearly done what the combined resources of the so-called 'chaps' had failed to do. Others tried to belittle what they had done purely because they were gay. But those who gave credit where it was due had to concede that Dave and Jeff had carried out an amazing feat.

Our crowd, who knew the full details, had nothing but respect and admiration for them. Merely to make a 'doubles' key was unparalleled. In fact, so much so that the prison authorities hadn't accepted that

Dave had made a 'double'. With the massive double gate now locked, they argued that they must have climbed over it, although the fact that they couldn't find any rope and hook did confuse them. They hadn't found the cell or gate key either and assumed that Dave had managed to hide them somewhere.

It would have been very embarrassing for them to admit that a con had got hold of a 'double'. It smacked of corruption in high places and the Home Office would want chapter and verse. And what security PO would want to admit that his was the first jail where a con had got his hands on a 'doubles' key?

Dave and Jeff, languishing in the punishment block, were largely oblivious to all the gossip and rumour. Dave was quite used to people knocking him. His answer was simply to shut them up by pulling off something quite amazing. That, in fact, was what he was working on at the very moment.

The warders had carefully searched Dave's and Jeff's clothing for the keys. They had also meticulously searched the area nearest the hole in the fence. They had found nothing, except the bolt croppers and the gloves. Having stripped them both naked, they were convinced that they weren't hiding anything. They could only assume that Dave had thrown the keys over the fence.

In this, they were quite wrong, for Dave still had them. When he had stepped behind the wall, out of sight of the warder with the dog, he had taken a metal tube out of his pocket. It was about four inches long and an inch in diameter, with a screw top. It looked like a shortened cigar tube.

There was already a length of hacksaw blade inside. Dave quickly dropped the three keys in with it and screwed the top on tightly. Dropping his trousers and pants, he squatted down. He pushed the rounded end of the tube up his arse. As his sphincter muscle closed behind the screw top, the whole tube disappeared from view.

It was now up inside his rectum and safe from anything but an intimate body search. Dave could retrieve it at any time. He often carried things about like this.

Locked in his punishment cell later that evening, Dave removed the tube. After wiping the outside with a tissue, he unscrewed the top and took out the hacksaw blade. Very gently, he started to saw at the exposed part of the top hinge of his cell door. Within two hours, he had sawn enough. He started on the bottom hinge. Another two hours saw him satisfied with the progress on this too. He put the blade back in the tube, screwed it shut and pushed in back up into his rectum. Then he lay down for a few hours' sleep.

The following morning, Dave slopped out, collected his breakfast and was locked up again. As was the case in the rest of the prison, the majority of the warders went off for their breakfast, leaving just one in the office. Dave immediately went to work on his door again.

He had left just enough hinge to support the weight of the door when it was opened. Now, in under 20 minutes, he cut through the remainder. With the hinges severed, he gently eased the hinged side of the door inwards. Once it cleared the jamb, he slid it sideways so that the lock and bolt both disengaged from the other jamb. He was out of his cell.

Moving silently to Jeff's cell, he quietly slid back the bolt and unlocked his door with one of the keys. They both padded noiselessly to the gate leading out of the punishment block. Dave inserted the gate key and turned, but it was a particularly stiff lock. As the levers sprang back there was a dull metallic 'clunk'.

This was one of the small sounds of the normally silent punishment block that the remaining warder was quite familiar with. After being in the quiet for a while, one gets to know every sound, even the small ones that register only subliminally. This was an important sound, though. It could be the first warning to a warder dozing, or doing a crossword, that a senior officer was coming in.

Alerted now, the warder came out of the office. He was astonished to see both Dave and Jeff halfway through the gate. Recovering quickly, he pressed the nearest alarm bell.

Dave and Jeff both stopped. It was no use running, since dozens of warders would be on the scene very quickly. A chase around the jail would be futile. They both filed back into the punishment block.

In due course, the news of this latest attempt reached us. I was astounded that Dave had managed to take his door off from the inside, and without making enough noise to alert a warder sitting in an office only yards away. Mentally, I kicked myself. I now realised what a treasure we had allowed to slip through our hands.

Both of Dave's escape attempts rated among the best I had ever heard of. Taken together, they demonstrated a skill, genius and resourcefulness that was breathtaking. If we had paid more attention to Dave's escaping skills rather than to his sexuality, a mass break-out in the early hours of the morning would definitely have been on. That, though, was the end of my first experience of Dave Martin.

Living in the long-term prison system is sometimes akin to travelling on the Circle Line. With only six or seven top-security jails, friends and acquaintances almost inevitably bump into each other again and again. Especially if they are troublesome prisoners who get moved about.

A short time after Dave was transferred out of Parkhurst, an incident took place that disrupted any further thoughts of escape that my friends and I had. Nearby Albany Prison staged a rooftop protest against the parole system. As a measure of solidarity, Parkhurst joined in. About 70 of us stayed out on the compound all night in protest. As one of the ringleaders, I was put in solitary for a month on bread and water, then transferred out to local prison. Within another month, though, I had been transferred to Long Lartin Prison in Worcestershire.

Long Lartin was very much a state-of-the-art, top-security prison, supposedly the most secure in the system. There were electronically unlocking doors, inbuilt alarms, CCTV cameras everywhere, trembler bells on fences, geophonic devices that would detect ground displacement if someone were trying to dig a tunnel out and arc lights that bathed the whole jail in brightness at night. No one had even got close to getting out.

On the positive side, though, the jail had a very relaxed and well-resourced regime. Workshop wages were good enough for inmates to be able to buy a whole range of stuff from the prison canteen. At weekends, some prisoners clubbed together to cook lavish meals in the little kitchens on each of the six wings.

There was a lot of time allowed out of cell for association and everyone got regular access to the sports field and yard. No only were radios allowed, but record players were permitted too, a significant concession not found in other jails. Much civilian clothing was permitted too. Consequently, although Long Lartin was a long way from being an alternative society – there were still too many things missing that one took for granted outside for that – it was possible to have a life of sorts. Many troublesome prisoners settled down here.

There were a couple of dozen Londoners in residence when I arrived, all of them doing very long sentences. Most of them were 'A-men', which defined them as a sort of elite, but the fact that they regarded themselves as the chaps gave them a leading role in the jail's life. Although we were greatly outnumbered by prisoners from other parts of the country, we were significantly more violent and always stuck together. An attack on one of us was usually treated as an attack on us all.

Several of these Londoners were old friends; others I knew of and they knew of me. To avoid too many of this type getting together and the control problems this would cause, the prison authorities spread them out among the wings. I suppose it was a backhanded tribute to my potential for causing trouble that I was placed on a wing with just one other Londoner.

Terry was about 40, the broken nose and cauliflower ears a sign of the professional boxer he had been in the past. Once a promising middleweight until poor eyesight ended his career prematurely, he was now several stones heavier and a bear of a man. He turned from boxing to bank robbery and had worked with several notorious 'firms'. His 12-year sentence reflected the seriousness of his offences.

Despite his size and fighting prowess, Terry was quite gentle and well mannered by nature. He also had a very well-developed sense of humour and loved to play pranks. We quickly became friends and relaxed into a familiar and supporting relationship that is one of the few good things about prison life.

I had only been at Long Lartin for about two months when Dave Martin arrived. Like me, he had been on a journey around the local jails, but his had taken a bit longer. He had the white and stressed look that is the hallmark of someone who has recently done a lot of solitary confinement.

Most ordinary people don't understand the impact of solitary confinement. I believe that its effects were so important in the moulding of the person Dave Martin was to become that it is worthwhile to briefly explain here. To the average person, to be placed in a small room where one is to be left on one's own for a long period might not seem to be much of a threat. One might imagine long periods spent reading, or just simply relaxing.

The reality is very much different. In psychological terms, solitary confinement is known as 'sensory deprivation'. In our normal environment, we are constantly bombarded with a multitude of stimuli. We interact with others, watch TV, cook, clean the house, play games and so on. In solitary confinement, all of these things stop, and stop abruptly. This tends to induce a sense of panic. You have to fight for control over a situation that you realise could quickly become intolerable. From moment one, there is a continuous fight to maintain control.

As reasoning individuals, we know that we can't stand this indefinitely. That is why, in controlled 'sensory deprivation' experiments conducted by universities, there is always a panic button that one can press when one has had enough. In solitary confinement, there is no panic button. No matter what you say or do, you will stay in solitary until your period is up.

Needless to say, some people 'crack up'. They might scream, or become violent when the warders open their door at meal or slop-out times. Then they will be beaten up, put in a canvas restraining suit and left on the floor of a 'strip' cell for days. Some never recover and end up certified and sent to mental hospitals. Most prisoners' greatest fear is to lose their minds while in prison.

The actual environment of the punishment block isn't conducive to mental stability either. It is a place to where the troublesome and mentally ill gravitate. The air is constantly rent by screams of anger and pain from those being brought down by the warders. And every so often, usually during a period of quiet, there comes the frantic scream of someone who has finally lost control. It reminds everyone else of their own mortality. For myself, I felt that if I screamed just the once I might never stop.

So, for a spirited individual, solitary is an awesome threat. You realise that you might have to make a stand against unfeeling and unjust authority just to stop them from breaking your will. But waiting just over the horizon is the awful prospect of several more months in solitary.

At Long Lartin, Dave was first placed on 'B' wing, where Alan, a friend of ours, lived. Alan was ten years into a very long life sentence and very much one of the chaps. He regularly dabbled in relationships with young effeminate prisoners, and was tolerated precisely because of his status. It seems that he took one look at Dave and it was love at first sight.

The feeling was definitely not reciprocated. Dave clearly saw himself as a chap in his own right now, albeit a gay one. To be a possession of another of the chaps wasn't attractive to him at all. Alan was persistent, but not threatening. Dave was adamant. The wing staff could see a situation developing and moved Dave on to 'C' wing, where Terry and I lived.

There was no ill feeling between Dave and me over the Parkhurst affair. In fact, we were quite pleased to see each other. For me, I would welcome the opportunity to have someone intelligent to talk to occasionally. For Dave, no doubt he would welcome the added status it would give him, vis-à-vis the other prisoners on the wing, to be seen to be on good terms with me. Such was the life he was forced to live.

Although straight himself, Terry was quite open-minded about gays. As with most other aspects of prison life, he refused to take it seriously and made a joke of it. Neither of us was about to take Dave into his life and become a close friend, and the feeling was mutual. He knew, as did we, that he would soon befriend a young and effeminate gay prisoner and they would become inseparable. That was the way he did his time. That and planning his next escape.

With regard to escaping, Terry was a few years into his sentence and could see the end of it. He wasn't interested. For me, there were a number of factors. First, Long Lartin's over-the-top security seemed quite impregnable. I didn't see the point of making an attempt just to get caught. I resolved to wait a while until I was transferred to another jail. As an 'A-man', I could expect to be moved every two years.

My second reason was that, in the first six years of my sentence, I had done two of them in solitary. I realised the damage it had done me, to both my mental and physical state. I was in for the long haul. It would do me no harm to have a couple of easy years at Long Lartin while I gathered my strength for my next determined escape attempt at another jail.

As expected, Dave soon befriended Eddie, a young and slightly effeminate gay prisoner. He had been the sometime companion of several of the chaps and was quite sought after, but, if not actually being mercenary, knew how to take advantage of a situation. He was putty in Dave's hands, though, and soon the pair were inseparable.

On every wing, the chaps had formed themselves into 'food boats'. They would club together and buy food from the canteen and cook it themselves. The culinary standards were quite high and many of the meals very attractive. It made a welcome break from the dull fare of prison food.

I was the only 'cook' on our 'firm'. Terry was always willing to do his share, but the results were inevitably dire. Consequently, I ended up doing most of the cooking. Together with all his other skills, Dave was an exceptional cook. It was Terry who thought of it first. He suggested that we allow Dave and Eddie to join us in a food boat. Both jumped at the chance. If nothing else, it meant that, as friends/acquaintances of ours, they would be safe from the many predators on the wing.

At first, everything worked out very well. With Dave, Eddie and me all doing our bit, while seriously discouraging Terry from doing anything at all, we turned out some excellent meals. Our food boat was the envy of the jail.

For all meals, even prison-prepared ones, the four of us would congregate in my cell. There, perched on chairs, the bed and the locker, we would eat and discuss the rumours of the day. With our different outlooks on life, it was both funny and stimulating.

In conversations, I had noticed a marked change in Dave. Gone was the shy understated personality of Parkhurst and in its place was something altogether more harsh and destructive. There was a clear and underlying arrogance, which caused him constantly to belittle others. All this was done in private, though, lest it get back to the subject and incur his wrath. Over and above everything else, Dave thought himself to be something very special. It all had an underlying bitterness that I was sure was a result of the solitary confinement. I had experienced similar feelings myself after long periods, but fortunately they had always abated.

Sometimes he would make outrageous statements. If talking about bank robbery, he would say something like, 'What you have got to do is walk in and shoot some old lady dead. Then everyone else will do exactly as they're told.'

This was ridiculous for a whole raft of reasons. Apart from any other considerations, by making the crime that much more serious, you would ensure that the police would look for you all the harder. Then, of course, the chaps were just as sensitive to the feelings of little old ladies as anyone else, and sometimes more so.

Or, as a means of diverting the police away from the scene of a proposed armed robbery, Dave advocated exploding a bomb on a bus several streets away. When you reminded him that there were innocent people on the bus, he would reply by saying that there were 12 innocent people on the jury that convicted him.

As an experienced bank robber himself, Terry might well have been expected to get annoyed. His easygoing character, though, took it all as a joke. 'What does he know?' he would say to me afterwards. 'He's never robbed a bank in his life and he ain't likely to.'

We both realised that it was just talk and that Dave didn't really mean it. I took it to be another symptom of all the solitary he had so recently done.

Occasionally, he referred to his sexuality, albeit obliquely. A favourite boast was that he had probably been with more beautiful women than most of the chaps. Once, he said that he got a lot of pleasure out of walking on to a new wing, picking out the most attractive and effeminate little raver that many of the chaps were after, and stealing him from right under their noses.

One day, though, he managed to go right over the top with Terry. In many ways, Eddie was quite a sad case. Orphaned at an early age, he and his brothers and sisters had been moved through a series of orphanages. It was here that he had been sexually abused. One of the few highpoints of his prison existence was when he received a letter from one of his brothers or sisters.

This day, Terry, Eddie and I were sitting in my cell eating our meals. Dave was yet to arrive. Eddie was perched on the corner of the bed, reading a letter he had just received.

Suddenly, Dave breezed into the cell. Seeing Eddie and the letter, he blurted out, 'Oh, got a letter, then? What is it? Good news, like your mother's died or something?'

There was a stunned silence, followed by a crash as Terry dropped his tray to the floor and jumped up. At first I thought he was about to punch Dave, who cowered back, but Terry was too much of a nice guy for that. Uncharacteristically raging, though, he shouted, 'I've had enough of this cunt,' and stormed out of the cell.

Like me, Terry had an aged mother. He was very close to her and, when all one's other friends had forgotten to keep in contact, it was always the old mums who stayed the course.

I immediately accepted that this was the end of our food boat with Dave and Eddie. By now, Dave was sitting quite crestfallen in the corner with his meal. I asked Eddie to leave for a moment while I spoke with Dave. I wasn't angry, more sad that the prison experience could turn people against each other.

'Dave,' I said in a reasonable tone, 'what the fuck's the matter with you? You weren't like this at Parkhurst. Why are you so bitter?'

Dave sat there silently, saying nothing.

'Why,' I continued, 'are you always trying to sound so tough and vicious. We both know that's not what you're really like.'

Still he sat there quietly.

Now I was starting to lose my temper. 'You're only doing a ten, Dave. Why don't you just settle down and you'll be out in a few years. Then you ought to find some secure building, a bank or a manufacturing jeweller's, find a way in and steal a million pounds, all non-violently. You've got the talent to do that.'

'I wouldn't want to get my money like that,' said Dave grudgingly.

'Who cares how you get your money, as long as it's not completely out of order? I'd steal a handbag if it had a million pounds in it,' I retorted. 'You know your trouble?' I was angry now. 'You won't be satisfied until you get your name on the front page of the *News of the World*.'

'I suppose I won't,' retorted Dave.

'Yeah, well, then you could be in the position I'm in, doing an endless sentence, and you just might find you can't handle it.' It could have been a prophecy.

After that, Terry and I carried on eating together and Dave stayed with Eddie.

Shortly afterwards, Eddie was released. It was just the opportunity that one of the wing predators was waiting for. Ray was undoubtedly one of the most dangerous men in the system and had spent several years in mental hospitals.

He was originally from Liverpool, but his twisted nature caused even the other Scousers to give him a wide berth. Very powerfully built, in many ways he was like a need personified. If he wanted something, he just took it, never mind the rights and wrongs of the situation.

When we first saw Dave fraternising with him, we knew he had made a mistake. For Dave, there was undoubtedly the added status that the friendship would give him on the wing. He could indulge his increasingly prima-donna ways and make disparaging remarks about others. But we knew that the piper would have to be paid. Ray was a confirmed prison homosexual. He had taken advantage of many weaker than himself. There was only one reason why he would befriend Dave, and that was to fuck him.

We knew it had all gone very wrong when Dave popped up in the TV room. He had always been absolutely scathing and dismissive of the 'mugs' and 'morons' who spent their association time watching TV. And he wasn't just watching the occasional programme: he went in as soon as the cells were unlocked for association and stayed until it was time for lockup again. The reason was obvious. He was relatively safe in the TV room. There were scores of other prisoners, and two warders sat just outside the door. Ray wouldn't attack him in the TV room.

Although I was by no means an avid observer of Dave's life, this little drama was being played out right in front of me. I realised his dilemma. He couldn't go to the warders and complain, because that would make him a grass and none of the chaps would ever speak to him again. He could hardly fight Ray, either, because he wasn't big enough or vicious enough. In similar circumstances, a weaker man might have asked to be put on Rule 43 protection. Under this rule, prisoners who are being intimidated by other prisoners can ask to be put in the punishment block. It wasn't much of an option for anyone. Call it 'protection' if you will, but it was still solitary confinement. And, anyway, no decent, honourable, proud con would ever do such a thing.

A couple of weeks passed and Dave was suddenly moved on to another wing. I still saw him about the prison and we acknowledged each other, even if we didn't stop and speak. Terry and I did hear reports about him from a couple of the chaps who lived on Dave's new wing though. He was up to his old tricks.

Within days, he had befriended Peter, a young London guy who was only 21. Although Peter had clean-cut good looks and something of a baby face, he wasn't at all effeminate and, to the best of everyone's knowledge, he wasn't gay. He had an easygoing personality and went out of his way to seek the approval of the chaps, whom he looked up to with some awe. From a criminal perspective, he was quite silly and his crime had been pure foolishness. He was also very easily led. He was forever getting into trouble with the warders, usually through doing something on someone else's behalf. Soon, he and Dave were inseparable.

Long Lartin was so hi-tech security-wise, that virtually everything was alarmed and linked to the central computer. Not only did all the doors lock and unlock electronically, but also every inspection panel on the walls and ceilings of the landings was fitted with an alarm. I suppose Dave just couldn't resist it. Within days he had bypassed the alarms and was taking the inspection panels off. Many of these led to ducting, which, while not leading outside, did run all over the wing. A favourite pastime of Dave and Peter's was to get into the ducting that ran above cells that gay couples frequented, and listen to what they were up to.

To the uninitiated, this might seem hilarious and harmless fun, but to people who were trying to survive in the jail it was an unnecessary complication. Many people had money, drugs, weapons and other contraband items hidden about the wing. It was like a constant game with the Security Department. There was a degree of 'live and let live'. Further, the warders didn't want to antagonise everyone unduly by conducting full-scale searches all the time. Occasionally, things were found and they were satisfied with that.

A serious security breach such as removing an inspection panel was another matter entirely. If they discovered something like that, it would be a direct challenge to them. You could expect them to close the wing down and search every cell from top to bottom. A lot of people would lose a lot of valuable things. Needless to say, quite a few cons on Dave's wing weren't too pleased by what they saw as unnecessary foolishness.

All of a sudden, I had a lot more to focus my attention on than Dave's antics. A violent incident on my own wing saw me and two of my friends remanded to the punishment block as part of an ongoing police investigation. We had been down there about a month when, late one night, Dave was brought down with his friend Peter. They had tried to escape.

A different code applies to the punishment block from the main prison. As it is a place where everyone is under considerable stress, old feuds tend to be forgotten and everyone tries to support each other. It was only natural that Dave and I speak again. Several of us sent canteen goods over to him.

Like mine, Dave's cell window looked out over the punishment block's small exercise yard. The very next time I was let out on exercise, I went straight over to his window. It wasn't just idle curiosity. I fully intended to try to escape again myself, even if it wasn't going to be from Long Lartin. Every bit of information about how the security worked was valuable.

Although he explained it to me several times, the technical detail of how he bypassed the electronics of his cell door was beyond me. But he had managed to open it himself, without its registering as being open in the central control room. He had already rigged Peter's door in a similar fashion and went in to join him.

All the cell bars at Long Lartin were made of manganese steel, specially hardened and supposedly uncuttable. Dave had taken his record player to pieces, fitted carborundum discs stolen from a workshop to the central spindle and made a very workable circular saw. Over a period of a couple of weeks he had ground away at Peter's bars. At the end of each session he would fill the cuts with a special filler that was also stolen from the workshops and paint it with quick-drying paint. As Peter was not a top-security prisoner, his cell bars didn't get the careful scrutiny that higher-security-category prisoners got.

The pair of them were quickly out of the wing, but now the plan really fell apart. The grounds were bright as day, lit from tall light masts. CCTV cameras scanned every square foot. Two 18-foot-high fences, separated by about 20 feet, ran around the perimeter. Each fence was festooned with rolls of razor wire hanging halfway up and barbed wire at the top. Geophonic detectors under the gravel path that ran along the inside of the first fence would pick up the sound of their feet. Trembler bells fitted to every panel would alert the control room if they touched the fence. In the circumstances, the rope and hook they had between them was grossly inadequate.

In reality, they stood no chance at all of getting away. It was just Dave doing what he enjoyed doing, namely, bypassing as many security measures as he could and winding the Security Department up in the process – that and adding to the growing legend that was beginning to be attached to his name.

A further and rather unexpected development was that Peter suddenly realised that he had been used. They wouldn't let Dave and him out on exercise together for security reasons, so the first time Peter was let out into the small yard he went straight over to Dave's window. I don't know what he expected, but his reception wasn't at all to his liking. Suddenly, he began screaming abuse at Dave, punching at his windows and throwing small stones from the yard at him. Several warders had to drag him back inside.

To those of us who knew the score, it was all so very obvious. Although Peter had never been known to be gay before, quite clearly a lot more had been going on than just a joint escape attempt. Equally clearly, Dave had used this relationship to inveigle Peter into escaping. He had never shown an interest in escaping before and was doing a comparatively short sentence. The fact that he was in a low-security category and his cell wouldn't be subjected to rigorous searches had clearly been another factor.

Shortly afterwards I was moved out to another prison, to await trial for the violent incident. I never saw Dave Martin again. But, from time to time, I did hear about his exploits. At Gartree, he joined together with a Midlands guy who, although in a high-security category, was generally regarded as a complete fool and definitely not one of the chaps. Despite Dave's now confirmed expertise in escaping, the deadly combination of his homosexuality and a desire to attract attention made the vast majority of serious people avoid him.

Once again, Dave and his accomplice had got out of their cells and away from the wing. They then broke into the workshop compound. Here they managed to get into a workshop and proceeded to try to weld together a ladder with which to scale the fences. For some reason they couldn't make the ladder. The workshop civilians had the surprise of their lives when they entered the workshop in the morning and saw Dave and the Midlander sitting there, drinking their umpteenth cup of tea.

For a period of several years, nothing was heard of Dave. Prison governors have almost unlimited powers regarding the prisoners under their control. The Rule 43 mentioned earlier has two sections, 43a and 43b. Under the former, the prisoner can request to be held in the punishment block, away from a tormentor, for his own protection. Under the latter, the governor can hold any prisoner in the punishment block, for an unlimited period, if he considers him to be a threat to the 'good order and discipline' of the prison. This is very much a catch-all term for what is, in effect, indefinite solitary confinement. The only appeal is to the visiting magistrates once a month, but, since they are invariably only the 'rubber stamp' of the governor, the prisoner can expect little relief here.

Not being able to curb his rebellious spirit and frightened now of his escape skills, governors resorted to holding Dave in their punishment blocks under Rule 43b. They frequently moved him from jail to jail, too. Solitary confinement as a fixed term is hard enough to bear, but at least you can count the days off, knowing it will come to an end. The unlimited nature of solitary under 43b is particularly onerous. You just can't see the end of what is an intolerable existence.

This, then, is the man they released directly on to the streets when he finally came to the end of his sentence in the summer of 1982. Small wonder that his parents are on record as saying that their son came home a changed man, full of hatred and bitterness.

None of us in the jail heard anything further about him, but then we didn't expect to. Criminally speaking, he wouldn't have moved among our friends and acquaintances. If attention-seeking gays are beyond the pale in prison, then they are even more so outside, especially where the serious business of crime is involved.

At first he got a job as a security guard. From a criminal perspective, having regard to his particular skills, this seemed a sensible course of action. Through his job he could identify worthwhile targets, then come back and bypass the security guarding them. This was his general intention, but only as a means to an end. While still in uniform, he burgled some of the shops he was being paid to protect, and stole jewellery and guns.

The key was the guns, because for Dave to achieve what he wanted most, to be regarded as one of the chaps, he had to be an armed robber. Again, in purely criminal terms, this was much akin to a skilled surgeon wanting to work as a butcher. But the macho image of the chaps was largely formed around armed robbery.

Dave would still have had a problem finding anyone to work with him, though. Certainly none of the chaps would have – especially when he announced his intention to carry out the robbery dressed as a woman. He was already a liability. As an untried and untested robber, he was highly unpredictable – no one could say what he would do in an emergency. The last thing any professional robber wants to do is to shoot someone unnecessarily. Further, should it come to a physical struggle, as it so easily could, the skinny Dave would be easily overpowered.

However, late in 1982, Dave robbed a security van with an accomplice, who shot and wounded a guard. Dave was dressed as a woman. This was both unnecessary and stupid. All it did was to 'hallmark' the crime and make it easier for the police to identify him. Very few women took part in the many thousands of armed robberies each year. And, from witness statements and possibly CCTV footage, it would soon emerge that the 'woman' was, in fact, a man in drag. Dave might as well have left a calling card.

Next, the pair robbed a bank of £25,000, with Dave wearing what was to become his trademark black-leather miniskirt and carrying a sawn-off shotgun. By now the police must have known who they were looking for.

A conversation with Dave during this period would have been revealing. Despite being wanted, he no doubt felt quite fulfilled. He had finally become what he had so much desired to be: a fully fledged armed robber.

It was at this time, flush with money from the robberies and out clubbing most nights, that he met Sue Stephens, a dark-haired attractive model. It seems that within a very short period of time he was desperately in love with her and, in fact, couldn't live without her.

This came as a considerable surprise to those of us who had known him well in jail. Not because he had fallen in love with a woman – we knew that he was bisexual – but rather because he had fallen in love at all. In jail, he had been totally in command of all his relationships and, if anything, was quite cold and mercenary regarding them. I took this to be further evidence of the damage all the solitary had done him. It tends to leave one with a deep and enduring feeling of loneliness.

No one knows whether Sue reciprocated these feelings, although her subsequent behaviour would suggest that she didn't. However, she has been reported as saying that she found Dave to be something of a 'dreamer'.

The relationship came to an abrupt halt when, late in December, Dave was ambushed and shot by robbery squad detectives. He was remanded to Brixton Prison on serious armed-robbery charges, and it looked as if he was going away again for a very long time. They hadn't reckoned with his escaping skills, though. Despite being in the top-security category, with all the extra security measures that entailed, Dave managed to escape from a cell at Marlborough Street Magistrates' Court, where he was appearing on remand. It was Christmas Eve.

Any other halfway sensible criminal would have headed for parts unknown, but not Dave. He immediately returned to Sue and the pair were inseparable throughout this period while the hunt for him continued.

Having had to shoot him to capture him the previous time, the police would now be treating him extremely seriously, you might think. Perhaps it was the 'gay' label that put them off. Certainly, the two robbery squad detectives who were checking out an address they had traced thought they weren't in any danger. As they walked along a corridor towards Dave's door, they failed to take notice of the tall attractive-looking 'woman' in a tight black miniskirt.

Dave reacted first. Pulling out a small-calibre pistol, he shot PC Nicholas Carr in the groin, then ran off. To shoot a policeman is one of the most serious of crimes. It brings retribution in the form of the most intense manhunt possible. I'm sure the symbolism of an officer's being shot in the groin by a transvestite armed robber was not lost on the Met. This powerful imagery no doubt prompted the next incident.

It didn't take the brains of Sherlock Holmes for the police to work out that the key to catching Dave Martin was to keep close tabs on Sue Stephens. They put her under constant surveillance.

On the evening of 14 January 1983, they were rewarded. A bright-yellow Mini pulled up outside Sue's address. There were two men in the front seats; the driver had the familiar long fair hair.

Sue and a female friend came out and got in the car with the two men. They all drove off in the direction of the West End, several unmarked police cars shadowing them. Thus, a full-scale operation swung into motion involving dozens of officers, many of them armed. They had shot him before and now he had shot one of them. They didn't expect Dave to go quietly.

The traffic heading towards the West End was particularly thick this night. The Mini and all the cars involved in the pursuit became entangled in a serious jam near Earls Court. In Pembroke Road, everything came to a complete halt. Taking advantage of this opportunity, the superintendent in charge of the operation ordered that one of his men get out and try to make a positive identification of Martin.

The plainclothes officer crept towards the Mini, trying to shield himself from view behind other cars. He had been told to be careful. No doubt he was mindful of the fact that the man they were pursuing was particularly dangerous. Probably for that reason, he didn't get too close. A profile and the long fair hair were enough for him to call in a positive identification.

The superintendent gave the word and several armed officers ran towards the car. They fired a volley of shots at close range into the body of the driver. As he slumped in his seat, the passenger beside him jumped out and ran off. Screaming, the two women cowered in the back seat.

Now the officers closed in on the form of the driver. He had managed to open his car door, but had then lapsed into unconsciousness. He lay, half in and half out of the car, his head nearly touching the road, the long fair hair discoloured by the streams of blood that coursed through it.

As the police gathered around the car, guns still at the ready, they surveyed the results of their handiwork. Seven shots had hit the driver in the body. Any fledgling feelings of euphoria were soon dispelled though by a very obvious fact. The driver wasn't Dave Martin!

A quick investigation revealed that they had shot an innocent TV producer named Stephen Waldorf. That he worked in the media, a group almost as powerful and as privileged as the police, meant that this couldn't be covered up. The following morning, banner headlines screamed out full details of the foul-up. On TV and radio, every bulletin carried a report of the event.

If Dave Martin had previously been only a very minor character on the underworld scene, that certainly wasn't the case now. Stephen Waldorf (who eventually made a full recovery and was paid compensation by the police) was the household name, but in the next breath came that of Dave Martin. The following Sunday, Dave was on the front page of the *News of the World*. If notoriety had been what he was seeking, he had it in spades.

Dave was now Public Enemy Number One as far as the police were concerned, and the most wanted man in Britain. Surely, nobody but a fool would stay around. Surely, the drumbeat heralding his inexorably approaching doom must have been audible to him.

Later, I wondered what was going through Dave's mind at this time, for, of all the things he was, he certainly wasn't a fool. Perhaps it was a subconscious death wish that drove him at this moment. However, he got straight in touch with Sue Stephens and arranged to meet her in a restaurant at Belsize Park.

Dave arrived early to look the place over, but it was a trap. Armed police ran from everywhere. As he fled down into the nearby Belsize Park underground station, Dave could only have thought that his Sue had betrayed him.

He fled ever deeper into the tunnel system, but the police were ready for that. They sealed off both ends of the tunnel. After a couple of hours of negotiations, his situation futile, Dave gave himself up.

Even with the hindsight of many years, the final acts of the tragedy still seem very strange. Remanded to top-security conditions in a special unit in Wormwood Scrubs, Dave embarked on a hunger strike and demanded to see his beloved Sue. For whatever reasons, she didn't come. Then he took an overdose of medicines he had saved up. Dramatic photos showed him being rushed to hospital by ambulance to have his stomach pumped out.

Sharing the same special unit at the Scrubs was Dennis Nilsen, the gay serial killer who had been sentenced to life in November 1983. Dave then embarked on an amazing relationship with him, which led Nilsen to declare that he was in love with Dave and, had he met him outside, he would never have started killing.

To those of us who had known him well, this was further evidence of just how strange Dave's thinking had become. The chaps despised cowardly sex offenders like Nilsen, a man who had lured his innocent and unsuspecting victims to their doom. In the long-term jails, given the opportunity, they would have beaten him senseless. We couldn't understand why Dave was even speaking to such an individual, let alone befriending him.

The actual trial was all too predictable. The judge made much of the fact that Dave had been on an armed robbery where a guard had been shot and that he, personally, had shot a detective. He was described as a 'very dangerous man'. The sentence was 25 years.

Who knows what Dave was thinking as the top-security convoy dropped him off at Parkhurst? It looked very much as if the wheel had turned full circle, except that this time Dave would be located in the ultra-top-security Special Wing. In its time, this prison within a prison had housed the Krays, the Great Train Robbers, IRA terrorists and other notorious prisoners. Its normal complement of no more than ten prisoners were watched day and night. Escape from here would be very difficult, if not impossible.

Despite the fact that all the other prisoners in the Special Wing were doing very long sentences too, Dave's elitist nature soon came to the fore. The prisoners always decided among themselves what they wanted to watch on the TV in the association room. Normally, an informal show of hands would suffice. Needless to say, Dave invariably liked to watch something more highbrow. A couple of times he had got up and just turned the TV over to the channel that he wanted to watch.

On this particular evening the vote had gone against him again. He jumped up to turn the TV over, but this time one of the other prisoners had had enough. He jumped up and physically confronted Dave, who, being no fighter of course, had to back down. He retreated to his cell with the insult of, 'You're only a fucking poof, anyway' ringing in his ears. It was a very public humiliation. As he slammed his door against a world that constantly belittled him because of his sexuality, Dave must have reflected that not even the armed robberies and the 25-year sentence had brought him the respect he so craved.

All long-term prisoners experience moments of despair, times when there seems no hope, and the pain of a meaningless existence becomes too much to bear. Most have contemplated suicide, however briefly. For the vast majority, the moment passes. Miserable as the situation may be at the moment, life is still the only game in town.

But not, it seems, for Dave. He made a rope out of a torn sheet, tied one end around the bars of his window and the other around his neck, then stepped off a chair to throttle, slowly, under his own weight. It couldn't have been an easy death. My bet would be that, in those last moments, he was thinking of Sue.

His latter-day arrogance apart, those of us who had known him well were deeply saddened. Whatever he had deserved, he hadn't deserved that. I walked again in my memories with the soft-spoken, shy, intelligent young man whom I had known at Parkhurst all those years ago. I tried to square that image with the strutting poseur who had so briefly blazed a path across the criminal firmament. And failed. I could only conclude that 'the system' had moulded him in its own image, then let him loose on the world.

No doubt there were those among the chaps, myself included, who felt guilty that they had so often put him down. For, in the final analysis, the passing of such a bright strong spirit diminished us all. And we were the weaker for it.

CHAPTER FOURTEEN

TIGERS

For quite a while, I had been intending to do a piece on the Tamil Tigers of Sri Lanka. Having spent so long without liberty myself, I seemed to have a natural affinity and sympathy for liberation movements. These invariably suffered from a poor press, with the international media usually supporting the status quo. I felt that my piece would serve a good cause, as well as cocking a snook at the powers-that-be.

From my research, I knew that Sri Lanka was ostensibly a paradise island, the size of Ireland, that lies off the southern tip of India. Its major selling points in the holiday brochures are the beautiful beaches in the south. Except for the occasional bomb outrage, the average tourist would hardly know that a virtual civil war is raging in the North.

This situation, like so many others of its ilk, had been largely created by us. As the former colonial masters when Sri Lanka was Ceylon, the British had handed over power after independence to the Sinhalese-dominated civil service. The Sinhalese are Buddhists and make up about 76 per cent of the population. The Hindu Tamil minority make up about 15% of the population and are heavily concentrated in the North. There was also a much smaller minority of Muslims.

Needless to say, the Sinhalese whom we had handed over to were reluctant to share power with anyone outside their immediate community. The Tamils strove for representation and equal rights, but were rewarded only with politically-inspired race riots during which many Tamils were massacred. This led the Tamils to demand their own state in the North, called Tamil Eelam, and the creation of a force committed to fight for it, the Liberation Tigers of Tamil Eelam, or Tigers for short. This war had been raging, at different intensities, for over 25 years.

Despite overwhelming international support from countries as diverse as the USA, India, China and Russia, the Sinhalese had never managed to defeat their outgunned but better-motivated enemy. On the contrary, displaying a commitment and fanaticism that the government couldn't match, the Tigers had won a string of victories culminating in the near taking of Jaffna, the major city of the North. This would have been a crushing military and political blow to the government.

Certainly not unique to Third World liberation movements, Tamil women had played a leading role in the fighting. This had arisen out of necessity, as so many of their menfolk had been killed. Ironically, the women's brigades had won a reputation for being among the fiercest fighters. Many of them had formed into suicide squads, throwing themselves in waves against entrenched positions. The government troops especially feared them.

I found this to be particularly fascinating, occurring in a Tamil culture that was largely non-violent. I hoped to interview some of the women's brigades as part of my story. The other interesting facet was that the Tigers had virtually introduced the suicide bomber as a weapon of urban warfare. Again, this was deeply ironic, occurring in a largely non-violent culture.

I also knew that, unlike in Colombia, the government denied the Tigers any concessions at all. There was a tight news blackout on the war, with journalists, even local ones, refused access to the front in the North. Increasingly losing the military war, the government seemed intent on winning the propaganda war through strict news management and censorship.

Quite obviously, I felt that didn't include me. However, I wasn't so naive as to think that I could go waltzing into a completely strange country without any help. There were two sides to this dispute, and I would need the assistance of one of them.

As luck would have it, the headquarters of the expatriate Tamil community in England was situated in Eelam House, over in Borough, Southeast London. A phone call elicited a request for me to put my application in writing. As I had done in letters I had written to other liberation movements, I mentioned that I was a freelance journalist and a member of the National Union of Journalists. I pointed out that the magazine I wrote for (*Front* in this instance) was a lifestyle magazine with a readership in the hundreds of thousands. Further, that by writing my articles in an 'adventurous' fashion I could reach an audience of young professionals who normally, perhaps, might not read a 'political' article. I concluded by saying, 'I am aware that this is an important time for the Tamil Eelam movement. I followed with interest the recent assault by the Tigers that nearly caused the fall of Jaffna. I would like to meet with you in the first instance, but I would also like to go to Tiger-held territory north of Jaffna to write my article.'

Liberation movements are just as much in the business of propaganda as the governments they oppose. They need all the publicity they can get, especially if it is sympathetic to their cause. I wasn't at all surprised when I got a phone call inviting me to a meeting.

I duly presented myself at Eelam House, a rather unimposing two-storey, office-block-type building, surrounded by a wire fence. Inside, though, was altogether more impressive, being done out like a Hindu temple. I was required to remove my shoes and was ushered upstairs to an office. Behind a large desk sat a short, plumpish, middle-aged man with a round pleasant face. He smiled broadly as he stood to shake my hand and introduced himself as Kumar.

I never determined whether this was his first or last name, so I erred on the side of caution by calling him Mr Kumar. Mr Kumar was politeness personified. He explained that he had been a journalist himself back in Sri Lanka, so he knew something about the profession. He went on to say that the situation in the Tamil-held North was very volatile at the moment and the government wasn't allowing any journalists up to the front line. I told him that I knew this, but was determined to find a way through.

He fixed me with a long studied look, as if weighing me up. I recognised the signs and realised that the situation called for openness on my part. I told him that I had recently spent over 24 years in British prisons, so I wasn't a particularly ardent supported of the government line. My article would be factual and unbiased.

The smile was once again on Mr Kumar's face. He wished me well with my trip, but added that to give me the contact details of Tamil activists in the North would put their lives in danger should the details be found on me. However, he did write down an English mobile number for me. He said that I should try to reach a place called Madhu

Road in the North. If I got there OK, I should call this number. I left feeling that I had made a very positive contact.

I didn't have any problem in pitching the story to *Front*. By now, they had every confidence that I would complete every assignment I set out on. This was all very well, but I was aware that, in magazine journalism, you are only as successful as your last story. It wouldn't do to take an international flight to Sri Lanka costing several hundred pounds, just to be stopped at customs and sent right back again. Clearly, I would have to have a cover story.

I could always be a tourist, of course, but that would work only if I stayed in the south, where the tourist resorts were. Once I went North, especially if a search revealed my journalist's card, I would have some explaining to do.

I scoured the Internet for details about northern Sri Lanka, particularly the area around Madhu Road. I noticed on several maps a small icon right on Madhu Road. When I checked the reference at the side of the map, I found it represented a Catholic Church.

So that was it, then. In a country full of Hindus, Buddhists and Muslims, where religious pilgrimage was almost a way of life, I would be a pilgrim – but a Catholic one. I wouldn't need the permission of the Pope, and the rabbi didn't have to be told. However, I did borrow a small cross and some rosary beads from a friend, just in case.

I landed at the capital, Colombo, and had minor misgivings as I approached customs. I needn't have worried, though. Tourists were so thin on the ground right now that any foreign face was welcome. Further, even though we had been the colonial power, many Sri Lankans still seemed to be involved in a love affair with England and the English.

Outside, I was surrounded by a baying mob of taxi drivers all vying for my attention. I was trying to be as low-profile as possible, so attention was just what I wanted to avoid. I jumped into the nearest taxi and told the driver to take me to the railway station.

Firmly in 'work mode' now, I was soaking up every detail of my environment. As a city, Colombo seemed to be mostly a slum. Ramshackle two-storey buildings lined the sides of roads full of potholes. All progress, vehicular or otherwise, was hindered by hundreds of cows. They wandered on pavements, in roads and even into shops, as if they owned the place. Which, it turned out, they did. The cow is holy to Hindus, and Sri Lankan Buddhists refuse to kill any living thing (except the occasional Tamil, that is). Ergo the cows, everywhere!

Above: With Edgar, our journalist and guide, who organised the tour of the working cocaine factory *(cocina)*.

Below: The four ELN guerillas arrive at El Baigre, one stop on our journey to the *cocina*.

Above: Danny holding bags of coca base at El Baigre.

Below: Danny and I posing for a photo with the ELN guerillas. Ernesto is far left, Elena bottom right.

The main factory building, a wall-less shed where the coca leaves are prepared and then cut into pieces with a strimmer.

Above: The chopped leaves are covered with cement and sprinkled with gasoline, then trod in by workers wearing Wellington boots.

Below: After the gasoline and cement have been trodden in, the mixture is shovelled into large plastic drums.

The drums are topped up with gasoline, then permanganate is added and they are left to stand for a couple of hours. The gasoline/permanganate mix is drained off, leaving the white viscous precipitate of coca base at the bottom of the drums. The coca base precipitate can be seen at the bottom of this jar.

Above: Outside the prison at Villavicencio, where I met the world's worst serial killer, Garavito.

Below: In the Habarana wildlife park, Sri Lanka, showing the bull elephant seconds before it charged at me.

Above: An Arab village in Gaza.

Below: Dr Jowed Tibi, Palestinian member of parliament, with two of his children in Khan Younis.

Above: The community centre in the Jewish settlement of Neve Dekalim, showing the blast wall to protect against rocket attacks.

Below: A walkway in Neve Dekalim, showing the concrete barriers used to protect against snipers.

Fort railway station was straight out of the films set in the days of the Raj. Old-fashioned steam trains puffed and whistled alongside platforms that couldn't have changed much in 50 years. All that was missing was Sir Ralph Richardson and a detachment of red-jacketed British troops.

I was already attracting many curious stares and a couple of people actually stopped me and asked if I was English, before welcoming me to the country. I was impressed both by their impeccable manners and their excellent English. However, once again I was concerned about attracting attention. I quickly took my place in the ticket queue.

I bought a ticket to Anuradhapura, 200 kilometres to the north. This was the site of an ancient city and the temples and ruins were world famous. It wouldn't be unexpected for a tourist to want to go there, I hoped. There were two surprises. A second-class ticket cost me only the equivalent of £1.50 for the 200 kilometres. I reflected that, back in London, £1.50 wouldn't take me one stop on the Underground.

When I saw the carriages, though, the ticket price made sense. They were dilapidated to the point of being nearly derelict. There was no glass in the windows, no curtains either, and the wooden benches were without cushioning and hadn't been painted for many years. Every carriage was thoroughly overcrowded. Even here, though, I was given privileged status. Two young men stood up from a bench seat and allowed me to slip inside and sit by the window, before reseating themselves.

The six-hour journey took me through dusty tumbledown towns and villages separated by vast expanses of jungle and scrubland. On the train or at any of the stations we passed I didn't see so much as one European face. Seated in the window, I was stared at from platforms and level crossings by curious faces. I felt about as undercover as Madonna.

The further north we went, the more the carriage emptied. After one stop, though, a young guy got on and sat next to me. He engaged me in conversation, then showed me his army identification card. It did wonders for my paranoia.

Either I was wrong about him, however, or Sinhalese agents aren't up to much. Suddenly, a ticket inspector appeared. On inspecting the army guy's ticket, the inspector saw that he was travelling in the wrong class and unceremoniously ejected him from the carriage.

I arrived at Anuradhapura, my face roasted by the sun and sandblasted by the dust. As I alighted on to the platform, I was nearly rugby-tackled by Raja, the local equivalent of wide boy Arthur Daley.

Raja professed to be a taxi driver, but hastened to assure me that he was also a tourist guide and could get me whatever I wanted. The wink isn't part of Sri Lankan culture, but his 'knowing look' was international. All the time he repeated, mantra-like, 'Wonderful people, the British; wonderful people, the British.'

I was tired, didn't want to attract any attention and was longing to sleep. Against my better judgement I got into his taxi.

The Milano Guest House was a slur on the good name of Milan and had no Italian connection that I could discern. The room for one was barely tolerable, even if the only air conditioning was an ancient rotating fan set in the ceiling. It was the bathroom for five that I had a problem with, especially as the other four were cockroaches. After a brief two-step with a couple of them in the shower, I retired to the bed, silently cursing Raja under my breath.

After 24 years of eating prison food, I had thought I was beyond being upset by a ruined meal. Breakfast at the Milano, though, was a culinary experience too far. I had asked only for chicken and rice, for God's sake, but the rice was soggy and stuck together in lumps and the chicken was all skin and innards. I seriously considered punching Raja full in his fat smiling face when next we met.

In the event, I resisted the temptation, rationalising that such behaviour would certainly bring me a whole lot of attention, probably from the police. When he arrived to take me sightseeing, though, I had paid for my room and was waiting with my bag all packed. I cut through his obsequious 'Good morning, sir' with a steely 'Take me to another hotel immediately.'

The Tissawewa Rest House was a quaint leftover from the colonial days. Its genteel decay was more than compensated for by scrupulous cleanliness and excellent service. I secreted the copy of *Front* I was carrying beneath some cushions lest its contents outrage the servants.

The large house must have been very beautiful in its day and, even though the white paintwork was peeling, there was still a feeling of sumptuousness about the place. The house stood in its own gardens and grounds, which were extensive. Hundreds of small, and not so small, monkeys roamed freely. Most had absolutely no fear of humans. In fact, the one caution I had from the staff was to make sure I closed my windows, otherwise monkeys could enter and steal things.

In such an idyllic setting it would have been very easy to forget what I had come for and just lounge around for a couple of days and relax. However, I was on a tight schedule. I would want to spend at least a couple of days with the Tigers, should I manage to contact them. That was why it was so frustrating to have to pretend that I was a tourist. I would have to waste good time doing 'touristy' things. Ergo Raja.

Later that day he took me on a tour of the ancient city. The temples were magnificent, their time-worn façades testimony to the architectural excellence of a bygone age. It must have been some kind of holy day, because thousands of pilgrims, wearing only white sheetlike clothing, swarmed everywhere.

Outside every temple were rows and rows of sandals that the faithful had removed before entering. Mine were the only pair of shoes. I still hadn't seen another European since I had left Colombo.

At the entrance of one temple stood three uniformed soldiers carrying machine guns. Raja informed me that they were guarding a special temple, inside which stood a holy tree. This tree was supposed to be thousands of years old and had been closely linked to one of the original prophets. I felt that this was worth seeing.

It didn't look like much, just a gnarled thin old trunk, bereft of leaves. It was surrounded by a circular railing, through which the faithful reached to touch the tree. Right next to it stood another soldier, also carrying a machine gun. Raja explained that the guard was necessary just in case the Tigers tried to damage the holy tree. I couldn't help but reflect on the ridiculousness of a situation where people would fight and die over an old tree.

A couple of hours in the heat and the dust was quite enough for me. I got Raja to take me back to the Tissawewa for a midday snooze. Later, he had organised a safari for me. I wanted to establish my tourist credentials as soon as possible, then move on to other, more serious, things.

The Habarana Wildlife Park was so absolutely massive that I was sure it didn't have a wall around it and was just a part of the countryside. The gate complex was impressive, with large barred gates and armed guards in uniform, but I guessed that was for the benefit of the tourists. I signed up for the basic 50-quid tour.

I have a theory about wildlife and safaris. I feel that any responsible parent would warn the cubs that the upright two-legged creatures might pull out a camera and take your picture. On the other hand, they also might pull out a gun and shoot you. So, to be on the safe side, whenever you see one, hide!

For the next two hours, with Raja sitting in the front of the open-topped jeep next to the driver and me in the back, we drove along the bumpy dusty trails of the wildlife park. Every living thing hid from us. On one occasion, far in the distance, we did see what looked like a water buffalo beside a lake, but when we finally got there the creature had disappeared.

I was quite unconcerned. I was content to go through the motions of being a tourist and safaris had never appealed to me anyway. But you could tell that Raja was deeply embarrassed. For a start, his incessant chatter had diminished to barely a trickle of half-hearted encouragements that there would be something just around the next corner. By now it was growing dark.

So far, I had been completely relaxed. It was just a safari and I didn't consider myself to be in any danger at all. The dangerous bit would come next when I tried to contact the Tigers. Further, I had assumed that, for all his insincerity, Raja knew what he was doing. I was just about to be rudely disabused of that notion.

Exiting a small forest of trees on to another large plain, we could see, a short distance away, another clump of trees. Among these were several elephants. I don't know if they tried to hide, but, as all the trees were quite small, perhaps they just weren't successful.

Seeing his chance to redeem himself in my eyes, Raja ordered the driver to get close to the herd. On the fringes, just outside the tree line, stood a very large elephant that I took to be a male, the bull, for it was much larger than any of the 20 or so others in the herd.

At first the elephant ignored us. It continued to pull clumps of grass from the ground with its trunk and stuff them into its mouth. At Raja's insistence, the driver drew closer. From 200 feet away, the animal looked big enough; from 100 feet away, it looked enormous. It completely dwarfed us and the jeep we were sitting in.

By now, however, although it was still chewing the last mouthful of grass, it wasn't intent on pulling any more from the ground. All its attention was on us. Suddenly, it started to paw at the ground with one of its front feet. At the same time, a deep growling sound came from its head, which it was now swinging from side to side.

Up until this moment, I had been merely a complacent observer of events. However, I was aware that elephants killed many people every year in Africa. It was just beginning to dawn on me that, should the beast charge, we could be in danger.

I might have read its mind. With a piercing squeal that immediately morphed into a full-throated bellow, it charged. Temporarily, the deafening sound paralysed all movement. I remember mentally remarking to myself how swift it was for such a large animal.

To give credit where it is due, the driver had always been aware of the danger we were in. Throwing the jeep into gear, he quickly reversed in a tight arc, then accelerated away. The jeep bucked like a wild thing as we raced across the bumpy terrain. I quickly became aware of another danger, that of falling out of the jeep. I clung on like grim death. So intent was I on holding on that I didn't even look over my shoulder. All I knew was that the elephant was very close behind and, sitting in the rear seats, I would be the first to feel the weight of its trunk.

After what seemed an age, the driver slowed. I looked behind and saw that the elephant had stopped a couple of hundred yards away. There would be no further pursuit. Perhaps it was the unexpected adrenalin rush, but, suddenly, I just couldn't help myself. I laughed and laughed. So much so that Raja looked at me quite concerned, then managed a weak smile in return. I continued to burst into fits of giggles all the way back to the main gate. As they dropped me off at the Tissawewa, they must have thought that I was quite mad.

Having now established my tourist credentials, I felt that I could venture into nearby Anuradhapura town and make some enquiries. A tuk-tuk, the local three-wheeled motorised taxi, dropped me off at the central square. The obvious people to ask were the taxi drivers, gathered around their tuk-tuks. However, taxi drivers in all cultures invariably work hand in hand with the police. I would have to be careful what I said.

I stressed the fact that I was interested in the Catholic church at Madhu Road. All the drivers threw up their hands in despair. Muttering darkly about 'Tigers'; several made imaginary shooting movements with imaginary guns. Clearly, none of them would take me. However, I did manage to elicit the information that a bus went from Anuradhapura to Vavuniya. Another bus would take me from here, along the Mannar Road, to within a few miles of Madhu Road and the Catholic church.

From my research, I knew that Vavuniya was a large garrison town and massively out of bounds to anyone who didn't have a good reason to go there. The next part of the journey would be fraught with risk. All the international aid agencies had accused the government of human-rights abuses at one time or another. I had read plentiful accounts of Tamil civilians being murdered out of hand. I did have my press card as a last resort, but in a war zone that would be no guarantee of safety. I wouldn't be the first journalist to be taken round a corner and shot in similar situations. And, in this instance, no doubt the government would blame it on the Tigers.

At nine the next morning I was on the bus to Vavuniya. Twenty-seven fellow passengers cast sly suspicious looks at the only European on board. I thought of Gordon at Khartoum and felt my stiff upper lip quiver.

Travelling quite slowly, we slalomed through several roadblocks without stopping. About ten miles from Vavuniya, the roadside bunkers started to appear, with armed soldiers posted every hundred yards. There was no turning back now.

As befits a garrison town, Vavuniya was absolutely swarming with troops. Hundreds of them, dressed in various uniforms, strolled about in groups. I slipped unobtrusively off the bus and into the nearest café.

As soon as I was confident that my arrival hadn't sparked a hue and cry, I emerged to locate the Madhu Road bus. The central bus station was easy enough to find. I bought a return ticket to Madhu Road and sat in the back of the darkened bus, waiting for its departure.

Time passed, and more and more people got on the bus. When we left, there were 46 passengers crammed around the 28 seats. I wasn't complaining: they were good cover for me. I hunkered down and tried to hide myself in the crush.

The earthwork forts and bunkers began immediately we left Vavuniya. Spaced every hundred yards along the road, each was manned by scores of heavily armed soldiers. Suddenly, we stopped at the first roadblock.

The success of any journalistic venture depends in large part on luck, or, in my case perhaps, on stupidity. As every living soul except me made to get off the bus, I was thinking how curious it was that everyone was going only to the first stop. Even if I realised it was a roadblock, I certainly didn't realise that one was required to get off and show one's papers. If I had, then perhaps that would have been the end of it. I sat at the back of the bus, waiting patiently for the journey to continue.

Accompanied by the 'clumping' sound of heavy boots, two very large military policemen climbed into the bus and made their way to me. I did have the presence of mind to pull out my passport and hold it out towards them. They stopped, took it off me with care, almost reverently – it was clearly a British passport – examined it, then handed it back. Not one word had been spoken. Whatever they had assumed, it was enough for them. All the rest of the passengers climbed back on to the bus and we continued our journey. But this time they were looking at me with a mixture of reverence and fear.

The view from the bus was one of preparations for war. Tanks stood cheek by jowl with gun emplacements, as jeeps bristling with armed men raced among them. Military-tented villages were dotted here and there. If this wasn't actually the front line, then we were very close.

Three more times we stopped at roadblocks and exactly the same procedure was followed. The fourth pair of military police at least had the initiative to ask me where I was going. 'The Catholic church at Madhu Road,' I said confidently, as if I had been going there all my life.

I alighted at the Madhu Road stop with a growing feeling of euphoria. If this indeed was Madhu Road, then surely it was just a question of nipping into the church, making the brief acquaintance of the priest, then nipping out through the back door into the arms of my new friends, the Tigers. In my dreams!

I had been sitting on the left-hand side of the bus and had got off on that side, too. As the bus moved off, it revealed the other side of the road to me. I took in a great mass of civilians squatting at the side of the road. I noticed the barbed-wire boundaries and guessed it must be some kind of transit camp. But transit to where? Surely they weren't all going to the Catholic church, too, were they?

Then I noticed the soldiers, at about the same instant as they noticed me. Twenty highly excited soldiers, some waving automatic weapons in the air, ran across the road and surrounded me. There was some confusion, what with the fact that they were all trying to speak to me at once, but the burning question was: What the fuck was I doing here? This was a highly restricted area and I didn't have the necessary papers.

'How did you get here?' demanded a young senior officer.

'On the bus,' I replied, thinking that it was a very obvious answer.

'Yes, but how did you get past the checkpoints?' continued the officer, shouting now.

'I just showed them my passport,' I said quite calmly and pulled said passport from my pocket and waved it at the officer.

The officer examined it quickly, then handed it back. Turning to one of the group of soldiers who had surrounded me, he said, 'Get him out of here before a senior officer sees him and we're really in trouble. Stop a lorry, anything that's going back to Vavuniya, and put him on it.'

'So how do I get permission to come to this area, then?' I shouted over my shoulder as I was led away.

'There's an office in Vavuniya,' the officer shouted back.

My escort of soldiers stopped a large dumper truck on the other side of the road. The driver and his mate were told to take me straight back to Vavuniya. We set off, but within five minutes we were halted by a stationary line of traffic in front of us. A few minutes passed and we could hear the wailing of sirens getting closer.

Suddenly, on the other side of the road, going in the direction we had just been, was a large United Nations convoy. Several armoured personnel carriers were painted in the UN colours and carried the legend 'UN'. Between them were two buses full of people, also with the UN logo. Clearly, this was some kind of UN-supervised personnel exchange between the two sides. I couldn't help but reflect that, if it took the UN and armoured vehicles to cross the ceasefire line, then I had been quite naive in thinking that I could do it on my own.

Back in Vavuniya I managed to find the office the officer had told me about. It was full of civil servants processing travel application forms. I managed to get an interview with someone quite senior. He looked at me quizzically when I mentioned that I had just been turned back from Madhu Road and laughed when I asked how I could get permission to go there. He said that it was completely out of the question.

Sitting in my room in the Tissawewa Rest House, I took stock of the situation. Although I had managed to go where no other journalist had been for over two years, I didn't have much to show for it. *Front* is specifically a visual magazine. I had taken a few photos of roadblocks and bunkers around Anuradhapura, but there was nothing to suggest that I was in the middle of a war zone. I would need some action pictures.

From a public phone in the centre of Anuradhapura, I called the mobile number that Mr Kumar had given me. I didn't recognise the voice that answered. I explained that I had managed to get to Madhu Road, but had been turned back. I emphasised that, for my story to have any impact, I would need some action photos. The voice told me to call back in one hour.

I was directed to a small shrine not far from the Tissawewa. As I waited, it wasn't only the intense heat that was making me sweat. I really didn't think that such a Third World country had the technology to intercept every phone call, but, should I be caught meeting with someone who was undoubtedly linked to the Tigers, it could be very serious.

Eventually, a tuk-tuk pulled up and the driver approached me. He bade me good day and called me Norman. Clearly, this was my contact.

I got in and we set off. Over the next hour or so, we drove along the highways and byways of Anuradhapura as my loquacious driver regaled me with stories of the armed struggle in the North.

I asked about the women's brigades and he told me of the recent battle for Elephant Pass. He described it as the greatest victory in Tamil history. Elephant Pass was a massive military base for more than 20,000 government troops. Built around a lagoon, the interlinked satellite bases that protected it were thought to be impregnable. One by one, over a period of six months, key satellite bases had fallen to onslaughts by women suicide squads. Finally, they captured the base that controlled the water supply. The 20,000 troops were now trapped without water. They fled, leaving masses of equipment behind them.

I suppose it was a tribute to the way the government managed the news and the international community cooperated with them that there had been few reports of this in the press. No doubt I should have felt privileged to be one of the first to hear about it at first hand. However, my mind was firmly on getting the photos and putting some distance between myself and this driver. Finally, he wished me farewell and handed me a small package.

Back in my room, I examined the photos. There were 20 of them and they were exactly what I wanted. I had heard that the Tigers had a pretty good propaganda machine of their own. They frequently filmed battle situations. Each photo had been taken in the heat of battle. There were enough dead bodies and blood to satisfy *Front*'s requirements. In the event, they printed several of them prominently on one page.

The editor expressed his satisfaction with my story, despite the fact that I hadn't managed to meet with the Tigers. For myself, I was disappointed. Even though no other journalist had managed to get past the government's blockade, I still felt that I hadn't delivered what I had promised. This was reflected in the somewhat childish tirade I concluded the article with. It was pure *Front* though.

'So next time some scumbag dictator bans the international press in an attempt to cover up his war crimes,' I wrote, 'he'd better watch out. *Front* just might show up at the front.'

CHAPTER FIFTEEN
THE DAY OF THE DEAD

The genesis of my Haiti story lay not so much in the fact that I was interested in voodoo per se, but more in that I was looking for a situation to put myself in that would freak out the average person. With Hallowe'en fast approaching, I figured that, of all the places not to be at midnight on that day, a voodoo ceremony in Haiti must rank at the top of the list.

However, I did have a passing interest in voodoo for personal reasons. Following the death of my girlfriend in front of a train several years previously (described in my book *Life After Life*), I had been subjected to a period of what I can only call haunting. There had been several very obvious poltergeist effects.

Subsequent to that, an old Jew, well versed in mysticism, whom I had met on just one occasion over a business deal, had warned a friend of mine to tell me that something was trying to take me over and that I should fight it. He had seemed a sensible old man, whom I had never seen before, nor was likely to see again. There was no reason for him to lie to me.

Last but not least, there was the small matter of the two lives I had taken. They do say that, when you die, you meet the spirits of all those you have wronged. So what of my own spirit? To have done those supremely evil acts, did that not have strong implications for the nature of my soul?

I knew that the priest/witch doctors of the voodoo religion were well versed in manipulating the spirit world. They also spent a lot of their time striving against evil spirits. Should I have such spirits in me, they would be just the people to ask what to do.

Call it a consultation if you will, but this was a matter that increasingly troubled me. The haunting situation had severely frightened me and I had been a man not particularly vulnerable to fear. So, on a very personal level, the coming visit to Haiti was going to be a severe trial for me.

Eoin of *Front* jumped at the story. The juxtaposition of Hallowe'en and Haiti had caught his imagination and he thought it would be a good story for the magazine. Further, a production company had expressed an interest in filming me on my next assignment. The story also caught their imagination. The upshot was that they would supply a cameraman for free, as well as paying half of all the expenses for the trip. In return they would want the rights to all the footage they had shot while in Haiti. It was an offer that *Front* couldn't refuse.

However, they did stipulate that they wanted some photos taken for the magazine. To this end they wanted our own photographer to go with us on the trip. They put me in touch with a young woman called Linda, who, apart from being a photographer, was also an absolute fount of knowledge about Haiti and voodoo. Over several years and dozens of trips, she had become an authority on the subject. She knew all the ritual of voodoo, had photographed countless ceremonies and artefacts, and had an extensive collection of voodoo dolls at home.

The meeting with her was something of a disappointment. As a venue for anything, the rundown African café in Hackney left a lot to be desired. I arrived early and Linda was late. I strenuously resisted the blandishments of the proprietor to order from the menu. I would have continued to do so had I been starving.

Linda was a somewhat scruffy young woman in her early thirties, with short cropped untidy hair. You could tell that her appearance wasn't among her priorities. She was pleasant enough, but underneath it all seemed to lie a deep sadness. I didn't know if she suffered from depression, but her general air was quite miserable.

In order to lighten the situation between two people who had just met and who would probably be working together under extreme circumstances, I did attempt some levity at times. Linda was totally impervious to it. She answered my light-hearted question as if it had been a request for factual information, without so much as acknowledging the intended levity behind it. After a while I gave up, resigning myself to the fact that maybe she didn't have much of a sense of humour.

However, she came across as a very pleasant person, and highly professional as well. She left me in no doubt that she knew Haiti and the subject matter, and that she was more than competent to take any photos we might need. She was also reasonably fluent in Creole, one of the two languages spoken in Haiti, the other being French.

Gary, the cameraman supplied by the production company, was as different from Linda as it was possible to be. A Canadian in his late twenties, he was as adventurous as I was and had been pursuing his passion for photography all over the world. The pair of us hit it off right away. The only misgivings I had were that sometimes I needed a sensible head to talk me out of throwing myself into desperate situations. All I would get from Gary was encouragement.

Unfortunately for me, all the international flights to Haiti went through Miami, since Haiti's airports were not capable of taking the big airliners. An overnight stay was required before continuing the journey in a much smaller plane. The problem was that the Americans had very strict immigration procedures. I knew that, because I had a serious criminal conviction, I could well be refused entry. Therefore, this was another assignment that could easily be nipped in the bud. I had nightmares of our paying for three tickets and my being sent back from Miami.

On the flight, Linda and I sat in adjacent seats. I had done some research on both voodoo and Haiti as a background to the story, but the two-hour tutorial I had from Linda more than filled in the gaps.

My first mistake had been in thinking that, for Haitians, it was Hallowe'en that they were celebrating. This is a very Westernised tradition, but, like so many other similar traditions, it is celebrated worldwide in other forms. Haitians specifically celebrate the Day of the Dead. There are numerous ceremonies in cemeteries all over the island with the biggest being in the sprawling central cemetery in the capital Port-au-Prince.

Voodoo has strong historical links with Catholicism and some Catholic ritual can still be seen in modern-day voodoo. However, originally, voodoo was a revolutionary movement by the slaves as a means of resisting their enslavement. At times, it was banned by the white slavemasters, but continued to flourish underground. Finally, the Catholic Church withdrew its priests from the island in protest at its continuance. This was when voodoo became the official mainstream religion. Today, millions practise it worldwide.

My second mistake had been in thinking that voodoo was some kind of black-magic cult. There are secret branches that invoke evil and use magic for bad intent. The sorcerers, or *boko*, do their work in cemeteries or at crossroads. They can make objects to bring harm, *wanga*, the most feared of which is *voye*, which can bring death.

But the vast majority of voodoo worshippers strive against evil, just as in Western religions. The celebrants worship a pantheon of spirits that rule different realms of life, under guidance from the voodoo 'priests', called *oungans* if they are male, and *mambos* if they are female.

Practitioners of voodoo believe that, at the point of death, the soul and guardian spirit remain in the body. A voodoo priest must force them out. The soul sinks into the abysmal waters for a year and a day to gain knowledge. Then it will be raised by the priest, using another ritual.

The spirits, or *Iwa*, can be invoked in a number of ways. Each one has its own symbols, songs and dances as well as its own symbolic drawing, called a *veve*. In ceremonies, *veves* are drawn on the floor to coax the spirits into the earthly plane. The priest will encourage the spirit into the material world with drumming, singing, dancing and magical chants. The act of possession is the supreme gift that the spirit can bestow on the celebrants, but no one knows whom the spirit will enter. When possessed, celebrants exhibit the unique movements and actions associated with that spirit.

I listened with interest as Linda explained all this. Before I had had my own experiences with spirits following my girlfriend's death, I would have dismissed the whole lot as so much mumbo jumbo. But, as a rational individual, I still hadn't been able to explain some of the things I had seen and heard. So, unless I was to deny the evidence of my own senses, something unseen and spiritual had entered this material plane. Therefore, why should I refuse to believe that a voodoo priest could conjure up spirits?

The more I talked with Linda, the more I got to understand her. Whether she was miserable or not, there was no harm in her. To the contrary, in fact. You could tell that she believed much of voodoo lore, although she didn't admit as much, and I didn't ask. In her own way, she would always strive against evil influences.

On the surface, she seemed like a troubled spirit, someone searching for something. Occasionally she would add a new item to her collection of voodoo dolls, and this would cause trouble. There would be bangs and crashes from the room where the collection was, and, when she went in, the new doll, or several near it, would be on the floor. Sometimes she had to return the doll to Haiti.

In further conversation, though, it emerged that her miserable state had a far more mundane cause. She had recently emerged from a very unhappy relationship. It seems that her boyfriend, for whom she cared deeply, had walked out on her. She had taken it very hard.

In view of the fact that we were being open with each other, I decided to make a confession of my own. It was also founded on sound practicality. As I filled in the US immigration form, I had to tick the box indicating that I had served a prison term of over five years. I had to consider the possibility that, on landing, I might be refused a visa and be held in the cells overnight, before being put on the flight to Haiti the following morning. In that instance, I wanted to establish where we should all meet in Haiti should we become separated.

Gary was intrigued and wanted to know more. I promised to explain later. Linda looked shocked. She wasn't curious, just put out that she had misjudged me, I think. However, always the consummate professional, she recovered and carried on with planning the trip.

Miami International Airport was a nightmare. I have been received into prisons with better grace. Massively long queues led to uniformed immigration officials who had unanimously discarded good manners long ago. I knew that the push of a button would bring up my criminal record anyway, so perhaps openness was the best policy. Handing over my press card at the same time as my passport and immigration form, I pointed to the box I had ticked acknowledging that I had served more than five years in prison.

If I had expected a reaction I would have been disappointed. The female immigration official scanned the form almost uninterestedly. With a curt 'Wait here', she walked away and out of sight behind a nearby screen. I assumed that she had gone to confirm that I should be refused entry. I turned to Gary and Linda, directly behind me in the queue, and shrugged wordlessly.

Almost as I turned back, the immigration official was there again. Without saying one single word, she stamped the form, handed it and the rest of my papers back to me and waved me through. I could only conclude that, what with all the other criminals already in America, they figured that one more wouldn't make much difference.

Miami itself was a disappointment. Admittedly, we didn't see that much of it on an overnight stay, but what we did see was characterised by massive freeways that proclaimed the realm of the car. As a result, almost no one walks anywhere. When Gary and I explored the vicinity of our hotel on foot, there were so few people on the streets that it was like a ghost town. Linda had already declared that she wasn't one for socialising – not much of a surprise there. So Gary and I dined alone that evening in a nearby restaurant.

The morning flight from Miami to Haiti was uneventful. I had no worries over immigration problems here and we were ushered through with a minimum of fuss. The few airport officials we did encounter treated us as if they were actually pleased to see us. I knew that there were very few tourists who came to Haiti. In the circumstances, that was hardly surprising. The US and Canada specifically advise their nationals not to go there under any circumstances. All the international aid agencies warn of the spiralling AIDS problem and the ever-present danger from carjacking, robbery and random murder.

Haiti was officially listed as a Fourth World country, and it showed. With Linda driving the hire car, we made our way through the deeply potholed roads strewn with rubbish that were the outskirts of Port-au-Prince. On all sides, decaying buildings formed a backdrop to our progress. Clapped-out cars, driven maniacally, clogged narrow streets that were completely without road markings. Traffic lights were very few and far between. I could see why Linda had insisted on driving. Only someone with experience of the place was liable to survive a journey by road.

We had gone only a short distance when Linda stopped outside a scruffy-looking store. It was one-storey high, like most of the buildings we had seen. Having said that she needed to buy some film for her cameras, she went inside. Gary and I followed her. While she was being served, I noticed some long-bladed knives in a display case. I picked out one that looked like a Bowie knife, complete with its own sheath. Saying that we could do with some protection in such a dangerous place, I expressed my intention to buy it.

The reaction from Linda was dramatic to say the least. As if stung, she spun around and confronted me. Face red and eyes dilated, she shouted that, if I bought it, that was as far as she went with us. When I asked, quite reasonably, what we should do if we were carjacked and in fear of our lives, she replied that we would just have to deal with the situation.

It was obvious that her mind was made up. It was equally obvious that, without her, we wouldn't get far with our assignment. To me it made little sense. I reflected that, should we end up on the wrong end of machetes wielded by local thugs, then perhaps her attitude would change.

Unfortunately, it set the tone for the rest of the journey. Never loquacious at the best of times, she drove the rest of the way in silence. It didn't really affect Gary and me. With him filming, I was doing pieces to camera, commenting on our surroundings. The obvious poverty was dire. 'If anyone sees someone smiling, we should stop and ask them what they've got to be happy about' was one remark that just about summed it up.

The Oloffson Hotel was a revelation. Although it had clearly seen better days, the graceful balconies with Gothic designs and acres of decorative lattices were quite beautiful. Linda explained that it was known as 'gingerbread architecture' and it certainly gave the impression of a fairyland gingerbread house.

The riotous unrestrained greenery that seemed to assault the hotel on all sides made for a perfect backdrop. I couldn't help but reflect, though that, while beautiful by day, it would be extremely sinister by night – a point remarked on by Graham Greene in his novel *The Comedians*, when he wrote, 'You expected a witch to open the door to you or a maniac butler, with a bat dangling from the chandelier behind him.' Greene had stayed at the Oloffson while writing his book, which is set in Haiti at the time of the murderous dictator 'Papa Doc' Duvalier and his equally murderous Tonton Macoutes, the secret police.

You could tell that it was home from home for Linda. The receptionist greeted her warmly and told her she would put her in her old room. As we set off for our separate rooms, Linda cautioned us about the frequent power cuts, but reassured us that the hotel's generator would restore power almost immediately.

That evening at dinner, it became clear that Linda intended to compartmentalise working and socialising. She didn't exactly ignore Gary and me, but she did maintain her distance. After initially introducing us to Richard, the hotel's owner, she retired to a table for four, where three people she obviously knew were already dining. In passing, she remarked that we would be going to see the voodoo priest in the morning.

In the event, the lack of Linda's company proved to be no loss at all. Social conversation with her was always awkward at the best of times. Further, the hotel's other guests all had interesting stories to tell. A mix of missionaries, peace corps volunteers, teachers, journalists, writers and artists, they were eccentrics all. This seemed to be a condition brought about by the environment, rather than any inherent character trait. I felt sure they wouldn't have behaved like it at home, wherever that was.

One staid middle-aged white woman, who was something high up in the peace corps, showed up for dinner on occasions with her black Haitian boyfriend, who could have been no more than 20. Not to be outdone, the elderly male missionary also had a young black boyfriend. Other customers came and went with various beautiful Haitian women on their arms. Not one word was said, not one remark made. The rules of polite company were scrupulously observed. It was all delightfully funny.

Gary and I table-hopped and, over a period of several days, got to know them all. They were a fount of information about all things Haitian. The power cuts and crime were the main topics of conversation, but on the day we arrived the talk was all of the intended civil protest to disrupt the 'Day of the Dead' proceedings. Riots were threatened, as were attacks on white tourists. To a government that was desperately trying to promote tourism as a source of revenue, this was a serious threat.

At breakfast, Linda introduced us to Milfort, a middle-aged, heavyset black guy who walked with a limp. He seemed to be a cross between a guide, a bodyguard and a translator for Linda, who said that we should employ him to accompany us everywhere. All personal differences apart, I fully realised that I was very much in Linda's hands as far as logistical and security considerations were concerned. Milfort joined us in the car.

Silva Joseph was a voodoo priest who lived in the rather inappropriately named Bel Air, a festering dangerous-looking slum in the suburbs of Port-au-Prince. Dressed in scuffed trainers, tracksuit bottoms and a grubby vest, the elderly wizened old guy didn't look much at all. However, as he squired us about his domain, you could tell that he was held in some esteem by his neighbours. All greeted him warmly and smiled at us.

The voodoo temple was clearly dual-purpose. Women and children were washing clothes, preparing food, eating and gossiping. Drying laundry hung everywhere. Linda pointed out the central post, which held up the pitched corrugated-tin roof. It was fantastically carved with symbols and figures. This was the *poto mitan*, or sacred post, around which all the ceremonies revolve. When the priest summoned them, this was the post that the *Iwa* would descend to enter the material world.

From a multitude of perspectives, not the least of them the visual one, this was something less than a gripping setting for anything. I was trying to visualise the photos we would get for *Front*. You could tell people it was a voodoo temple until you were blue in the face, but the ultimate reality was that it looked like some ramshackle old tin-roofed shed with lots of washing drying. Couple that with the old boy in his tracksuit bottoms and grubby vest and you would have a spectacle that fell far short of the mystical.

I intimated as much to Linda and she pointed out the altar in a nearby alcove. I had completely missed it. Black-faced extravagantly dressed dolls with horns jockeyed for position with dusty old skulls. Bright multicoloured objects of indiscernible origin filled the spaces in between. This was much more impressive.

With both Linda and Milfort translating, we explained to Silva what my particular problem was. I may be troubled by evil spirits. He took this in as if he heard it every day, as no doubt he did. He said that he would conjure up his own personal spirit, Mazaka La Croix, to check me out. Then, if there was anything troubling me, he would drive it out with a magical bath. The conjuring up of his personal spirit would cost £50 and the magical bath another £100, a lot of money in Haitian terms. There was nothing particularly mystical about his prices!

In a similar, businesslike vein I told him I would need a receipt. Voodoo priest or no voodoo priest, absolutely no one was immune from the rules of *Front*'s accounts department. I paid a deposit and agreed to return the following day, the 31st, the Eve of All Hallows, or Hallowe'en.

Lying in my room that night, I mulled over what I was about to do. I wasn't complacent about stirring up the spirit world, but I felt absolutely no fear. I was quite confident about my spiritual condition. I knew I was a strong spirit, one that had progressed from an evil orientation to a good one. I had performed that most incredible of feats. I had turned around my heart and had come to a comparative state of grace. I totally rejected evil in all its forms and was sure that it couldn't touch me. Further, after all the years of pain, much of which I still lived with, I had no fear of death. Needless to say, I didn't share these thoughts with Linda.

We set out for Bel Air the following afternoon. To my question of why the ceremony wasn't being held at night, Linda answered that to be out after dark in Port-au-Prince was a sure invitation to be murdered. With absolutely no street lighting, even the police stayed in their police stations after dark.

If it was a special day for me, it certainly wasn't for the usual inhabitants of the voodoo temple. Washerwomen, playing children, crawling infants, chickens, a goat and several cats wandered in and out. Damp washing still hung everywhere.

Silva, still dressed in the same clothes, welcomed me warmly, then retired into a small dark room next to the altar to prepare himself. Strange chanting could be heard for several minutes. Suddenly, a double handclap announced that I could enter.

By candlelight, I sat down in a chair next to Silva. He seemed to be in some kind of trance, staring about the room wildly. However, he did have the presence of mind to shake hands with me. Then he stared directly into my face for a while, before taking out a pack of cards and dealing some on to the table between us. All the while Gary filmed the proceedings while Linda snapped away with her camera.

I'd like to say that he came close, but he didn't. First, he asked if I had had trouble with a black person recently. I hadn't, but sitting in a voodoo temple in Haiti surrounded by black people, I would hardly have admitted to it if I had.

I suppose he was warmer when he said that I was very ambitious, but he kept coming back to the question about the trouble with a black person. I scoured my memory. I had exchanged hostile looks with an officious ticket collector on the London Underground the previous week, but I was sure that wasn't what Silva was referring to.

After about 20 minutes, during which time the room became unbearably hot, Silva pronounced me clear of evil spirits. However, there was another problem. It seemed that there was a powerful female spirit called Erzili Frieda, who wanted to get close to me, but couldn't because of my jealous girlfriend. The latter part was certainly close enough. I was sure that Marsha would deter even the most powerful voodoo spirit.

According to Silva, this female spirit was becoming increasingly angry, and this was blocking me for good fortune. He strongly advised that I should let her come closer. To facilitate this he recommended that I take a magical bath, which he would administer personally.

I had to hand it to the old guy. I was sure the pitch for the magical bath would come in somewhere – he certainly wasn't going to miss out on the extra £100. But this was quite ingenious. Anyway, as the spectacle of the magic-bath ceremony was sure to be more impressive than what I had just been through, I agreed. It was usually naked, nubile, young women who appeared in the pages of *Front*. Surely, I'd be a welcome change.

I was told that there was some preparation to be done and that I should come back in a couple of hours. On my return, Silva's appearance had smartened up dramatically. Gone were the grubby vest, crumpled tracksuit bottoms and scuffed trainers, and in their place were a pristine white shirt, immaculately pressed black trousers and highly polished black shoes. Also, all the women, children and assorted animals had gone, and some of the washing had been taken down, Clearly, Silva meant business.

He welcomed me again, then withdrew into the altar room with his assistant to prepare once more. Candles were lit, incantations uttered and a large white porcelain bowl was placed on a chair in front of the altar. Into this was poured a foul-smelling brown liquid. I was then told to strip naked and stand on a board in front of the altar.

Now I had realised that for a bath, magical or otherwise, a degree of nakedness would be required. What I hadn't realised was that I would be stark naked. However, you can't spend 24 years in prison and still be shy about personal matters. That had been among men, though. Linda was still a woman. I was going to have to stand stark naked in front of her.

All modesty apart, there was also a very sound practical reason for my caution. Of all the baleful spirits that might be watching over us at this moment, the one firmly to the front of my mind was that of Marsha. What would happen if she ever saw my article in the magazine? There I would be, stark naked for all the world to see, and the byline for the photographs would contain the name of Linda, clearly a woman. It would take an army of voodoo priests to protect me from Marsha's wrath.

My ruminations were suddenly disrupted by a small explosion and a sheet of flame. Silva had set light to the liquid in the bowl. It burned brightly for several seconds before he snuffed it out with a towel. He spun me around several times, all the while uttering incantations. Then, with Silva holding a candle just below my chin, I had to say a silent prayer to Saint Nicholas for what I desired.

Having filled his cupped hands with some of the liquid from the bowl, Silva proceeded to rub it all over my body, from the top of my head, to the soles of my feet. Suddenly, my flesh seemed as if it were on fire. My face burned so fiercely that my eyes filled with tears, temporarily blinding me. A hot flush spread through my insides. I involuntarily clutched at my groin in agony as a small droplet of the liquid entered the eye of my dick.

Not surprisingly, every bit of my complacency had disappeared. I was now taking the experience a lot more seriously – I hadn't expected it to hurt me physically. I wondered what trial Silva had in store for me next. I didn't have to wait long to find out.

After telling me to hold out my left hand, Silva poured some of the liquid into my upturned palm. I was told that he was going to set it alight and that I should snuff out the flame and rub what remained of the liquid over my scalp. What he didn't tell me was just how difficult it would be to snuff out the flame.

With the palm of my left hand literally a ball of flame, I flapped my arm about in a vain attempt to put the fire out. The rush of air seemed to make the flames burn more fiercely. The pain was excruciating. I briefly contemplated slapping my hand against my side, but this would only have burned a more tender part of my body. It didn't reassure me to see that Silva was now looking quite concerned.

Suddenly, the flames went out. I don't think it was of my causing, more that the liquid had all burned up. It was a very sore left hand that I rubbed across my scalp. As I looked at my palm, two very large blisters came up right before my eyes.

Silva told me to get dressed and not to wash or bathe for the rest of the day. He handed me a bottle containing what remained of the liquid and instructed me to rub it over my body at 7 a.m. on a day that I had hard work to do. I took a silent oath to remain idle for the rest of my life.

In the car back to the hotel, Linda told Gary and me what to expect at the Day of the Dead ceremonies in the morning. For Haitians it was the festival of Gede. The Gede are a family of spirits who are guardians of the dead. They are presided over by Baron Samedi and his wife, Gran Brigitte. The 1st and 2nd of November are national holidays in Haiti. There are prayers, offerings, sacrifices of animals and birds, ceremonies and processions. However, serious as this might be, humour is an integral part of the proceedings – as if by mocking death, we can lose our fear of it.

At breakfast, there was reassuring news from the hotel staff. Although the police had shot dead nine people in violent protests in recent days and there had been talk of another disturbance in Port-au-Prince's main cemetery on Gede, targeting tourists and other foreigners, the director of the National Cemetery had just announced that there would be no trouble after all.

On Linda's advice, we set out early for the National Cemetery. A portly middle-aged Canadian academic had arrived the previous day and had asked if he could come along with us. We agreed, reasoning that there would be more safety in numbers. Mentally, I steeled myself. Protest or no protest, I had been warned that the coming experience would be an ordeal.

If the buildings of Port-au-Prince had been merely decaying, the fabric of the cemetery was in an altogether more parlous state. Rusty gates hung haphazardly from broken hinges and the low once-white wall was cobwebbed with cracks caused by subsidence.

Around the entrance milled a seething mass of celebrants. Some wore white sheetlike robes, while others were dressed like Baron Samedi, with black trousers, purple scarf, black hat and white shirt. Many cradled a skull in one arm, while holding a black walking stick in one hand.

The sight of two police cars and several officers was reassuring, but Linda cautioned that they would stay outside and, once we went in, we would be on our own. Of the five of us, at this point Milfort was the most skittish. He had a worried look on his face and was constantly looking about him as if he expected a sneak attack at any moment. To be truthful, I had never had much confidence in his powers of protection. At his age and in his condition, it didn't seem as if he could have much of a fight. However, perhaps fear and respect were based on other things locally.

With Milfort leading the way, we entered the cemetery. We were immediately confronted by hordes of beggars of all ages. From young children, to aged crones, including women with infants in their arms, they cried in unison, '*Blanc, blanc, un dollar*' over and over again like some ritualistic chant.

I was firmly in battle mode. I didn't feel afraid. I had told myself that, whatever happened, I couldn't afford to show any fear. People pick up on fear. As just four white faces in a sea of black ones, we wouldn't have stood a chance if the mob had turned on us. I also knew that to give anything to one beggar would only encourage the others the more. I stared fixedly in front of me and pushed through the crush.

Suddenly, two young men in their early twenties were in front of me. Thrusting their faces into mine while walking backwards they shouted, '*Blanc, blanc, un dollar.*' I ignored them as if they weren't there. As they saw that I wasn't going to give them anything, their tone became even more aggressive and they began shouting something like, '*Blanc, cacka; blanc, cacka.*' I knew that *blanc* meant foreigner, but *cacka* was new to me. However, it was obviously some term of abuse.

I hazarded a guess that *cacka* meant shit. Now they definitely weren't going to get anything.

Each of our party, except Milfort, was being subjected to the same treatment. Linda was taking it all in her stride. Twisting and turning, she seemed to weave her way through the mob. Gary actually seemed to be enjoying himself. With his cine camera held tightly in his arms, he filmed our progress and zoomed in on the most vociferous of the beggars.

The Canadian academic, though, was suffering badly. Clearly frightened, he made the mistake of giving money to some particularly persistent children. The baying mob immediately pressed forward, pinning him against a tombstone until Milfort rescued him.

White-faced and literally shaking with fear, the academic rushed close to us and kept both hands firmly in his pockets from then on.

As we battled our way towards the centre of the cemetery, most of the beggars dropped away. This gave us more opportunity to examine our surroundings in detail. We passed groups gathered around graves lit with candles, who were chanting, giving offerings and drinking the local fermented cane-sugar drink, *kleren*. There were friendly welcoming looks, but there were also hostile stares. Assuming an air of confidence I didn't really feel, I pressed on.

Suddenly, we came to a large white cross blackened with the soot of hundreds of candles that surrounded it. Scores of celebrants milled about. This was the cross of Baron Samedi and served as the focal point of the cemetery celebrations.

The more *kleren* that was consumed, the more frantic the chanting and singing became. From time to time, men would appear dressed as Baron Samedi. One gambolled through the throng, cracking jokes. He stopped right in front of me, tweaked my nose and, as I raised my hands in a reflex action, he reached down and tweaked at my dick. Linda assured me that it was nothing personal, just the lewdness and humour of Gede.

By now, about an hour had passed since we had entered the cemetery. We felt that we had seen enough and that to stay longer would be to press our luck. With the assistance of two young men who had attached themselves to our party and who had protected us from the worst of the beggars, we forged a path back to the entrance. As we reached our car I gave them five dollars each. Thus ended a thoroughly unpleasant experience, one that left me exhausted from all the tension. I returned to the hotel and slept for several hours.

The following day, we drove down to the coastal town of Jacmel to witness their Gede celebrations. Linda explained that we wouldn't have to worry so much about security considerations, which would allow us more opportunity to observe the proceedings objectively. I gathered that she hadn't enjoyed the experience of the previous day either.

The genteel decay of the French colonial buildings of Jacmel was a refreshing change from the urban collapse of Port-au-Prince. There was still grinding poverty, but the beggars who accosted us in the cemetery were much more restrained than those of the day before.

That evening, we witnessed two Gede ceremonies that could hardly have been more different. The first was presided over by an enormous white woman called Carol. She stood all of six foot three in her stockinged feet and must have weighed 16 stones at least. She was fat in places, but the overall impression was one of a great strapping woman. Similar to some of the ex-pats who frequented the Oloffson, she seemed to have several young Haitian males in attendance.

Carol was an American with a master's degree from the University of Massachusetts, and it showed. The carefully choreographed ceremony, held in a roofed temple with no walls, owed more to show business than to spirituality. Lounging about in her street clothes as she articulated the cult of voodoo with considerable clarity, Carol sounded believable. Done up in her priestess's outfit of flowing blue robe, blue turban, sporting a pink silk scarf and wielding a massive machete that must have been a yard long, she looked quite ridiculous.

Carol, supposedly a fully initiated priestess herself, advertises voodoo holidays on the Internet. During some of these holidays, she initiates would-be voodooists into the priesthood. At the height of the ceremony, which consisted mostly of Carol thundering about the earthen floor wielding the machete with both hands, she pointed out Dave, a short, fat, bearded Jewish guy from Syracuse, whom she had personally initiated.

Voodoo priest Dave, in a Baron Samedi outfit he might easily have borrowed from a fancy-dress shop, swayed gracelessly to the beat of the drums. Woody Allen would have made more of the role. Whatever. We Jews are quite familiar with the role of the voodoo priest – we call them rabbis. And Dave is only doing his bit for the cause. For with George W Bush in the White House, what America desperately needs right now is more kosher witchdoctors!

Thus far, I hadn't been at all impressed by the degree of spirituality of the ceremonies conducted by the voodoo priesthood. Those carried out by both Silva and Carol seemed to be merely voodoo for tourists. As far as spiritual experiences go, they had left me cold and unmoved. I could only hope that the ceremony later that evening would be different.

The initial proceedings hadn't gone well. We had met with the priestess in a rundown restaurant she owned in the slum quarter of the town. The bargaining over how much we should pay to witness the ceremony was drawn out and, at times, bitter. Clearly, she wanted to get as much as she could out of us. Again, this tended to detract from the supposed spirituality of the event.

We made our way through narrow labyrinthine alleys, in pitch blackness, as we went ever deeper into the heart of the slum. The thought did occur to me that, should we lose the priestess who was leading us, we would never find our way out again. That served to make us keep up. We arrived at the temple shortly before midnight.

As a place of worship, this temple was entirely more impressive than any we had previously seen. It was fully twice as big as the one Silva Joseph practised in and was lit by hundreds of candles. If it was also of dual use, we saw no evidence of it. The central pole was massive. It was decorated with fantastical carvings and paintings, and hundreds of strange, ritualistic objects hung all over it.

The priest's assistant was busy marking out the mystical drawings for Gede in cornflour on the bare earth floor. At cardinal points he set lighted candles and bottles of rum. Several drummers sat in a group in a corner, while scores of celebrants in their street clothes thronged the margins of the temple. Some wore Christian crosses on chains around their necks.

I did feel that we were intruding, both as the only whites present and as outsiders. Quite clearly, we weren't sincere practitioners, merely curious observers. We weren't exactly welcomed, but there was no real hostility either. With Gary filming and Linda snapping away, I decided to make myself inconspicuous and settled down in a corner.

Suddenly, the voodoo priest appeared, clad all in purple. He seemed quite young, certainly no more than in his late twenties. He gave a signal and the drums began to beat. He was joined at the centre of the temple by the priestess, now clad all in white. A chorus of several other women, dressed in white flowing robes, circled them and the central post.

At first, it was just call and response, initiated by the priest. Then, as the beat and the intensity increased, the singing and dancing began. At the margins, the congregation swayed rhythmically, occasionally calling out and joining in the singing.

I was trying to observe proceedings objectively. Not diverted by the demands of participation, I was coolly appraising every event, however minor. I didn't want to miss anything. Hopefully, my account would be a definitive one on the true nature of a voodoo ceremony.

However, much as I tried to remain objective and above the proceedings, slowly, inexorably, I felt myself being drawn in. The drumming was so loud now that it seemed to be inside my head. Myriad smells assailed my nostrils. The temple seemed to have grown several degrees hotter and I was sweating profusely. My very consciousness, previously casting about to take in every little thing, seemed to be focusing more and more on what the priest and priestess were doing.

As the drumming reached fever pitch, the women of the chorus seemed to experience some kind of seizure. One after the other, it sent them reeling and stumbling across the temple. Just when you thought they were about to fall, they were caught and supported by the rest. According to voodoo lore, they had been possessed by the spirits of Gede.

Then, after a quick swig of rum, they would break away, dancing wildly and spinning round and round in a fashion that would have made any ordinary person dizzy in seconds. The most amazing thing, though, was that, no matter how fast they spun, or how wildly they danced, often with their eyes closed, not once did their feet come close to knocking over one of the candles or bottles that had been placed on the mystical drawings. There was no rational explanation for this.

By now, the whole room and everyone in it was convulsing to the deafening beat of the drums. Whatever was happening (and I still haven't really worked it out), I was caught up in it. I felt elated, enthused, excited and moved, all at the same time. I wouldn't attempt to try to quantify the experience with words such as trance and possession, but I had certainly attained some kind of higher state, spiritual or otherwise.

I like being in control. My awesome self-discipline, built up over 24 years of incarceration, was designed to achieve just that end. So to be out of control, or rather, to be controlled by other forces, was completely alien to me. I experienced a brief feeling of panic. I had to get away.

I stumbled out into the night, disoriented and confused. Never have the shadows of a darkened street seemed so ominous. I clearly remember that, as I waited for the others, I was hoping that whatever had touched me in the temple would find no foothold in me. I had come to Haiti to *get rid* of any spirits that might be troubling me, not to find one and take it home with me.

All mysticism aside, the Haiti assignment was a considerable success. *Front* ran my story in their next issue, accompanied by a score or so of dramatic and exotic pictures. Central among these was one of me naked. Well, not showing me completely naked. It was shot from behind, from the waist up, with Silva's altar in the background and the porcelain bowl just above my head. And there, on the byline for the photography, was Linda's name.

It was a ticking bomb. Should Marsha ever discover the article, all the spirits of Gede wouldn't be able to protect me from her wrath. Now that's what I call living dangerously!

CHAPTER SIXTEEN
MY SPIRIT BEAST

Although I felt that I had brought the Haiti story to a successful conclusion from a journalistic perspective, from a spiritual one it still left many questions unanswered. The fact that Silva Joseph had told me that I was free from evil spirits was neither here nor there. I was sure that he would have told me whatever it took to get the most money off me. And, now that my curiosity was well and truly aroused, I found myself casting about for other ways to test my spiritual wellbeing.

The answer came from an unexpected source. Since our Colombian adventures together, Dan and I were now good friends. We frequently emailed each other and occasionally talked on the phone. During one of our phone conversations, I mentioned in passing the trip to Haiti and the voodoo ceremonies, especially the 'priests'.

'Why don't you do something on the Colombian shamans?' suggested Dan. 'They're good at driving out spirits. You can drink the local *jage* [he pronounced it yah-hey] too. It's a special potion. I've done it.'

I had heard of the shamans, of course, but mostly in connection with the Red Indians of North America. My research revealed that shamanism is one of the oldest forms of religious consciousness on the planet. In many cultures the shaman has multiple roles, the most important being his mediation between the temporal and spiritual worlds, although he is also important for his healing powers. In his visionary state, under the influence of the powerfully hallucinogenic *jage*, many believe him capable of communicating with the spirit world.

Jage is used extensively throughout Central and South America. Depending on the area and the culture, it can also be called *ayahuasca*, *caapi* and *yaje*. The potion is made by boiling the bark of the banisteriopsis vine (*Banisteriopsis caapi*). Because of its psychedelic effects it has also been called 'the vine of the dead', the visionary vine' and 'the vine of souls'.

Bearing in mind that if I did the story I could end up drinking the stuff, I was curious to know exactly what was in it. I didn't doubt for one minute that Dan had taken it, but he virtually ran on cocaine in the way that a car ran on petrol. It had probably been just one more psychedelic experience to go with all the rest. I was a novice where drugs were concerned. It might have an altogether different effect on me, one that I might have difficulty in recovering from.

The answers from my research weren't reassuring. *Jage* includes other jungle plants as well as banisteriopsis. On boiling, they break down into the powerfully hallucinogenic alkaloids harmine, harmaline, ditetrahydroharmine and dimethyltryptamine (DMT). These compounds have effects similar to LSD, mescaline and psilocybin. DMT has been found to occur naturally in mammals, but is usually broken down by the naturally occurring monoamine oxidase (MO). *Jage* also contains MO inhibitors.

Not surprisingly, the drinking of *jage* has several severe effects, not least of them nausea, vomiting, dizziness and diarrhoea. It also leads to euphoric, aggressive or sexually aroused states. The vomiting and diarrhoea are part of the purgative process that drives evil spirits and toxic matter out of the body. This is often accompanied by visions of creatures and plants, even by Europeans who have never seen such things before. Occasionally, one sees oneself as the spirit form of whatever jungle creature one is. Some experiences can be beautiful, others can be terrifying.

Quite clearly, any normal person would have to think twice about taking such a potion. And I was a very long way from being a normal person. Despite my proud boast of having turned around my heart and renounced evil in all its forms, my character previously had been, at times, savage. What if I took the potion and saw myself as one of the more terrifying creatures? What if I reverted to my former savage self?

I accepted that the only damage I could do, deep in the Colombian jungle, would be to Dan and the unfortunate shaman. But the thought of roaming the rainforest in some semi-demented state, thinking I was an animal, concentrated my mind wonderfully. As things stood right now, I wasn't expecting much of an epitaph. In that eventuality, even if I were to write it myself, it wasn't the stuff of great obituaries.

Front went for the story immediately. Although I emphasised that I was going in search of my spirit beast, their main interest seemed to be in this powerfully hallucinogenic sex drug called *jage*. No doubt their entire readership were regularly drunk, stoned, wrecked and otherwise bombed out on a variety of illegal substances, and aspired to be even more so. The idea of some superdrug that you could get by merely boiling up a bunch of leaves would certainly fire their imagination.

The production company had been pleased with the footage they had got from the Haiti trip and had made it into a short film, with me as the presenter. They also wanted to cover the upcoming Colombian shaman trip. Their intention was to make a five-minute video, incorporating both trips, and take it to one of the TV networks. Once again they funded half the cost of the trip, but this time Gary would be taking photographs for *Front* as well as filming for the production company.

The production company booked and paid for the tickets. It was only when Gary and I got to the airport that we saw that our Bogotá journey would break in Miami for a change of planes. Having passed successfully through Miami before, I wasn't so much concerned about not being allowed in. It was the two-hour window between our plane landing in Miami and the Bogotá flight taking off that concerned me. Gary said that I was being alarmist and that two hours was plenty of time to make a connection.

We landed in Miami right on time. Then we spent 40 minutes out on the runway. When we finally got to the docking gate, there was another 40-minute delay before we could disembark. Then there was a delay in getting our baggage off the carousel. With 15 minutes left before the takeoff of the Bogotá flight, we were racing through the airport, trying to reach the boarding gate in time.

We burst through one check-in, with a flight attendant shouting after me that I would have to check my large suitcase into the hold. I ignored her and just made it to the gate. Gary had a small bag and was passed straight through. I was stopped and told in no uncertain terms that my bag was too big for hand luggage and I would have to go back and check it in. This, in effect, condemned me to miss the flight. Realising this, Gary shouted that I should get on the next flight and he would meet me at Bogotá Airport.

I explained at the airline desk what had happened. They apologised and put me on their next flight. This didn't take off until the following morning, though. I spent a very frustrating night in the airport hotel worrying if I would be able to connect up with Gary again. It was his first time in Colombia and Dan wasn't the most reliable person in the world. I had known all along that I would have a problem in stopping Dan and Gary partying all the time.

My worst fears seemed to be realised when I landed at Bogotá around noon on the following day. No one was there to meet me. However, just as I was about to get into a taxi and head for a hotel, another taxi pulled up and Dan and Gary jumped out. It was as I had thought. They had hit it off together and gone out on a bender the night before. In the morning they found that the cheap hotel they stayed in wouldn't take Gary's credit card. So they were delayed while they ran around trying to raise the money. It didn't augur well for the upcoming trip.

Our flight was to Leticia, the southernmost town in all Colombia and the only one on the Amazon. Dan explained that there had been an agreement between the surrounding countries of Brazil and Peru to give Colombia a town on the great river. The result was the long thin tongue of land that stretched southwards to meet the Amazon, with Leticia at its point.

Leticia was typical of all Colombian jungle towns, the two-storey shabby buildings separated by dusty, potholed streets. Along these trundled rusting old cars, surrounded by a sea of motorbikes, scooters and cycles, some carrying several passengers.

It was both hot and humid. The temperature had reached 91 degrees Fahrenheit and it rained heavily for several hours at a time. The Hotel Anaconda was the best in town, but, once again in Colombia, *best* was to be a comparative term. There was no hot water and the aircon wheezed consumptively. We were the only guests. The civil war had killed the tourist trade in an area known for its Amazon trips.

Ironically, the town was very safe, with regular patrols from the nearby army base. Peru was just across the river, which was patrolled by the Peruvian Navy. Brazil was barely two miles down the road. Smuggling is the name of the game here, drugs for the world's markets out of Colombia and weapons for the indigenous guerrillas coming the other way.

I had already lost a day, so I didn't want to waste any more time. The following morning Dan introduced us to Jorge, a young guide he knew from a previous trip. We struggled down to the river with our kit and some provisions and climbed into a long canoe powered by an outboard motor. I was fully alert and in work mode now. I knew that the cultural element was going to be supremely important. I needed to see the people, the creatures and the plants, all in their natural environments. Only then would I be able to understand the true import of any visions I might see.

The Amazon was mighty and magnificent. Only a few hundred yards across at Leticia, it widened until it was difficult to see either bank. At a shout from the boatman I turned and saw dolphins, both blue and pink, dipping in and out of the water. Myriad fantastically coloured birds swooped and called all around us. Along the bank grew thick vegetation, unbroken by any sign of human habitation. As an experience it was quite breathtaking.

It started to spot with rain. Moving swiftly, the boatman unrolled a waterproof canopy and headed for the shore. It wasn't panic, but all his previous movements had been slow and measured. I wondered what he was concerned about. I was just about to find out.

Suddenly, the heavens opened. Rain, in very large droplets, poured down in such quantity that we couldn't see a yard ahead. The surface of the river seemed to boil, churned up by the falling rain. Seconds earlier, the sky had been clear and the sun was shining brightly. Lesson one was that the weather can change very quickly on the Amazon.

By now, though, we were moored in a little tributary. Jorge suggested that it was a good opportunity to eat. We hunkered down in the canoe, eating what the hotel had prepared for us. A wind had sprung up, whipping the thick reeds so that they thrashed against each other. Together with the sound of the rain, the noise was awesome. As the elements warred around us, one could only feel very small and insignificant in the grand scheme of things.

As quickly as it had begun, it was over. Once again the sky was clear and the sun shone brightly. Steam rose from the land where the freshly fallen rain had pooled. We set off, out into the main stream again. We had been travelling for only an hour, and Monkey Island was still another three hours away. In Amazonian terms, this was only a short distance.

Dan explained that Monkey Island was a project started by an American 20 years previously. He had built long wooden dormitories for tourists to stay in while they observed the thousands of monkeys that inhabit the island. Or that's what he said his intention was. He disappeared when customs found five tons of cocaine in a shipment of wood he was sending back to the US. The place had lain derelict for many years now, occupied only by an Indian family who scraped a precarious living from the very few tourists who visited.

I was eager to get close to the monkeys. I had been doing bits to camera with Gary as we travelled, but the birds and the dolphins had all been so far away. As we glided into the bank, the Indian and his whole family were waiting for us. Soon we were standing in a large clearing, but I couldn't see any monkeys. 'Where are the fucking monkeys then, Dan?' I asked petulantly.

Dan gave me his 'long-suffering' look – he knew me and my impatience quite well now. 'In the fucking trees, Norm,' he replied, pointing in the general direction of the surrounding forest.

Then I saw them. In fact, the monkeys *were* the trees. There were so many thousands of them in the branches that the trees seemed to be the same colour as the monkeys' fur. The grey army sat watching us to see if we were dangerous to them. As the Indian pulled out bunches of bananas they recognised the signs. They swarmed to the ground and ran towards us. They were all quite tiny, none larger than a domestic cat and most the size of kittens. Some were mothers, with mouse-sized young hanging round their necks.

Completely fearless now, they swarmed all over us. They were clinging to my clothes, my shoulders, and one was sitting on my head. I laughed hysterically, all the while peeling bananas as fast as I could, only to have them snatched from my hands by the tiny manikins. Under the circumstances, it took five attempts for me to do a piece to the camera.

Dan explained that our next mission was to photograph me with a young crocodile, but for some as yet unexplained reason this could only be done at night. We had several hours to kill. Dan announced that in the meantime we would go fishing. I had been fishing only once before in my entire life and I found it to be extremely boring. You sat about for hours with virtually nothing happening. As I articulated these thoughts, Dan gave me another of his 'long-suffering' looks. 'You'll see,' he replied cryptically.

We pulled into another small tributary and climbed out of the canoe and on to the bank. Jorge busied himself breaking off small branches from nearby bushes and tying a fishing line and hook to each. We now had four 'fishing rods' that wouldn't have looked out of place in the hands of garden gnomes. It was my turn to show the 'long-suffering' look. I turned to Dan, indicating that I was doing this only to humour him. He smiled, but said nothing.

'What are we fishing for?' I asked laconically, as Jorge fixed a small piece of fish flesh to the hook of my 'rod'.

'Piranha,' replied Dan deadpan.

I pulled my feet back from the water's edge as I lowered the hook and bait into the water.

For several seconds nothing happened. Then the water seemed to boil as dozens of small snapping silver fish thrashed about, trying to get the bait. As a reflex action I pulled the hook and bait from the water. Several piranha sailed clear of the water after it. They were only small, but seemed to be all sharp pointed teeth. I suppressed a shudder as I contemplated what would happen if I fell in. At this point, life in the Amazon looked vicious and deadly.

Now it was I who was hooked, though. I fished frantically, pulling a fish from the water at every attempt. Soon all the bait was gone and it was getting dark. Time to find the crocodile.

Night fell surprisingly quickly on the Amazon. It seemed as if one moment we were fishing in broad daylight, the next it was gloomy, and the very next moment darkness was upon us. We climbed back into the boat and pushed out into midstream. At the direction of the boatman, Jorge made his way to the prow and pulled back a tarpaulin. Underneath was a large battery similar to the ones in cars. He fiddled about for a couple of seconds and then a powerful beam of light shot out, lighting up the river in front of us.

Crouching over the light, Jorge directed it back and forth, first lighting up one bank with its beam, then the other. In between, the river was revealed to be an unrelieved black mass.

The effect was quite surreal. Almost like a picture projected on a screen, the lit-up section of the bank revealed every detail. 'Won't that frighten everything away?' I whispered to Dan.

'Jorge knows what he's doing, mate,' he replied. 'The idea is that the light paralyses them. It's a thing with crocodiles. They look into the beam and freeze. You'll see.'

Up until this point, it had all been something of a jolly outing. I hadn't felt that I was in much danger, unless, of course, the canoe sank. Suddenly, though, during one sweep across the river, two deep-yellow lights lit up about 50 yards in front of us. They weren't as bright as car headlights, but their deeper glow had an intensity that you might find in car sidelights.

'What the fuck's that, Dan?' My tone was curious rather than frightened. Dan exchanged words with Jorge, who focused the beam right on the centre of the river. Once again the two yellow lights lit up the darkness.

Now there was a distinct tone of caution in Dan's voice. 'It's a crocodile,' he said hoarsely. He paused to exchange a few more words with Jorge. 'A big one,' he added, his voice dropping a couple of octaves.

Under power from the outboard motor, we had been flying along at a good rate of knots. Dan had already warned that travelling on the river at night was dangerous, because of the many partially submerged logs. These were trees felled by loggers and allowed to float downriver. Dan had cautioned that to hit one of these at speed would be disastrous. The canoe would shatter and we would all be thrown into the water. Previously I had only been concerned about having a few chunks bitten out of me by the piranha. Now I would be breast-stroking with a large crocodile.

My thought process was disturbed by a shout from Jorge. Quite involuntarily, I jumped. What could it be now? The beam was fixed on the right-hand bank and Jorge was pointing at something. I followed the direction of his finger and saw, right in the middle of the beam, a baby crocodile, frozen into inaction.

We coasted into the bank. As we neared land, Jorge motioned me towards the front of the canoe. Explaining through Dan, he handed me the light and told me to keep it focused firmly on the baby croc. While it was gazing fixedly into the beam, Jorge would circle around behind it.

Much as I tried to focus my attention on the baby croc, a small part of me was asking where its mother was. Surely this was incredibly dangerous. It must be close by and all animals attack when they think their young are threatened. Knowing what the answer would be, though, I didn't bother to ask.

Suddenly, out of the darkness, Jorge could be seen in the beam. The baby croc was oblivious to him. He crept up on it and grabbed it just behind the jaws with one hand, while holding its hind quarters with the other. Then he held it up to show us. This croc-in-miniature bared its teeth for Gary's camera. Now it was my turn.

My thoughts firmly with big Mummy Croc, I gingerly made my way up the bank and into the glare of the beam. I stood and took Baby Croc off Jorge. Partially blinded, I did my piece to camera. 'Could my spirit beast be that of the crocodile?' I posed the question, while fervently hoping that the answer was no.

After that, the rest of the journey home was something of an anti-climax.

The following morning I discovered that there was a makeshift zoo barely half a mile from the hotel. All the animals were kept in wooden-fenced pens or rough pits in the ground. It was a whole lot easier to see them here than it was to chase all over the Amazon on the off chance of seeing one. And a whole lot safer. However, there wasn't much of a selection.

The crocodiles lay, three-quarters submerged, in the mud of their large pool. They seemed as if they were asleep but, in fact, were ever watchful. As you moved near the fence surrounding the pool, you could see their eyes following you.

An Indian threw a chicken on to the bank. It fluffed up its feathers and pecked at the ground, oblivious to the danger. Silently, without a ripple to give it away, the crocodile slid in close to the bank. Then, it came out of the water accompanied by a spray of droplets, its jaws snapping on the hapless chicken, and it slid back under the surface, all in one swift smooth movement. There was something inherently evil in this merciless creature. Once again I prayed that it wasn't my spirit beast.

In a murky pool lay two anacondas. Because of the mud it was difficult to see how big they were. An Indian keeper in his street clothes reached into the pool and grasped one anaconda around the head and neck. With his other hand supporting its middle, he lifted the creature clear of the pool. It was still partially curled up, so it was difficult to determine how long it was, but it seemed to be well over nine feet. In places, it was as thick as a man's leg.

The Indian beckoned me closer. I didn't have any phobias about snakes and, anyway, the creature looked quite docile. With a swing of his arms, the Indian draped the anaconda around my neck. While still keeping hold of the head, he motioned me to put one hand just below his and my other to hold the body of the snake. More than anything, I was conscious of the green slime from the pool running down my neck.

Gary filmed away while I did my bit to camera. If one had to be an Amazonian animal, one could do worse than to be an anaconda, I was thinking. Growing more confident now, I was aware that, although the Indian was out of shot, you would still be able to see his hand, just above mine, holding the snake's head. I gripped the head tightly and motioned for him to let go.

He shook his head determinedly. I was sure I'd got the hang of this and I motioned for him to let go again. He adamantly refused and, if anything, gripped tighter.

Dan was watching the whole episode and shook his head, a rueful smile on his face. 'You do make me laugh, Norm,' he said afterwards. 'You come over here thinking you can do anything the natives can do. See that Indian. He's grown up around anacondas. He's been handling them all his life. He wasn't just holding its head. He had two fingers pressed against certain muscles in its neck that paralyses it. If he'd let go it would have bit half your head off. Its jaws open incredibly wide and it has very long sharp fangs. If the bite didn't kill you, then the poison from its fangs surely would.'

I took this all in and told myself that perhaps I should slow down a bit. Dan was right, of course, but I so wanted to do a good piece that I was ignoring many of the dangers. Anyway, I consoled myself with the fact that I had done a good piece to camera with the anaconda round my neck.

In a pen near by were several tapirs. They seemed to be a cross between a furry pig and an elephant. The size and shape of the body was definitely pig, but the elongated snout belonged to the elephant. It was friendly though and, as I massaged its neck, it closed its eyes in ecstasy. Suddenly it brayed, flinging the snout upwards to reveal long curved teeth. It looked absolutely ridiculous, like an animal cobbled together out of the parts of several others. It had better not be my spirit beast. Rather be a crocodile and feared than a tapir and laughed at.

That evening, we looked through the footage we shot on the day. I smiled with satisfaction when we reached the anaconda sequence, then gaped in amazement. Halfway through, the anaconda disappeared and there I was, stroking the ridiculous tapir. It was the legacy of Dan's little tin. I had thought that Gary looked a bit off his face during the day's shooting. Quite obviously, he taped over the anaconda sequence by mistake.

He dropped his head as I went into a spontaneous rant. I shouted that we'd come thousands of miles to get that sequence and others like it and we wouldn't get another chance, so would he kindly shape up and stay straight until we'd finished filming. Dan sat in a corner quietly, knowing that it was as much his fault for giving Gary the stuff.

It was now the morning of the day. I woke early and lay there thinking about what I had committed myself to. The dangers from the various

Amazonian animals seemed as nothing compared with the upcoming experience with the *jage*. From my research and from what others had told me I knew just how powerful a potion it was.

I had never been much of a drugs person. I had puffed cannabis occasionally and, a few times in the mid-seventies, I took LSD, from which I got experience of hallucinogenics. But that was something called California Sunshine and, as its name implied, was all warmth and light. Even so, people had had bad 'trips' on it, so much so that some had ended up in mental hospitals. For me, it brought about a major personality change. So I was in no doubt about the effects and dangers of hallucinogens.

Jage, however, was something else entirely and had another order of magnitude of strength. Again I kept coming back to the fact that I was far from being a normal person. Some of my experiences in life had been pure horror; some of my previous states of mind pure purgatory.

I had been advised not to fight the *jage* and to go with it passively. But what if the visions of my personal demons sent me crazy? What if I ran screaming into the jungle and got lost? What if the near-death experience was so real that it brought on a heart attack?

However, I was nothing if not a realist now. I always assessed a situation and, if it couldn't be avoided, I dealt with it. It had got me through the 24 years of incarceration. I knew that I was committed to take the *jage* now. It was far too late to back out. So I put all the fears out of my mind and told myself that I would just have to deal with it.

Once I was up and moving I felt much better. Food interacts with the *jage*, colouring the visions and increasing the vomiting, so it was necessary for me to fast for most of the day. I ate just a light breakfast of scrambled eggs. By the time I took the *jage* that night, my stomach would be empty.

Jorge was waiting outside the hotel with a driver and his four-wheel-drive jeep. Once we hit the outskirts of Leticia all the roads disappeared, leaving only rough tracks. The jeep navigated across water-filled holes and around fallen trees. A normal vehicle wouldn't have lasted five minutes in this terrain.

We drove for about half an hour, then stopped in a clearing at the edge of what seemed to be impenetrable forest. Quite clearly, even the jeep could go no further. The rest of the journey would have to be made on foot. But how? All I could see was thick jungle vegetation surrounded by viscous muddy swamp.

Jorge walked to a fallen tree and climbed on to it. Dan followed. I wondered what they were up to, but followed in their footsteps. We all walked along the trunk of this massive fallen tree. To my surprise, at its end was another massive fallen tree. And after that another. It was a log 'road' made out of fallen trees.

Walking was very difficult, because the surface of the trees was covered with slime. Dan called out to be careful. The shaman's wife had fallen and broken both wrists recently and the shaman himself often fell. So saying, Dan skidded on the slippery bark, overbalanced and had to jump into the swamp. He stood there, up to his knees in mud, and we all laughed.

Then it was my turn. The surface was absolutely treacherous. One foot slipped and I overbalanced. Next minute I too was standing, knee deep, in the swamp. Although we laughed, I was aware that it was very dangerous. A bad fall could result in broken bones and the Amazonian jungle is no place to break a leg! I focused my full attention on the act of walking.

I couldn't help but remark on how expertly the log road had been made. The end of each log virtually touched the start of the next. Yet it would have been impossible to get heavy equipment in here to move the trees once they had fallen. Clearly, they had been cut exactly right so that they had fallen in these positions. I marvelled at the skill and knowledge that this must have involved.

Half an hour and several falls later, we emerged into a wide clearing. Right in the middle was a large hut made of trees. It was perfectly circular, each straight, upright tree trunk closely abutting the next. About 10 feet above ground level the sloping, conical roof started. It had been thatched with great care. Dan told me that this hut was called a *miloca* and that it served as a meeting place for the local community.

The shaman walked out to greet us. Wilder was 46 years old, but was bald and his face prematurely aged. He looked 20 years older. Life in the jungle must have been hard. He was very friendly, though, and welcomed us while shaking our hands vigorously.

He invited us into the hut and introduced us to his wife. She looked up and nodded to us, her hands full with the meal she was preparing. I noticed some unfamiliar vegetables and, near by, a dead monkey, its fur all blackened and singed. Quite obviously, it was monkey for dinner. I was thankful that I had to fast for the *jage* ceremony.

The interior of the hut was rudimentary in the extreme. Carefully crafted timbers supported the roof and wall, but the floor was just earth. Various pots and pans stood on makeshift shelves. When asked,

Wilder explained that it took him ten months to build the hut. And the log road? He said it took 25 years!

We walked back outside with him and he showed us the vine, growing close by, that we would be using. He cut a portion off and beat it to a pulp before putting it into a pot of boiling water with other plants he had cut earlier. It was left on the fire to cook. Wilder explained that he prepared the *jage* that we would be using tonight in the same way yesterday. It was better to let it stand for a day.

Back outside, Wilder pointed out other plants, telling us which leaf cured which illness and which plant used in conjunction with which bark could cure another. Although he had no formal education, he was an absolute fount of knowledge. He explained that he was from the Huitoto tribe, who have no written records. Knowledge is handed down from father to son over generations. Wilder said that he had been learning now for 46 years, yet there was still much to learn.

He went on to explain that the *jage* ceremony I was about to experience was millennia old and descended from the Incas. He emphasised that it wasn't he himself who was powerful, but God. It was God's power, passing through Wilder that cured people.

He pointed to two small bowls on the floor in front of him. One contained a viscous liquid he said was pure nicotine extract. He dipped his finger in and licked it. The other was dried powdered coca leaves. He took a pinch and put it in his mouth. According to the lore, both are sacred to God and the Huitoto. They make the hut powerful, attracting divine power down into it, which Wilder then channels. Fortunately for me, the ingesting of either wasn't necessary for the ceremony. I passed on Wilder's offer.

It was quite dark now but there was still an hour or so until the ceremony. Wilder went off to prepare. I noticed Dan and Gary standing over by the shaman's wife. Both were giggling over something. I walked over and saw that the wife was about to cut off the dead monkey's willy. I suppose it was funny, but not *that* funny. I guessed they were both off their faces again. I felt like a teacher on a school outing.

I called them both over to me. I looked at their now serious faces and suddenly it was I who felt guilty. 'Look, fellas,' I said, trying to sound as reasonable as possible, 'I don't really give a fuck if you get off your faces. But do me one big favour. Keep an eye on me tonight. If I go into one and try to run out of the hut, grab hold of me. I don't want to run off and get lost in the jungle, OK?'

I guess the image of Norman running loose in the rainforest was too much for them. Both burst into laughter and couldn't stop. I knew I was wasting my time and would have to hope for the best.

I wandered outside to mentally prepare myself. Despite the effects of the *jage*, I wanted to stay focused. This wasn't just a hedonistic experience: I would try to write a definitive account of it. I was well aware that, with some drugs, you forgot all about the experience once you came down.

It was pitch black outside. There was no moon, but even if there had been its light wouldn't have penetrated the canopy of leaves. There were jungle sounds, but the overall impression was one of stillness. I stood, legs apart, eyes closed and face tilted slightly upwards. I felt the power of the forest all around me. I'm not one for melodrama, but I found myself raising my arms towards the heavens. I was sure I felt the power run into me.

Suddenly, I was aware that I was completely at ease here and feared nothing in the jungle. A small voice whispered that, whatever spirit I am, I'm a powerful one. Another voice warned that perhaps this should concern me.

The ceremony was about to start. I went inside and Wilder introduced me to Ernesto, a young Colombian guy who was also to take part in drinking the *jage*. Wilder was wearing a blue tunic-type top and his head was covered by a white cloth. There was a raised wooden platform in the corner of the hut, which was holy ground. Only the shaman and the celebrants sat on this. Ernesto and I squatted cross-legged opposite Wilder while he prayed over a small urn containing the *jage* brew.

Wilder warned us that, when we wanted to go outside to vomit or to use the toilet, we must ask his permission. He emphasised again that this was holy ground. Jorge would then guide us through the darkness. He crawled across and tied a piece of white cloth around Ernesto's forehead as well as around mine, explaining that this was to protect against evil spirits. Then he summoned each of us in turn to drink the *jage*.

The urn was blackened with age, its top encrusted with old dried *jage*. The brew itself had an indescribable smell, one that was distinctly unpleasant. Although the taste was foul, there was no residual flavour in the mouth, only a warm feeling at the back of the throat.

This was now the holy phase of the ceremony and all light had to be extinguished. Wilder stressed that light was our enemy and would distort the effects of the *jage* for the worse. He consoled us by saying that we would 'see' more in the dark, anyway. I reflected that, with no light, there would be nothing for Gary to film. I further reflected that

Dan's little tin would probably get a right hammering. I resigned myself to the fact that I was largely on my own now.

I sat in the pitch-blackness, waiting for the effects of the *jage* to kick in. A few feet away, but invisible to me, Wilder chanted, sang, talked and whistled a strange, breathy, un-shrill whistle. Time passed, but I had no way of telling how much. I was fully conscious of all that was happening. It occurred to me that sitting in absolute darkness isn't the most stimulating environment for the mind. I became incredibly bored and realised that it would be a very long night.

Suddenly, I was aware that the speed of my thought processes had accelerated phenomenally. Ideas zoomed in and out of my mind like bullets. There were some flashes of light, but no colours, and no visions of anything Amazonian.

My breathing slowed, then slowed again. I guessed that this was the start of the near-death experience. The knowledge did nothing to lessen the horror of the effect. Everything was ultra-real and I was able to think forward to the next step, then the next. I actually began to experience the process of suffocating to death. I couldn't imagine a more painful terrifying end. I knew that I had several more hours of this and cursed myself for ever taking the *jage*.

I breathed normally again and all at once my mind was a computer screen. Schematics of my personal relationships popped up for me to examine. I was supersensitive to emotion. Marsha and I had been having some problems lately, but the schematic glowed with warmth and light. I could see that she loved me dearly, and I her.

Another schematic was of an old friend I hadn't seen for a while. There was warmth in it and I resolved to contact him again. Another schematic was cold and dark. Someone I had considered to be a good friend cared nothing for me. I wouldn't contact him again.

Underneath all this, something was gnawing at my consciousness. I focused on it and realised that I wanted to be sick. 'Permessos, Wilder,' I cried out and heard his mumbled reply. On unsteady legs, I stumbled out into the darkness with Jorge holding my arm. But it was a false alarm.

Back on holy ground, I was terminally bored. Then I discovered sex. I had been thinking of Marsha and we started to make love. But it seemed very real and exciting, as if for the first time. A succession of erotic episodes flashed through my mind like convincing porno movies. The thinking of it seemed almost as pleasurable as the real thing. Suddenly, I remembered being told that the shaman could see what I was seeing. I reflected that I was certainly brightening up the old guy's life tonight.

My bowels intruded. I stumbled through the darkness and rain, into the filthiest toilet I had ever encountered. I squatted over a rough-hewn wooden toilet bowl and the diarrhoea poured out of me. The sounds, the smells, the whole experience were all so very real. I looked up and was reassured that Gary and Dan had both come outside with me. Then I noticed the camera and saw that Gary was filming the sequence. It was hard to look dignified, sitting on the toilet with one's trousers round one's ankles, but I was beyond caring.

The sex scenes were not so enjoyable now because I was closely monitoring my stomach, which was bubbling audibly. I rushed to the toilet again, pulling my trousers down as I went. In my haste, I crapped all over the back of the seat. Trying to clean up the mess with tissues was probably the worst experience of my life. I guessed that most celebrants did this. The thought that I had been sitting in the shit of hundreds of others did nothing for my composure.

Back inside, it was just a question of fighting the boredom now. Visual or aural stimulation might have triggered something, but the darkness and silence seemed to deaden even thought. I reflected that *jage* would never catch on back in London. Sex with your partner might be interesting, but it would have to be in a place with two toilets.

Finally, after what seemed like an age, Wilder said it was over. He took the cloth from my head and led me to a hammock. I climbed in and he covered it with a mosquito net. I was very comfortable, but my mind was still racing at a thousand miles an hour. I'd have had more chance of falling asleep running up stairs.

Morning finally arrived and I had counted every second. A cockerel crowed and light filtered through the doorway. When I stood, my legs were still unsteady. As I moved my arms, their outline seemed to lag behind like dark thread. I was tired, I badly needed a shower and I longed for food.

I went to wish Wilder goodbye, but, strangely, his eyes wouldn't meet mine. He shook my hand and wished me goodbye, but looked at the floor. I felt too uncomfortable to care and perhaps I was misreading things through the effects of the *jage*.

It did bother me, though, and it gnawed at me all the way back to the hotel. Previously he had been a man of impeccable manners. What could I have done to upset him? For the more I thought about it, the clearer it was that he wouldn't look me in the eye.

A warm shower and clean clothes worked wonders. I felt more like my old self as I joined Dan at the breakfast table. Straight away, I asked if Wilder had said anything to him about last night and told him about Wilder's refusal to meet my gaze. Dan looked ill at ease, guilty even, and busied himself with his breakfast.

My suspicions were fully aroused now. 'Oi, Dan,' I said chidingly, 'you're supposed to be my mate. If something was said, you're entitled to tell me about it. I'd do it for you.'

'Norm, I was going to tell you,' said Dan, and paused. It couldn't have been for effect. Taking a deep breath he continued, 'Wilder said that it was extremely unusual for you not to vomit,' he said. 'It's always part of the *jage* process. Everybody does it.'

'And?' I questioned. 'That can't be all of it. What's his explanation?'

Now it was Dan who couldn't meet my eyes. He took another deep breath and continued. 'Wilder doesn't know for sure,' he said, 'but he thinks that the evil spirits inside you are so strong that you need to keep what you might vomit inside you just to control them.'

You could have heard the proverbial pin drop. Dan and I finished our breakfast in complete silence. Later, I reflected that, from a spiritual perspective, it was the worst news I could have heard.

In spite of my own reservations, back at *Front*, all was joy and light. For them, the spiritual perspective was something you drank with tonic. They exulted over the photos of me with the anaconda and baby crocodile. They laughed at the ridiculous tapir and its long trunk. The photo of me sitting on the toilet brought the house down. They were all to be included in the article. I laughed along with them, but inside I was far from amused. Wilder's words still haunted me.

CHAPTER SEVENTEEN
PARKER OF THE EXPRESS

The last three years of my life sentence I spent at Ford Open Prison. After 20 years living in the long-term jails, I now tended to keep myself very much to myself. I associated only with people I knew to be both serious and sensible. Ford was renowned for being a trap for the unwary. Being so close to freedom, some people took liberties and found themselves back in closed jails. I was determined that it wouldn't happen to me. To some it might have seemed that I was anti-social, but there was a sound logical reason why I ignored the vast majority of Ford's inmates. In prison, associating with the naive or foolish can get you into trouble.

Each Friday, the Jews of Ford congregated in the synagogue, which was located at the end of one of the prefabricated huts that served as living accommodation. Comparatively speaking, there was quite a high percentage of Jews at Ford. No doubt this was because, in general, they didn't commit the most serious and violent crimes. Also, they were well-behaved 'model' prisoners. These are the type of people who get sent to open prison.

Needless to say, apart from our shared racial ties, they didn't have much in common with me. They had difficulty in comprehending how someone could commit murder and they most certainly couldn't comprehend how one could survive over 20 years in jail for it. They were struggling to do their own, comparatively very short, sentences.

However, I wasn't looking for their approval. I went to synagogue for my own reasons, ones they probably wouldn't have understood. I wouldn't join in the majority of their conversations, especially when they went on about the dreaded P-word. All prisoners long for parole, but experienced sensible ones know that to go on about it all the time is to drive oneself mad. In prison, the P-word isn't mentioned in polite company.

But the Jews of Ford were obsessed with it. Every bit of news about someone new getting parole was discussed with relish, which inevitably brought them round to discussing their own prospects for the umpteenth time. Then, in a process similar to mutual masturbation, they would assure each other that they would get their own parole very soon.

Further, many of them went out of their way to curry favour with the authorities. This didn't exactly endear them to the other prisoners, whose general attitude was that one should try to do one's time like a man, without grovelling.

There was one man though who was very different. Gerald Ronson was doing nine months for what had been called the 'Guinness Affair', an alleged fraud. Outside he had been a rich, powerful and influential businessman. Inside, he put on no airs and graces at all. Originally a working-class boy from the East End of London, he knew something of the code of putting up with adversity without complaining.

In the synagogue and about the prison, the other Jews fawned on him. Gerald took it all in his stride, neither taking advantage of it nor rebuffing people. He steadfastly refused to get involved in discussions about parole. Further, not only didn't he go out of his way to curry favour with the authorities, but actually refused privileges offered. It's all very well espousing principles in theory, but it's actually suffering for them that shows integrity. Gerald was determined to do his time with dignity.

Initially, I virtually ignored him along with all the rest. However, I was intrigued by this man who had no experience of prison, yet was determined to stand up for himself. As a strong Jew myself, in a world where Jews were often characterised as being weak, I could identify with another strong Jew. In a similar vein, I believe, Gerald was intrigued by this Jewish guy who had survived over 20 years without cracking up. Our friendship grew out of this mutual respect.

He was released long before I was, but we stayed in touch. When I got out I would pop into his office occasionally and we would discuss how we were both faring. He had largely rebuilt his business empire; I had just had a bestselling book. Often we would laugh about old times in Ford.

By now, though, I was growing increasingly disenchanted with writing for the lads' magazines. It was getting ever more difficult to come up with new ideas and, logistically speaking, it was proving impossible to do more than one article a month. As each article paid only around a thousand pounds, I wasn't earning much money, either. I felt that it was time for me to move onwards and upwards.

On one of my occasional meetings with Gerald, I asked him if he knew anybody in the newspaper industry, because I wanted try my hand at 'proper' journalism. He said that he was friendly with Richard Desmond, who had recently bought Express Newspapers. He would ask him if there were any opportunities.

A few days passed and I got a phone call inviting me for an interview. The *Express* building on Blackfriars Bridge was both massive and intimidating. This would be a very different prospect from working for *Front*. The scope for gonzoism would be absolutely minimal.

I presented myself at the reception and asked for the person who had phoned me. A few minutes passed and a smartly dressed, middle-aged man appeared. He introduced himself as Phil McNeil and suggested that we should go to the pub across the road for the interview, since the big office where he worked was hardly suitable.

He had asked me to bring a sample of my work. I had agonised over the suitability of several pieces, but the inescapable conclusion was that they had all been written in a manner that was suitable for a light-hearted read. Most were thoroughly irreverent; many were outright rude. However, that didn't mean that they didn't have some merit. I eventually chose the article on Iraq. It was funny, and humour isn't that easy to do. Further, it showed that I had the initiative to go to a strange country and get a story. As we settled into our seats in the pub, I handed the article over, complete with the copy of *Front* that contained it.

Soon he was smiling, then laughing. He handed the magazine back, saying that it was a good article. He asked me what I wanted from the *Express*. This took me somewhat by surprise. I was under the impression that newspapers sent their journalists to cover the story of the newspaper's choosing. But clearly this was some kind of test. They wanted to see if I could come up with an interesting story of my own to cover. I was sent on my way with the instruction that I should present them with a proposal for a story.

Now I was back on familiar ground. This was exactly what I had been doing for the lads' magazines, but now I wasn't restricted to 'adventure' stories. I had the whole world to choose from and every type of news article one could think of.

Knowing what it had taken to survive in an extreme environment for over 20 years, I was intrigued by how some people handled stressful situations that others found unbearable. Clearly, they were special people with phenomenally strong spirits. An article about people like these would probably capture the imagination of the *Express.*

The papers and the news were full of the ongoing conflict in Israel. An average of two suicide bombers a day were blowing themselves up in crowded places. No doubt the media spared us the more horrifying details and all photographs were taken from a distance. However, for sheer horror and carnage, it would be hard to imagine a worse scene than the aftermath of such a bombing. The screams of the injured and dying; survivors searching for loved ones; blood and body parts, even of young children, strewn about. It was a nightmare tableau straight from Hell.

To witness such a thing once would be to live with it in one's memory for the rest of one's life. So what of those who had to deal with it on a regular basis? What about the men and women of the Israeli ambulance service who had to respond to the emergency call? How did they sit about the ambulance station knowing that the next call could bring another living nightmare? What sort of people could be strong enough to put up with that?

Phil McNeil liked the proposal. He told me to go ahead. Thirty phone calls to Israel later and I had set up meetings with people I thought would have a valuable viewpoint on the story. I experienced no resistance whatsoever. Everyone in Israel admired the work of Magen David Adom (MDA), the Israeli equivalent of the Red Cross.

The direct flight took me to Tel Aviv and I picked up my hire car at the airport. The two-hour drive to Jerusalem was a baptism of fire for me. Israeli drivers are easily the craziest in the world, a reflection, perhaps, of their being in a constant state of war for decades now. It was a relief to get to my hotel.

Despite the fact that Tel Aviv is the capital, I had chosen Jerusalem, because that was where the majority of the bombs were going off. I found that, comparatively speaking, Jerusalem is tiny. You could virtually walk across it in half an hour. Yet, at this time, an average of two bombs per day were going off here.

Not surprisingly, it had had a devastating effect on the city's 'café society', to the extent that it no longer existed. Open shopping malls were largely deserted and the closed ones were subject to the strictest of security measures when you entered. Almost everywhere had an armed guard on the door. After work, everybody seemed to go home. The vast majority of cafés and restaurants were quite empty.

Although Jerusalem resembled a ghost town from a 'café society' perspective, there was nothing of a siege mentality among the people. Those I met in the hotel and in the streets seemed to be going about their business in a remarkably normal fashion. The concierge at the hotel summed up the general view when he told me that one had to get on with one's life, no matter what. You couldn't live like an animal in a hole, otherwise the terrorists had won.

Initially, this didn't strike me as either very brave or noble. Probably, like the vast majority of people, I had come to Israel with my views on the situation largely already formed by the weight of opinion in the international media. Jewish or not, I had considerable sympathy for the Palestinians and their predicament. Further, I was firmly of the opinion that the heavy-handed measures of the army didn't help matters. Merely a mention of the Israeli Defence Force (IDF) served to conjure up images of heavily armed troops shooting children for throwing stones.

However, as I lived day by day under the constant threat of being blown to pieces, I began to get a better insight into the collective Israeli mind. I didn't doubt that a large proportion of the population had been thoroughly traumatised by fear. And in such a fraught state of mind they had come to ignore, connive at or even support some of the excesses of the IDF.

I shared their experience of having to go out to go about one's business. And, while out, one also had to eat or have a cup of coffee or buy something. I tried to pick small restaurants and cafés that were either deserted or had only a couple of customers. I reasoned that a suicide bomber would pick a 'richer' target, one where there were more people.

As I sat there, I found myself becoming ever more concerned as the place filled up. Once that happened it really was just a matter of chance whether a suicide bomber walked in or not. And, what with Jerusalem being such a small city, that chance seemed quite broad. Bearing in mind some of the dangerous places I had already been, I could hardly be described as timid. However, I was always relieved to get out of the restaurant or café and get back to the hotel. I couldn't help but reflect that many Israelis lived every day of their lives like this!

I had only a week to get the story. It was actually the *Sunday Express* I was working for, rather than the daily edition. So, if everything went to plan, my story would be in the following Sunday's edition. I felt under considerable pressure. Whatever I wrote would be subjected to close scrutiny. The generalisations that sufficed for the lads' mags wouldn't be good enough here. All quotes would have to be attributable, all statements supported by evidence. As far as I was concerned, this type of journalism would have to be entirely more scientific, objective and accurate.

Not wanting to waste any time, I started out on my first contact. Dikla Amar's name had been given to me as someone typical of MDA workers. She had sounded very young when I had called her from England. I called her again from the hotel and she agreed to meet me in a café in a nearby shopping mall.

The *Sunday Express* obviously had a network of people they regularly worked with in Israel, so they hadn't sent a photographer with me. I had already spoken with their agency photographer. Now I phoned him again and asked him to meet me at the café. It occurred to me that, in some respects, this assignment would be easier than those carried out for the lads' mags. There, one had to find the unusual and get it to hold still long enough to photograph it. And not once, but several times. Now, the written copy was the important thing. At a stretch, an archive photo would suffice.

The café was situated in an open mall that was a pedestrian precinct. I had already walked through it a couple of times before on brief forays from the hotel to explore my new environment. Although there were no armed guards on the many entrances, a few of the bigger shops did have them. There was nothing whatsoever to stop a suicide bomber from entering the mall and walking into the majority of the shops and cafés, though.

Further, this mall was exactly the type of target the suicide bombers went for. In fact, I had heard that it had been bombed a couple of times previously. There was no lasting evidence of this, no burned-out premises or boarded-up windows. I understood that the Israelis always repaired places very quickly and then carried on as normal. I suppose it would have had a devastating psychological effect on people to walk about a city with lasting physical scars of previous atrocities.

As someone who had survived in dangerous long-term jails, as well as working in dangerous countries, I was very much keeping my wits about me. But previously the danger had seemed to be that much more easy to recognise and to take precautions against. Here, though, the danger seemed to be completely anonymous and unpredictable. I felt totally vulnerable to the random nature of chance. For someone who likes to be in control of the situation, that was quite unnerving.

Like all the other places I had passed, the café where we were to meet had yards of glass frontage. I reflected that, even in the event of a place near by being targeted, this would turn into shrapnel and injure the café's customers. I tried to put this from my mind as I waited for my contacts.

Dikla and the photographer arrived within seconds of each other. Neither seemed to have trouble in identifying me and both joined me at my table. The photographer was middle-aged and balding, with a short neatly trimmed beard. He introduced himself as Nick and said that he had been told to take just a couple of shots of Dikla, as this would be all that was needed to go with the story. As he unpacked the shoulder bag he was carrying and went about setting up the shot, I turned my attention to Dikla.

She looked very young, barely out of her teens, and it turned out that she was just 20. She was short, slim and quite beautiful. Her long black hair framed a pretty face without makeup. These were the surface details that I took in as I first weighed her up.

But it was immediately apparent that something was very wrong with this pretty young girl. On closer examination her face was unnaturally pale. Her eyes, although intelligent and clear, seemed somehow lifeless. Her whole demeanour, while not being cowed or broken, was somehow resigned, as if she lived with a terrible secret. There was an utter and complete absence of humour and joy. She looked like someone who had recently suffered a bereavement.

She was pleasant enough, and cooperative, without being enthusiastic. No doubt she felt it to be her duty to give an account of her work to a visiting journalist. I did wonder if I would have to pick my words with care, lest I upset her and trigger an emotional reaction. But I could discern that, underneath, there was a steely resolve and considerable strength. There would be no tears from this girl – she was long since past that stage.

Dikla told me that, as a religious Jew, she had opted for MDA as her national service, rather than go into the army. She immediately confessed that, in many ways, it had been harder for her. She may not have been put in the position where she would have to kill, but, with MDA, death and destruction had become a regular part of her life.

She spoke quietly, undemonstratively, almost in a breathy whisper. It was very much like a confession. However, there was no obvious release for her, just satisfaction in the knowledge that she was having to relive her nightmares for a good cause.

'The first time I attended a bombing I guess I was in shock, so lots of things didn't register,' she began. 'What did strike me, though, was the immediate silence. People who were quite badly injured were sitting there stunned. One young boy of about eight was sitting next to his mother, who was dead in her chair. He wasn't making a sound. It was only as we helped him up that we noticed that his hand had been blown off.

'Another thing that you never get used to is the stench of burned flesh. From that moment I have never eaten meat, because it too seems to have something of that smell. I can't go to barbecues now. After that first bomb, I hardly ate for two weeks.'

I had placed a small tape recorder on the table, but I was also making notes. From time to time I looked up and into her eyes, as if to reassure her. I hardly had to prompt her at all. It didn't flow out of her like some cathartic, emotional release, but, in a measured way, almost matter-of-factly, she enunciated those memories that she thought the most important.

'Because we work in neighbourhoods where we live, we sometimes find friends among the victims. At the recent bombing of the Sharro restaurant, the sister of a close friend phoned me to say that she believed her sister was in there. So I looked for her and the Superman T-shirt she was wearing, but many of the bodies were very badly burned. It was only later in the ambulance when I noticed a scrap of the T-shirt on a badly burned body that I realised it was her.'

But were there any positive aspects to her work? I asked.

'You have to look for positive things. Say like when a mother is searching for her child and finds him alive and well. Then there is the knowledge that you are doing something positive, helping people when they desperately need help.'

And did what she saw make her angry?

'I have learned to control my emotions. I just go through the motions, letting the professionalism take over. If the terrorist survives, we treat him in the ambulance just as we treat the victims. But I don't let myself get too close to the victims, because if they die later you suffer all the more. Personally, I feel that I have become a colder person now.'

So how did she keep going?

'We in MDA support each other, but there really is no other option.

It's not that we have got used to the bombings, but we know that after this one there will be another and another, so we have to go on.'

And if she had a message for those who might read my article, what would it be?

'I would say that the hardest thing to bear is the hypocrisy. When innocent women and children were killed in Northern Ireland in the Omagh bombing [in August 1998], there was universal condemnation. So why is the international community so silent about these suicide bombings in Israel?'

That seemed like a natural point to terminate the interview. We sat in silence while the photographer took several photos. We left simultaneously to go our different ways. Never did the sunshine seem so bright, never the breeze so cleansing. Darkness is the place for nightmares, yet even so some of Dikla's nightmares lingered with me. For a long time afterwards, I couldn't help but think of that pretty young girl and her head full of ugly memories.

Through my research I had found out that the MDA did have a proper counselling programme for its members. It was designed and operated by a Dr Daniel Gottlieb, a clinical psychologist. He lived out in the suburbs, though, and it would involve a 30-minute bus journey for me to get to him. I was just about to be introduced to the Jerusalem public-transport system.

It was early evening when I set off for the interview. The streets were busy with hundreds of people hurrying home for work. It looked like a scene at the end of a day's work anywhere in the world. Elsewhere, though, the worst drama that could befall travellers would be that they might miss a connection and be a little late getting home. Here, they were running a gauntlet of suicide bombers and might never get home at all. Several buses had been targeted in recent weeks.

A policeman carrying a machine gun stopped me as I entered the bus station. 'Have you got a machine gun with you?' he asked, as if it were the most normal of questions.

The idea seemed so ridiculous that I nearly laughed. Yet outside in the street I had seen many people carrying sub-machine guns. At least half the population seemed to be armed, so it was a very reasonable question. I answered in the negative and he waved me through. The incident did nothing for my composure, although it was reassuring that there was such a high level of security.

That assurance soon disappeared. Once we were out on the road, it immediately became apparent that, while they might secure the bus station, it was practicably impossible to secure the bus. At the first stop, dozens of people got on. No one was monitoring the queue and there were clearly Arabs among the new passengers. I say 'clearly' but in reality it wasn't clear at all. To an outsider, many of the Israeli Jews looked like Arabs, and vice versa.

The other thing that concerned me was that everyone seemed to be carrying a large bag of some sort. From military-type duffle bags to ordinary shopping bags, they either stowed them in the hold underneath the bus before they got on, or struggled onboard with them. How was anyone to know that one of the bags didn't contain a bomb? Many buses had been bombed in this way recently.

Once again, it was all down to random chance. There were no precautions you could take and no strategy to be adopted. You just had to sit there and hope that it wouldn't happen to *this* bus. You were running a psychological gauntlet, and every journey would be the same. Thus, suicide bombings claim many more victims than the ones immediately caught in the blast. It was with considerable relief that I got off at my stop.

Dr Gottlieb looked like the clinical psychologist he was. Articulate, intense and very much in control, he described how he had set up a programme for MDA workers called Critical Incident Stress Debriefing. It involved group counselling, where the whole team discuss their feelings about the most recent incident. There is a very strong bond in MDA that prevents members discussing things with outsiders.

'There are a whole gamut of reactions,' said Dr Gottlieb. 'They range from anxiety, fearfulness and crying, to insomnia, eating disorders and obsessive behaviour.'

I settled back into a comfortable armchair as Dr Gottlieb described how the mind tries to deal with extremely stressful situations. He went on to detail case after case of people who had cracked under the pressure. Much, it seemed, depended on the individual. Often there was extreme irony. Someone who had gone through a series of terrible incidents would be pushed over the edge by something comparatively trifling. Everyone had their breaking point, it seemed. It was his job to recognise when the individual had reached theirs.

'The average Israeli family is very large and extended, as are their social relationships,' continued Dr Gottlieb. 'Comparatively speaking, Israel is only a small country. When a suicide bombing happens, almost everyone knows someone involved. Or knows someone who knows someone. This makes it all very personal and threatening.'

It had certainly become very personal and threatening to me. I had been sitting in the comfort and safety of Dr Gottlieb's armchair. An hour or so had passed and it had grown dark. I wasn't looking forward to the prospect of the return bus journey at all. I asked Dr Gottlieb if he could call me a taxi back to central Jerusalem. He said that he could, but that it would cost me the equivalent of about £50. I didn't want to take liberties with the *Express* expenses account on my first assignment, but I felt that, in the circumstances, it was more than justified.

I knew that, at some stage, I would have to go to a hospital. I didn't want to go so far as to interview victims in their hospital beds, for that would have smacked of intruding into personal grief. However, the ambulance crews weren't the only ones who had to deal with the almost daily horror. What of the hospital staff who met the ambulances once they arrived at the hospital?

'Of course the pressure is intolerable,' said Dr Avi Rivkind, head of triage, at the prestigious Hadassah Hospital. He meets the ambulances straight from the bombings and decides who goes where for what. Not only does he witness the most terrible things, often his decisions are life-or-death ones.

Amazingly, he was a very cheerful chap. He smiled constantly and often laughed uproariously at his own jokes. Not in a distasteful way – he clearly took his job very seriously – but, in the midst of so much horror, I guessed that it was his way of dealing with it.

'Statistically speaking,' he continued, 'road accidents kill many more Israeli children than suicide bombings. But the media spotlight is on the latter, which increases the emotional pressure.'

In some ways he was encapsulated in his own, artificially created little world. For him, the hospital was like sanctuary. Whatever happened outside, whatever one's personal suffering and feelings, it was all left outside. He concluded, 'We treat the terrorist with as much care as we treat his victims. Sometimes patients ask us why we bother to treat him at all, but we ignore this, which helps us to rise above things. Even now there are two surviving terrorists in the same ward as their victims, albeit with a police presence at their bedsides.'

Dr Dorrit Nitzam of the Facial Surgery Department felt both helpless and exposed, and it showed. Her face was drawn and she seemed tired. She had a permanent worried expression. She felt exposed in that anyone could be a victim and helpless in that the authorities seemed powerless to stop the bombings.

However, she paid tribute to the strong sense of community within the hospital and confessed that, without it, she would have found it very difficult to carry on. Jewish and Arab staff worked together without friction and, in the Mother and Baby Unit, Arab and Jewish children played together under the approving gaze of their mothers. 'I suppose that helps me to keep going, that and a sense of professionalism,' she added.

Even the security forces weren't immune to the pressure from the unrelenting horror. Lieutenant Colonel Rafowicz Oliver knew all about the feeling of helplessness. 'We can only stop so many, but some inevitably get through,' he said. He looked worried when he spoke of a new breed of terrorist who will stop at nothing to carry out their mission.

'The other week there was a very bad bombing outside a synagogue. The bomber hung around for an hour to pick the most opportune time to kill the most people. He could even have planted the bomb and got away. Or one might have expected him to arrive at the scene and, full of emotion, run over and detonate. We expect everyone to have some will to live, but this guy was so cold and calculating. There is no psychological profile to fit someone like him, so we can't identify him, so we can't stop him. And this disturbs me.'

With this last interview, I calculated that I had more than enough material for my piece. I didn't fool myself by thinking that the *Sunday Express* was going to give me a couple of pages for a major spread. I knew they would cut bits out anyway for reasons of space. I wrote my article, entitled it 'Who Helps the Helpers?' and emailed it to the *Express*.

However, in the process of doing the MDA story, I had stumbled on an even more moving and unusual story. As I questioned the various interviewees about how they coped with the horror of their particular role, they began to tell me of another organisation whose work plumbed altogether new depths of horror.

This organisation is called in Hebrew Zihui Korbanot Asson (ZAKA), which roughly translates as 'Identification, Victims, Tragedies'. But ZAKA is more commonly known by the name of its helpline, 'Chessed Shel Emet' or 'True Kindness'.

It is an integral part of both Jewish and Islamic religious law that the body in its entirety be buried in the same place. By their very nature, suicide bombings scatter parts of victims over a wide area. The police, ambulance service and fire brigade are stretched enough without having to hunt down every scrap. ZAKA has stepped in to remedy this situation.

The organisation, whose 700 volunteers are spread in towns and cities all over Israel, is divided into six separate districts. Although it claims to be a secular organisation, in practice it comprises mostly Orthodox Jews. Certainly, its actions correspond with the ancient Jewish principle of respect for the dead and the sanctity of Jewish burial. However, the organisation extends the same respect to the bodies of the Arab suicide bombers, collecting every piece of the body and returning it to the relatives.

As one might imagine, not everyone is up to the task of crawling about on their hands and knees at the scene of the latest suicide bombing and picking up the tiniest pieces of flesh, hair, bone and blood. There is a rigorous selection procedure. Successful volunteers are all Jewish men over 25 and married. This is deemed to be a recipe for stability and maturity. Supposedly, it will help to protect against the ravages of the unimaginable horror of the situation. Unlike in the ambulance service, where there is a motivation to save lives, here the main motivation is an ancient principle – which is perhaps why secular Jews don't last very long in ZAKA.

Not surprisingly, there are many failures. A third fail at their first sight of a whole body, dead of natural causes. Another third fail at the scene of their first violent death. The remainder soldier on, although the crisis point seems to be eighteen months. Over the past four years, there has been nearly a 100 per cent turnover.

The organisation is professionally run. Many members are ex-volunteers with MDA and all have training in first aid, so they are able to assist the medics at the scene. There is a course on Jewish law, dealing with all 613 religious regulations. Volunteers in ZAKA are allowed one exemption over other Jews: they are excused their daily prayers while burying the dead.

Bearing in mind that the locations of most violent deaths are crime scenes, volunteers must understand how to preserve evidence. For this reason, there is a course with the police Forensic Department. As their duties extend to consoling members of victim's families, they are also trained to be skilled counsellors.

So what kind of people are they, these men of steely determination and strong stomach? Does it take scripture-quoting, cold-hearted zealots to do such work? Who could put up with carrying out such a task just the once, never mind the eighteen months that some of them last? If I was interested in strength in all its many forms, I had to find out what drove these men.

Contacting ZAKA was easy enough. I was given the name of a member, and I phoned him and arranged a meeting. Ironically, Schlomo Bloch was perhaps the most unusual of all ZAKA's members. At 25, he was the youngest volunteer and the only one not married. He had joined before the stipulation was made. A recent immigrant from France, he was slim, of average build and intense as befits his role, but not overly so. He managed the occasional strained smile, but his normal expression was that of a man on a particularly onerous mission.

We talked in the cramped premises of a ZAKA station, located in the basement of a dwelling house. Stretchers, shovels, buckets and plastic bins, the tools of ZAKA's trade, were tucked away in alcoves. Large, burly, Jewish men in wide-brimmed black hats, white shirts and black trousers bustled in and out. All were polite and friendly, if serious. They seemed to ooze strength and fortitude. In some ways, they reminded me of the frontiersmen of the Old West, God-fearing, family-oriented men. There was no trace of zealotry.

'I was looking for something to do, some way to play my part. For a while I was with MDA, but I felt a calling for this work. I felt I was strong enough,' Schlomo said. 'I've had many moments of doubt, though. Like others, there have been many times when I nearly gave up. I particularly found the smell of burned flesh hard to take. Sometimes, hours afterwards, I would sit down to a meal and think I smelled the same smell on the meat. My stomach would turn and I would walk away from the meal.

'At other times I haven't been able to sleep and have called other volunteers, talking for long hours into the night. For some, it is too much, even though they want to go on. Their wives or friends have called to complain of a massive change in the person since they have become a volunteer, a change that is affecting their families.

'In those cases, we don't call the person so much, then not at all. We let them keep their yellow ZAKA flak jacket so they feel they still belong and haven't given up.'

Early attempts to provide some support failed when, over a period of a whole year, not one volunteer went to see a psychiatrist ZAKA had hired, because no one wanted to show weakness. Nowadays, help comes in the form of a hotel booked for a weekend, where they can discuss their problems in a group.

So what sustained Schlomo Bloch? He was young, unmarried, had been working for ZAKA for eighteen months now and had become one of the main organisers. 'Despite the general antagonism between religious and secular Jews, ZAKA is respected across Israeli society, and I am proud of that. We are the only Jewish organisation respected by the Arabs. During the intifada, they stopped the young children throwing stones at us when we returned terrorist bodies to Arab villages. Following a tragedy in a village hall where we salvaged the bodies of several Arab women, Yasser Arafat himself praised us and sent us a gift of two camels. Last year our founder, Yehuda Meshi-Zahav, was honoured at the United Nations and ZAKA was proclaimed the best volunteer organisation in the world.'

'So has the universal acclaim altered the original objectives of the organisation?' I asked, and instantly regretted it.

But Schlomo wasn't offended. 'Not for myself and, I'm sure, not for anyone I've spoken to.' He paused and dropped his eyes modestly. 'I've always believed that the best favour is the one done with no thought of return. That is why I feel that our work is the essence of true kindness.'

I wrote up this story too, titled it 'True Kindness' and sent it off to the *Express*. I didn't really expect them to print it, but I was so moved by the story that I felt people should know about it. For hours afterwards, I kept remembering Schlomo's words and of how he had felt strong enough to do the work. That inevitably started me wondering whether I was strong enough to do it. I felt that I was. I had managed to motivate myself to do most things. Also, in this mercenary and selfish world we live in, I was deeply impressed by these men who put themselves through so much hardship, purely to help the relatives of the dead. As Schlomo had said, it was the essence of true kindness.

I arrived back late on the Friday and Phil McNeil told me to come in on Monday afternoon. He said I should look out for my pieces in the Sunday edition. He had said 'pieces', so I knew they were going to print both articles.

Early Sunday morning, I went to my local newsagent and bought two copies of the *Sunday Express*. I hurried home with them unopened. It wasn't a centre-page spread, but the articles were *near* the centre and they *were* spread over two pages. The MDA article occupied the whole of the left-hand page and the ZAKA article took up two-thirds of the right-hand page. The former had a photo of Dikla Amar, the latter, one of ZAKA at work at the scene of a bombing. And there, right at the top of the page just below the headline, was a tiny photo of me and the byline 'From Norman Parker in Jerusalem'.

On Monday afternoon, I presented myself at the *Express* and Phil McNeil came down into the lobby to meet me. This time he got me issued with a pass and I went up in the lift to the big office he worked in. He walked me through this and into the editor's office. I didn't know it for a fact, but I guessed that this was a significant honour.

The editor, a balding, harassed-looking man in his early forties, shook my hand warmly. 'Norman, I want to congratulate you on a brilliant journalistic debut,' he said.

I could hardly have expected more praise if I'd written his lines myself. He went on to say that he hoped I would keep up the good work.

On the way down in the lift, Phil was talking about my next assignment. There had been serious riots in North Belfast; they wanted me to leave that evening.

Unfortunately, Marsha had other ideas. 'But you've only just got back,' she wailed. 'If I'm not going to see you, there's not much point, is there?'

I could definitely see my new job costing me my relationship. In the event, I reached a compromise.

Hitler once said, 'Compromise is weakness' – but he didn't have Marsha to contend with, and, anyway, look what happened to him! The compromise was that I went the following day. Like most compromises, it fell between two stools. The *Express* wasn't pleased that I was going a day late and Marsha wasn't pleased that I was going at all. I found myself wondering whether the average journalist was single.

I researched the background to the story and found that, on the evening of 3 April, a Protestant mob numbering over 400 had attacked a police line between them and the Catholic community in the Limestone Road area of North Belfast. During the ensuing riot, which lasted several hours, 23 blast bombs were thrown and there were five shooting incidents. Even by the standards of Northern Ireland, it was a sustained and vicious attack on police officers.

The local police commander, Assistant Chief Constable Alan McQuillan, had said that it was a miracle that no one was killed and accused the Protestant Ulster Defence Association (UDA) of being behind the attack.

Straight away, I realised that, although I had been to Northern

Ireland before to do the Gerry Kelly piece and had very good contacts within the Catholic community, this time I would be dealing directly with members of the Protestant community. If anything, my contacts with the Catholics would work against me and, should anyone connect me to the story about Gerry Kelly and our friendship, it could place me in danger.

I had phoned Anne and, once again, went and stayed with her. I figured that the Falls Road was a good base from where to do the Catholic side of the story. Further, I knew there was considerable contact between both sides – perhaps I could be pointed in the right direction regarding whom to speak to on the Protestant side.

Anne was pleased to see me again and made me welcome. She said that people had enjoyed my piece on Gerry, even if they didn't much care for the magazine that it had been in. She went on to say that Gerry had got some abuse over the piece in the Protestant community. There were articles in their papers saying that *Front* was a 'porn' magazine and that Gerry Kelly was now a 'porn star'.

Apart from regretting any embarrassment I had brought to Gerry, I now had to confront the reality that, far from not knowing about *Front* and the article, the Protestant community were well aware of it. So no doubt my name might ring a few bells too.

It was generally agreed by most people I spoke to that the peace process in Northern Ireland was more advanced now than ever before. There had been isolated clashes between Catholic and Protestant communities in other areas, but with nothing like the regularity and intensity of North Belfast. So the first thing I had to investigate was the peculiar mechanism that perpetuated extreme sectarianism in this area.

My first stop was to see Gerry. He greeted me warmly and downplayed my apologies regarding any embarrassment the *Front* article had brought him. He assured me that he regularly got criticised in the Protestant press, anyway, no matter what he did. However, he looked considerably more reassured when I told him I was now writing for the *Sunday Express*. I asked him about the recent riots.

'Look, Norman,' he said, 'what you've got to realise is that the UDA is a deeply sectarian organisation. It has a monolithic rather than a hierarchical structure, which allows individual commanders to run their areas like fiefdoms. They are anti-peace-process, anti-Catholic and totally into controlling what they see as their areas.'

I asked if there was any meaningful contact between the two sides. 'There was,' replied Gerry. 'For four weeks before the latest disturbances we had initiated a telephone system whereby influential Loyalists and Nationalists could be contacted to express concern over potential flashpoints, so that each side could deal with their own. A week before the riot, the UDA cancelled the arrangement, citing pressure from within their community.'

'So are the Nationalists totally blameless in all this?' I asked.

'No, of course not, and I've never ever said that we are,' replied Gerry. 'However, there are two issues here. Firstly, the Nationalists are fully in favour of the peace process and are reasonably pleased with the progress we have made. Secondly, we are much more in control of our own people. Not through fear, but through grassroots organisation.'

When I pressed him on percentages, he conceded that Catholics were responsible for some attacks on Protestants, but he put it at only about 10 per cent of the total violence.

I was well aware that my article would be relatively small, so space was an important consideration. It meant that most commentators would be restricted to a couple of lines of quotes and I would need a variety of viewpoints. To that end, Gerry gave me contact numbers for three influential people in the Protestant community, as well as two other Nationalist spokesmen.

With regard to why North Belfast remained so violent, Sinn Fein councillor Eoin O'Bruin said that there were both historical and practical reasons. North Belfast had sustained more than 25 per cent of the total number of victims of violence throughout the province. Further, the easiest route for the Loyalist death squads was through Catholic areas in the north of the city.

Demographics have also played a large part in the decline of the Protestant communities in this area. De-industrialisation has led to social fragmentation, with young Protestants leading the outward flight to places like Ballymena, Coleraine, Craigavon and Newtownards, all predominantly Protestant towns. O'Bruin argued that young Catholics are more communal by nature and stay to reinvigorate their communities, which are expanding and have a growing need for housing. Of the 1,700 people on the urgent waiting list of the local council, 1,400 were Catholics.

Assemblyman Alban Maginness of the SDLP for North Belfast had identical views to Gerry Kelly. He blamed the UDA for 90 per cent of the violence involving attacks on Catholics. 'It's all about the UDA controlling their areas,' he said. 'They want to prevent Catholics from moving into vacant housing. Further, some UDA members actually believe they can halt the peace process.' Quite significantly, he mentioned that there had been four sectarian murders of Catholics in the area in recent months.

Thus far, I had heard only the Nationalist view of the riots and the situation surrounding them. For another, and no doubt opposing, view I would have to go into North Belfast and speak with Protestant commentators and politicians. This was breaking new ground for me.

A phone call put me in touch with Danny Mahood of the rather grandiosely named Ulster Political Research Group (UPRG), an advisory body to the UDA. Following his directions, I met him outside a shop housing his organisation. It was a dilapidated building in a row of similar premises. Its name smacked of academia, science and statistics. There was little of that about the premises, or Danny Mahood for that matter.

An untidy overweight man in his fifties, he was friendly enough, in a gruff sort of way. But, if he was a Loyalist political leader of some description, then clearly such people were cut from completely different cloth from any other politicians I had met, anywhere. If a political requisite is to put people at their ease, win their sympathy for your cause and impress them with your knowledge of the situation, then he failed miserably. He came across as coarse, inarticulate and not particularly intelligent. I could only conclude that this didn't reflect very well on the parent organisation, the UDA.

As I walked with Danny Mahood through the Loyalist estates, they seemed a mirror image of the Nationalist areas of West Belfast, but with different flags, painted kerbs and painted murals immortalising the dead Protestant volunteers. Both sides had suffered so much through this conflict.

The streets were very quiet and almost deserted. Mahood explained that the Queen Mother's funeral was on TV (this was April 2002) and, this being a Loyalist area, everyone was watching it. As we neared the Limestone Road/Tiger's Bay area, he pointed to rows of derelict, burned-out houses at the interface between the Catholic and Protestant communities. He said that this was evidence of the many attacks on Protestants by Catholics.

Halfway down the Limestone Road, there was a police presence of three armoured police Land Rovers and an armoured car, guarded by two British soldiers from a Highland regiment. There had been no disturbances for several nights now, but Mahood put this down to the presence of a squad of UDA volunteers who had been on duty. 'Much of the violence is recreational,' he said. 'It's started by yobbos and inevitably draws the paramilitaries in.'

We turned into a small estate and entered the kitchen of one of the flats. There I was introduced to John White, also of the UPRG, but a close friend and comrade of Johnny Adair as well. I knew Adair to be the controversial leader of a Loyalist group violently opposed to the peace process. He was also violently opposed to certain other Loyalist groups. There had been many intra-Protestant acts of violence recently.

A tall balding man in his forties, John White had served over 16 years in jail for sectarian murders. Again, when it came to political skills, he showed the same lack as Danny Mahood. But with White there was also an underlying air of menace. I reflected that perhaps wartime situations threw up a particular type of leader, but immediately rejected that because the actual fighting stage of this war was supposed to be long over.

White admitted that the North Belfast area was particularly problematic, conceding that the North Belfast Brigade had sustained 25 per cent of all Loyalist casualties in the conflict. However, like Mahood, he said that there had been many attacks on Protestants by Catholics recently. He argued that it was all a matter of presentation. 'The PR machine of the Nationalists invariably gets their message across far better than that of the Loyalists,' he said. He compared the situation of the Protestant community in North Belfast to that of the Israelis, who he felt were also a misunderstood and unjustly criticised people. I had noticed the Israeli flags flying in the courtyard. Having so recently visited Israel, I couldn't help but conclude that the Israelis wouldn't welcome the comparison.

I approached my next interview with growing trepidation. If Mahood and White were typical of Loyalist representation, what could I expect from the next interviewee? Billy Hutchinson had been a notorious killer in the Loyalist death squads and had served nearly 20 years for his crimes. He was now the Member for the Legislative Assembly (MLA) for the Loyalist Progressive Unionist Party (PUP).

The venue for the meeting was the parliamentary building at Stormont. As I was ushered past all the security, I reflected on the irony that so many of the province's elected political representatives, on both sides, had served long periods in jail. I was shown into an office off the main hall and into the presence of Billy Hutchinson.

Immediately, I felt at my ease. There was no air of underlying threat or bluster that had been the case with his colleagues. This confident, clearly intelligent man in his late forties had a definite feeling of gravitas about him. I recognised the signs from my own prison experience. While inside, he had obviously matured.

When I put to him what others had said, he agreed with most of the statistics, but not the underlying causes. 'Working-class Protestants in North Belfast have been very poorly represented in the past by Unionist politicians,' he said. 'These were only interested in the middle and upper classes. As a result poor Protestants have become marginalised and now have a growing sense of frustration.'

This was the first criticism by a Loyalist, implied or otherwise, that I had heard of the Loyalist position. As some of the more extreme Loyalist demands were hardly defensible in terms of social justice, I felt that this reflected well on his political maturity.

As for O'Bruin's argument, he conceded that young Catholics were more community-minded, but added that young Protestants were more individualistic.

Having now got the opinions of those on either side, I went in search of those caught in the middle, namely the police and the security forces. Both the police and the soldiers I approached in Limestone Road said that they weren't allowed to speak to the press. Assistant Chief Constable McQuillan was unavailable for comment. Of others who were available for comment, none was willing to be quoted, which I took to be a reflection on the degree of fear generated by the UDA. Nevertheless, a picture of that organisation did emerge.

The previous year, the then Northern Ireland Secretary, John Reid, had declared that the UDA were no longer on ceasefire because of their continued violence. It was pointed out to me by those not willing to be quoted that, despite the 23 blast bombs, 30 petrol bombs and five shooting incidents on the night of the riot, as well as 300 additional bombings previously, all filmed by the hi-tech CCTV surveillance cameras mounted on the police vehicles, not one single Loyalist had been arrested!

I had now reached certain inescapable conclusions. These brought me face to face with a dilemma that I knew I would have to face before long while working for the *Express*. Politically speaking, we were very strange bedfellows indeed. The *Express* was a solidly pro-establishment, right-wing newspaper. My politics were decidedly left of centre and my attitude was rabidly anti-establishment. In many ways I was merely delaying the inevitable.

I was sure that my conclusions were correct. What other reason could there be for no one's being arrested for all those blatant offences, right under the noses of the police? So, unless this was to be my first step on the road to becoming a professional liar and propagandist for the establishment, I would have to write the truth. This was my conclusion.

It has long been acknowledged, even by the Special Branch, that the Security Services have deeply infiltrated the UDA. This raises two interesting possibilities. Firstly, that the UDA perpetrators of this violence are Special Branch assets who are too valuable in other ways to be arrested. Or, in a policy totally at odds with British Government policy, certain members of the security establishment are pursuing their own agenda and trying to halt or slow down the Peace Process.

The *Sunday Express* didn't print the article. There could have been a number of reasons for this, not least the fact that there had been no more riots and the story was rapidly becoming old news. However, they didn't phone me to offer me any more assignments and, when I phoned them, they were decidedly cool.

I was determined to find out the reason. I had made some good and widespread contacts in the time that I had been out. When pressed, one or other of these could usually come up with information. This was the case now. It seemed that it was all related to Richard Desmond asking that I be given an interview. The hacks at the *Express* had assumed that I was to be the first of his many placemen who would gradually take over the *Express* at the expense of their own jobs. Ergo, no more work for me!

I did consider going up to the *Express* and telling them that I didn't know Richard Desmond, had never so much as spoken to the man and wouldn't recognise him if he walked in the door. So I definitely wasn't one of his placemen. However, I guessed I would be wasting my time. The *Express* had already made up its mind.

CHAPTER EIGHTEEN
JEW BOY

Hot on the heels of the early demise in 2002 of my newspaper-journalist career came a further disappointment. By now, the TV-production company had put together a five-minute tape of the highlights of my Haitian and Colombian trips, the voodoo and the shaman. Craig, the director of the production company, had managed to secure an interview with the head of current-affairs programming at Channel 4.

Craig was optimistic. The guy we were going to see had been something of a young Turk himself. He had come from nowhere, brought some good programmes to the network and now was the head of a department. Craig expressed the opinion that, as the guy had already seen the promotional tape, we must be in with a chance.

In the event, it was all depressingly familiar. Despite liking the tape and my presentation, his conclusion was that he would like to see me doing something on domestic British crime, rather than foreign topics. There were a couple of programmes already that did exposé-type stuff, where the presenter went undercover and secretly filmed his contacts talking about nefarious activities. In many instances, the contacts had been arrested and charged after the programme had been aired.

So I was back to square one. First, I didn't want to be part of the treachery whereby someone who is thinking they are talking in confidence suddenly has that confidence betrayed. Second, within a very short period of time, everybody would know that I wasn't to be trusted and no one would speak to me. I would lose the good reputation I had built up as well as the trust of all my contacts, not to mention my friends. This, then, wasn't an option I could even consider.

They do say that bad things come in threes and this was certainly the case with me. With so many other things going wrong in my life, my relationship with Marsha now entered a particularly precarious phase. It resulted in my having to move out of the flat we shared.

Much as I tried to deal with it, I couldn't deny that it had a major effect on me. Despite the awesome self-discipline and strength I had built up to survive the 24 years, it seemed that, when it came to emotional matters, I still had weaknesses. It was very frustrating. I could go without all sorts of physical things and motivate myself to do quite amazing feats of denial and endurance, yet this simple mental feeling of loss tormented me.

I rationalised that the weakness was there because there had been absolutely no emotional dimension to my life in prison. The whole reason I had survived where other strong men had gone under was that I had handled the loneliness better. Metaphorically speaking, I had retreated into my castle, pulled up the drawbridge and stood on the battlements, observing that great body of the human race that I was no longer part of. It made me feel safe, and so strong.

However, even though I told myself I liked this 'cold' state of being, I was self-aware enough to know that it was an unnatural state, one that, however long-enduring, was only temporary. What I hadn't realised was that, once the emotional floodgates were open again, it would be so very hard to close them. Or even to maintain any control over events.

I needed to get away and, thankfully, *Front* came to the rescue. Impressed by my journalistic 'tour de force' in Israel, they agreed to my doing a piece for them on the situation in Gaza – specifically, how the two opposing sides, Arab and Jew, were confronting each other.

This was a story I wanted to do for spiritual as well as intellectual reasons. I needed to see if life in any of the 'settler' communities of Gaza was different from that in normal Israeli society. I knew that some of the extremely orthodox settlements were thoroughly bigoted and racist, but what of the less orthodox ones? Now that my relationship with Marsha was over, there was nothing to keep me in England. I was looking for a place in the world and perhaps I might find it in one of the settlements.

To be frank, I had been disappointed with what I had seen on my previous trip to Israel. I hadn't needed Schlomo Bloch to tell me about the general antagonism between religious and secular Jews. I had experienced it myself. It had been only a minor incident, but it had upset me out of all proportion to its significance.

It was when I was in Jerusalem, searching for the premises of ZAKA. All around me was evidence of the internationality of Jews. Russian Jews, wearing big fur coats, bustled past dark-skinned Oriental Jews dressed in clothes you would normally see on Arabs. Such amazing diversity. I stopped a tall Jew who was obviously very orthodox. The tight-fitting black suit, tall black hat and ringlets that framed a long angular face attested to someone who took his religion very seriously indeed. Politely, I asked him if he knew where a certain street was.

He stopped and shrank back as if I had physically assaulted him. He gave me a look of utter contempt, as if to say, How *dare* you even talk to me? He glared, stepped round me and hurried off muttering out loud. It was a complete and utter rejection.

I can't say that I agonised over the incident, but it did disturb me. Over the following days, the more I thought about it, the more it bothered me. It seems that I had been rejected because I wasn't Jewish enough. In view of my personal history, I found that deeply ironic.

My father, Charles Solomon Parker, was Jewish, as were his parents and grandparents going back generations. My mother, Anne Louisa Bitmead, had been a Church of England Christian when she met my father. However, she had taken instruction from the Beth Din for six months prior to the marriage and had been a converted Jewess when she married my father.

Now I don't know how 'Jewish' this would have made me, but other events intervened. For some reason, unbeknown to myself, my father had fallen out with all of his side of the family. One of the practical effects of this was that neither he nor my mother attended the local Brook Green Synagogue in Hammersmith. Needless to say, I didn't go there either. In fact, I knew nothing of my Jewish 'heritage'. I was enrolled in a local state school and 'wore' the normal Church of England religion in exactly the same superficial way as I wore the school uniform. I did it because everybody else did it. Thus, the only 'heritage' I had of my Jewish background was a rather large Semitic nose.

The other practical effect of my father's alienation from his side of the family was that I knew nothing of my Jewish uncles, aunts and cousins. Every morning when I went to school, I passed the synagogue where they all prayed. I actually passed the house of my uncle Benny, not knowing that it was his house and that my relatives lived there. So I was quite blissfully unaware of my Jewishness. This was a situation that didn't last for long.

Hammersmith was a poor, working-class area, with a minuscule Jewish population. There was a large immigrant Irish Catholic community. In the main, they lived cheek by jowl with their English counterparts with a minimum of friction.

I can't remember when it started, but, on occasion, I was attacked by older, bigger boys. It wasn't done in any organised, enduring fashion, but sometimes I was kicked or punched or chased and called 'Jew boy'. The assaults were relatively minor, if their effects weren't. I can remember worrying long and hard over why I should be singled out for such treatment. Why was I 'Jew boy'? I wasn't Jewish and knew nothing of the religion. And, even if I had been Jewish, why would that be cause for someone to attack me?

There was no obvious ideology behind the assaults. It was just a term of abuse to someone who was deemed to be different, in my case by virtue of my Semitic nose. When I complained to my father, he said that I would have to stand up for myself. Yet I had observed him in similar, threatening situations where he had unconditionally backed down. I could only conclude that he was a physical coward.

For myself, it was all very well to say that I should stand up and fight, but, when my opponent was much bigger and stronger than I, there could be only one outcome.

Disgusted with what I saw to be my father's lack of courage in dealing with life's threatening situations, I grew up with but one ambition in life. I wanted to be 'not-my-father'. Whatever else I achieved, I was determined not to be like him.

By now, I had found that the dynamics of every threatening situation involved both power and violence. I would make myself strong and violent. I didn't intend to attack anyone without provocation, but anyone who attacked or threatened me would find out that this was one little 'Jew boy' who wouldn't take it lying down.

If this may seem an excuse for my later extreme violence, it isn't meant to be. However, in retrospect, weighing up all the factors that led to two killings, countless other acts of violence as well as my spending a total of 28 years in prison, I can only conclude that it was a mitigating factor. It started me out on that path.

For many years, I still lived in denial. Spirituality wasn't at all important to me at this stage. Following a successful armed robbery, I booked into the prestigious Princess Grace Hospital and had expensive plastic surgery on my much-hated nose. Ironically, the majority of my friends said that they could hardly tell the difference. It had been largely in my mind.

Quite strangely, my most liberating spiritual event was being sentenced to life imprisonment. On reception I was asked what religion I was. Most Jews deny their religion in prison out of fear of prejudice. I answered that I was Jewish. I may not have known much about the Jewish religion or Jewish law, but I clearly felt it to be my legacy. I would live in denial no longer and, in my presently homicidal phase, woe betide anyone who would threaten me just because I was a Jew.

All this came back to me as I ruminated about the experience with the Orthodox Jew. The irony wasn't lost on me. As a boy I had been attacked because I was Jewish, albeit only 'partly' so. Now, as a man, I had been rejected because I wasn't Jewish enough. I looked forward to my coming experience with the 'settlers' in Gaza. I had been told that some of their communities were idyllically tolerant and supportive. If I was searching for something, I just might find it there.

There have been Jews in the narrow coastal strip of Israel since biblical times. The first kibbutz was established at Kfar Darom in 1946 as part of a plan for settling the inhospitable Negev Desert. Now there were 18 fortified settlements comprising some 7,000 souls. Mostly they grew hothouse vegetables and flowers on 2,600 of the 10,000 acres under their control. Around them lived more than a million Arabs. If there was a front line in the war between Jews and Arabs, then it was here in Gaza. Never were the American settlers of the Old West faced with a more implacable foe.

I drove down from Jerusalem and crossed into Gaza at a place called Kissufim. If I had been in any doubt about the danger of the situation, Kissufim Crossing would have brought it all into perspective. Massive concrete bunkers straddled the road, along which convoys of armoured jeeps hurtled at breakneck speed. Flak-jacketed IDF personnel were everywhere. Watchtowers with powerful searchlights dotted the landscape, as armoured bulldozers piled up earth in protective embankments. With a squeal of metal, a tank appeared in a cloud of dust and crossed the road.

At the IDF roadblock, my passport was checked. They didn't ask where I was going, since Gaza isn't a closed military area. Anyone is free to come here, although I guessed that there were stringent restrictions on Arabs. No doubt the danger of the situation was enough to deter most. I had already been warned that the roads were very dangerous. There have been many attacks on both the IDF and settlers. In effect, other than the Palestinians, no one else comes here. In my hire car, I could only be mistaken for a settler. Just recently, a roadside bomb had destroyed a tank, killing three soldiers.

The land looked flat and barren. Perhaps this was artificially so. Vegetation had been cleared from the side of the road to prevent ambushes, and natural hillocks had been levelled for the same reason. A high concrete wall separated the Palestinian carriageway from that of the settlers. Evidence of new building was everywhere. Roads, bridges, fortifications, in various stages of construction, abounded. I concluded that rumours of withdrawal were premature.

Electrified fences announced the beginning of the settlements, but, for the moment, these weren't my destination. I was looking for a place to stay and there were no hotels at all in the area. No tourists came and friends and relatives of the settlers stayed in the settlements with them.

I turned off on to a dusty road that led towards the sea. Almost at the very end was what had once been a holiday camp. Scores of small, thatched-roofed, two- and three-roomed, hutlike buildings stood in rows separated by narrow walkways. In many places, these had been partially obscured by windblown sand, evidence of the general neglect of the site.

Not surprisingly, apart from a couple of IDF soldiers, I was the only guest. I roused the caretaker from what had once been the reception building and he showed me to a cabin at the far edge of the site. It was circular in design and comprised just a bedroom and a bathroom. It was clean, though, and everything was in working order.

The caretaker handed me my key and left. He hadn't asked what I was doing here, or even how long I intended to stay. Further, there was no advice on where it was safe to go and where it wasn't. I resigned myself to the fact that I would have to find that out for myself.

I unpacked, stowed my gear in the lockers available and left the cabin to explore the immediate locality. I wandered the walkways of the deserted former holiday camp, looking for the exit. The wire fence surrounding the site was plain and rusty, without barbed wire and sagged in places. It would keep no determined intruder out. There was no check on anyone entering or leaving the camp. The caretaker was nowhere to be seen.

On the road outside I turned right. Left would have taken me back up to the junction where I had turned off. Apart from earthwork fortifications nestling in the lee of tall watchtowers, the landscape was quite barren. Several fields away, a few crude farmhouse-type buildings could be seen. I guessed these belonged to local Arabs. Other than that, there was no sign of human habitation and no humans to be seen at all.

A 200-yard stroll took me to the end of the road and an equally barren coastline, except for one amazing construction. As someone with long experience of security establishments from the inside, I could only marvel at what stood in front of me.

It was obviously a base from where to observe and protect that part of the coast. Tiers and tiers of interlocking and overlapping barbed-wire fencing circled the rocky outcrop on which it had been built. Tall watchtowers festooned with searchlights jutted everywhere. Each section of the fence, which was numbered, had a fierce dog on a chain linked to a bar alongside the fence. This allowed it to have a free run for about 30 feet. As I walked past, a good 50 feet away, one barked fiercely and ran after me until the extent of its chain ran out. Then it stood on its hind legs, forelegs against the fence, baring its fangs and growling.

I was impressed. Purely as an academic exercise, I sat and examined the base's defences to see if I could find a way in. In so doing, I picked up on small details I had missed in my first assessment. There were trembler bells on each section of fence, the mere touching of which would set off an alarm. A neat path had been cleared outside the perimeter, close to the fence. From my experience of the security jails I guessed there to be geophonic detectors beneath the path. One footstep would be enough to set the alarm off.

The more I looked at it, the more impregnable the base seemed. There were layers upon layers of security measures that had clearly evolved over years of experience. Equally clearly, whoever it was designed to keep out was resourceful, determined and very dangerous. I couldn't help but reflect that such an enemy would make short work of the puny neglected fence around my holiday-camp cabin.

Whereas to the right of the base lay a gravel beach, to the left ran a road. Another couple of hundred yards' stroll took me to a deserted holiday complex, which lay right on the coast. This had obviously been an upmarket version of where I was staying. The large reception building was adjoined by equally large recreation buildings. Substantial chalets, in pastel colours, lined the surrounding cliffs.

The road ended a few hundred yards further on. There was a large deserted residential building right on the edge of the beach and, just beyond that, a roadblock of some kind. But it was facing outwards, to check on anyone coming in. I could see the backs of two IDF soldiers next to their armoured jeep. I turned and headed back up the road. Thus far, my first impression of Gaza was that it resembled some post-apocalyptic film set. Deserted and dilapidated habitations stood cheek by jowl with defensive preparations for some unseen and deadly enemy. I could only hope that the settlements were more hospitable.

One legacy of my long years in prison was that I was now a creature of habit. The following morning, I was up at six. I changed into my shorts, vest, cap and running shoes and set out for my early-morning run. I certainly hadn't seen any runners out on the roads of Gaza as I drove in, only armoured convoys and cars driven at speed. But that didn't mean that I was going to abandon the habits of a lifetime.

My route would be up to the junction where I turned off, along the main road to the first roundabout and back the way I had come. In all, it was a run of about two miles. It would take me past all the various earthwork defences and watchtowers. I didn't know what they would make of this new phenomenon, the early-morning runner, but in the absence of a local gym my morning run was all I had to keep me fit. I would just have to hope that the IDF manning the defences didn't think that I was a fleeing terrorist and put a bullet in me.

At 10 a.m., I drove to the nearby settlement of Neve Dekalim for my first appointment. As I approached the fortified gate lodge, I took in the electrified perimeter fences topped with barbed wire, the CCTV cameras and the other electronic security measures. I reflected that it looked very much like Long Lartin, Gartree and Albany, those long-term top-security prisons where I had spent much of the previous three decades. This time, though, the security was designed to protect people, not to keep them in.

They examined my passport at the gate lodge and waved me through. Clearly, they had been expecting me. I parked next to a modern-looking concrete building that was the administration centre for Neve Dekalim and also the seat of the regional government for all the Gaza settlements, the Hof Aza. Inside it was spacious, cool and minimalist, but thoroughly functional. As I approached the reception desk, my contact was waiting for me.

Debbie Rosen was a matronly-looking woman in her early forties, who juggled her role as public-relations representative for the settlement with the full-time job of being mother to six children. I had been warned that Neve Dekalim was home to religious Jews, but not extremely orthodox ones. Debbie was wearing a two-piece business suit in sober colours and had what I was to find out was the de rigueur small hat perched on her head.

At first sight it seemed a strange outfit. Clothes like that hadn't been worn in England since the early fifties. They were smart, if somewhat dowdy by modern standards, and not the slightest bit stylish. But this was clearly the intention.

If I was now expecting a moralistic prude, I was agreeably surprised. Debbie was delightfully warm and friendly. She quickly put me at my ease by reassuring me that, although this was a religious settlement, they were very tolerant of others' views and not in the least judgemental. I had been dreading the questions of whether I was Jewish and where I worshipped back in England. I could answer yes to the first, but I was afraid that the negative to the second would reveal me to be not very much of a Jew at all.

As we sat in her small office, she related the recent history of the Gaza settlements. It was one steeped in violence and bloodshed. She had lived in Neve Dekalim for the past 16 years. In that time, the population had grown to its present size of 1,400 people. This was despite the regular attacks on the settlers and the constant bombardment by mortars. She pointed to the collection of pieces of mortar shells on a nearby shelf. 'During the last 19 months of the latest intifada nearly a thousand mortars have landed on the settlements, causing much damage and many casualties,' said Debbie matter-of-factly.

Death here, though, comes in many forms, and not necessarily just from the sky. For Miri Amitai, it was a roadside bomb that shattered the school bus, killing her and another teacher, while wounding nine children. Gabi Zaghouri was machine-gunned to death in a roadside ambush as he drove his delivery truck. An anonymous sniper picked off 18-year-old Itamar Yefet as he waited at a checkpoint. Nisan Dollinger knew his killer, a Palestinian labourer who had worked for him for 11 years and regularly ate at his table. But it was another anonymous stranger who recently crawled under the fences of the Atzmona settlement, with no doubt in his mind that this would be a one-way trip.

He must have cut the barbed wire surrounding the settlement just before midnight. He had avoided the IDF patrols and those of the settlers, before skirting the electrified fences. In the first exchange of fire, he wounded a settler guard in his patrol car. The lights of the classroom would have attracted him, but his information was good anyway. He knew exactly what his target was.

He burst in, spraying the rows of children with his AK-47. As he ran among the dormitories he also threw grenades. But the settlers were alerted now. Several exchanged fire with him as he ran about in the confusion. He died by the library, but in the 20 minutes he had been loose in the settlement he had killed five children and wounded another 23.

As someone who had lived in and survived some of the most dangerous long-term jails, I was experienced in weighing up the dangers of my environment and preparing against them. But how could you prepare against this? At Parkhurst, I had secretly made a knife and walked tall, confident that I could handle whatever came my way. There could be no such confidence in this situation, though. Violent death and injury came in so many different guises a normal reaction would be constant paranoia. Yet Debbie, while by no means being blasé about the situation, seemed to take it all in her stride. I felt myself warming to this woman.

For a while, we walked among the buildings of the settlement. We were greeted by everyone we met. The men looked quite incongruous in their long beards and skull caps, but carrying assault rifles. The women all wore long, sensible, unstylish dresses and covered their hair with small hats. They came from all over Europe and all over the world. The most recent arrivals were from France, victims of the latest upsurge in Gallic anti-Semitism. Once again, Jews were fleeing persecution in Europe.

In the distance, on a hilltop, Debbie pointed out the Palestinian city of Khan Younis. She explained that this brought added security considerations in the form of sniping from high buildings. This was reflected in the architecture of the settlement. Massive blast walls shielded the community centre and the industrial zone. At the girls' school, students now slept in small concrete units. Massive reinforced slabs protected a crucial walkway. It all served to make me feel very vulnerable when I stepped out into the open. I couldn't ignore the feeling that I just might be in a sniper's sights.

The people of the settlement went about their business, though, despite the ever-present threat. Terrorism apart, the community was virtually crime-free, although there had been a spate of bicycle stealing recently. Drunkenness, drug taking and brawls were unheard of. Divorce was rare and the average family had six or seven children.

In the evenings, the kids thronged the neat, graffiti-free streets. By day, they were ferried to school in convoys with heavily armed personnel carriers.

The reality was never far away, though. The IDF have a massive presence here. They man the gate lodge and patrol the perimeter. Hilltop forts are dotted about the landscape, interspersed with watchtowers. Armoured convoys race along the roads between them.

By now, it was time for my next interview. We returned to the Hof Aza for my meeting with the mayor. Avner Shimoni was middle-aged and overweight, and his clothes were indistinguishable from those of any of the other settlers. Clearly, he was a man who didn't stand on ceremony. He was friendly, but his message was also uncompromising. 'In many ways life is idyllic here, if only we didn't have the terrorism,' he began. 'The government should send the army into the Palestinian towns of Gaza, just like they did in other parts of the country in Operation Defensive Shield. That's the only way to root the terrorists out.'

I heard the words, but I wasn't convinced that he believed in the wisdom of what he was saying. He looked tired, almost resigned to the continuing war of attrition. And, in the final analysis, he was an elected politician. Outwardly, he would have to have some sort of solution to the problem.

I asked if this wouldn't just make the situation worse. Every time the IDF had gone into the Palestinian towns and cities, innocent civilians had died in the crossfire. This had provoked a backlash in the form of increased attacks on Israeli civilians and further damage to the international reputation of Israel.

He studied me closely for a few seconds as if trying to determine whether this was a genuine question or merely another uninformed attack on Israel. Whatever his conclusion, he didn't really have an answer to what was probably an insoluble problem. His reply of, 'Well, we can't just sit here and do nothing' smacked of desperation.

As I emerged from the meeting, Debbie was waiting for me in the hallway. To my surprise, she had arranged a whole series of other meetings for me, both in Neve Dekalim and some other settlements. She was nothing if not thorough. It would enable me to have a broader view of life for the average settler.

The first stop was at the house of her friend, Rivka Goldschmidt, in the nearby settlement of Ganei Tal. An intense but friendly woman in her fifties, she worked as a teacher in the settlement school. She and her husband Michael had been farming here for the past 24 years. As we talked, we walked among the long greenhouses. I noticed that many of the workers were Arabs.

'When we first came here there was nothing but desert. We have worked so hard, now they want to take it all away from us,' said Rivka with passion. She blamed Arafat. 'We always got on well with our workers before the Palestinian Authority came. They would tell you as much, but they are afraid to do so. The Palestinian Authority isn't democratic, it is brutal and corrupt. It is the same with the so-called refugee camps. Every government of Israel has offered refugee villagers solutions, but Arafat wouldn't let them go. They are worth more to him as propaganda in the camps.'

I commented on the sorry state of the Palestinian villages we had passed on our way to the settlement, but Rivka had an answer. 'Those villages and the ones throughout Gaza are called the Al Mawasi. They are Bedouin villages and they have lived the same way for centuries, long, long before we came. It is an exaggeration to call them a people, because they are made up of many different tribes.'

'Couldn't the same be said about us, Rivka?' I replied. 'Up in Jerusalem I saw Jews from all over the world. Russian Jews in big fur costs, dark-skinned Abyssinian Jews. Aren't we many different tribes?'

We had now entered a particularly big greenhouse and were joined by Michael, Rivka's husband. The question went unanswered. She introduced me as an English journalist. I shook hands with Michael but there was no warmth in his greeting. If anything there was a hard sarcastic look on his face that fell just short of a sneer. 'I suppose you're one of those journalists who have come to Israel with his mind already made up about how badly we treat the Palestinians?' he began with absolutely no preliminaries whatsoever.

For a fleeting second, I felt my anger flare and I was about to reply, in just as hostile a fashion, 'Yeah, that's about right.' But that would have been the anger speaking. Instead, I said, as levelly as I could manage, 'Israel doesn't get a very good press around the world, you know. It isn't surprising that people come here with preconceptions. I'm trying to keep an open mind, though.'

There was no radical change in Michael's attitude, but at least his tone became more reasonable. 'I mostly export flowers to Europe,' he continued. 'I have built the business up and now I employ dozens of Palestinians as labourers. When we came here 24 years ago there was nothing but desert. The local Arabs asked me what I was going to do here. When I said that I was going to grow flowers and vegetables they laughed. When I told them I was also going to grow tomatoes they said I was mad. They said that nothing would grow here. It took a lot of work, but now Israel leads the world in soil technology. I can grow anything in my greenhouses.'

'So you're not going to give up this land willingly, then?' I asked, looking him straight in the eye.

He replied with a sardonic smile on his face, as if to indicate that I was being the confrontational one now. 'If I thought it would bring peace, I would give it up tomorrow. But I know that it wouldn't. The Palestinian Authority want every last Jew out of Gaza first, then the whole of Israel. So to give up anything would be a sign of weakness. And the worst thing a Jew can do is show an Arab weakness.' It seemed a good point at which to end the interview.

Egypt was only two miles away, so Debbie and I drove to take a look. Debbie pointed out the town of Rafah, which sat astride the border and was divided by it into half Palestinian and half Egyptian. 'It was created like that after the first Camp David agreement,' said Debbie. 'You can see what Sadat thought of the Palestinians: he ejected them all from the Egyptian side. Yet no one says a word about that.'

On the way back to Neve Dekalim, we passed Atzmona, the scene of the recent machine-gun attack that killed five children and wounded 23. Debbie advised that it wouldn't be convenient to visit, as the special security police from Jerusalem were still investigating and the whole settlement was still in a state of shock. There was a strong suspicion that one of the Palestinian workers had set up the attack. 'The Palestinian Authority make them inform,' said Debbie. 'Otherwise they won't let them come to work for us.'

Back at Neve Dekalim, Rachel Sapperstein was waiting for us. The 65-year-old former English teacher from New York swept me up and took me on a tour of the Ulpana, a school for 230 teenage girls where she still taught. She seemed filled with energy and was clearly still a formidable lady.

She said that mortars regularly dropped on the school. She pointed out the massive blast walls that had been erected and the small reinforced dorms where the girls now slept. On a classroom wall were photos of Miri Amitai, the teacher killed when the roadside bomb shattered the school bus, injuring nine children. Poignant letters from her students surrounded the photos. Rachel wasn't deterred, though, even though her husband was wounded in a recent incident. 'Every night there is shooting and bombing, but they won't drive us out,' she said pugnaciously.

That evening, I had dinner with Rachel and her husband at their house. Debbie had arranged it and she told me that there were other dinner engagements on subsequent nights. It seemed that everyone wanted to have the English journalist as their guest.

All the settlement houses seemed virtually identical single-storey chalets, except for the fact that they ranged from one-bedroom to three-bedroom. There were no grandiose residences and no slums for that matter, either. The Sappersteins' residence was tastefully furnished, but there was no ostentation.

They made me very welcome and I soon relaxed in their company. Over dinner, we talked about life in the settlements, then ranged over many different topics. I found them to be determined and passionate, but not bitter or fanatical. Everything was discussed in a very civilised manner. At times, I mentally had to remind myself where I was and that a mortar could come crashing through the roof at any moment. However, I knew that both my hosts were aware of that and weren't perturbed by it.

The following morning, Debbie introduced me to Dror Vanunu, the settlement's resident journalist. A slim young man in his late twenties, Dror wrote newsletters and generally conducted an email campaign keeping supporters all over the world informed about the situation. He also had a wife and two young children to support as well as security commitments. It made for a very hectic life. Our interview was conducted virtually at a run, with Dror hurrying from place to place and me in close pursuit. Clearly, he was a man on a mission.

He seemed fascinated by the fact that I was an international journalist. I had a copy of the *Sunday Express* with my two Israel articles in it. He read and reread them several times, photocopied them and asked if I had any more of my work with me. Not surprisingly, I hadn't brought any of the lads' mags with me, and my prison-based books had seemed similarly unsuitable.

That evening, dinner with Dror and his wife was conducted against a background of an account of the settlers' continuing struggle with both the government and the Palestinian Authority. At times, it seemed hard to discern whom Dror thought to be the greater enemy. Before I left, he offered me free access to his files on all the incidents in the settlements.

I had asked to accompany the IDF on one of their patrols through the settlements. Debbie had set it up for the following day. I was under no illusions about the trip. Whereas the settlers had largely a defensive role, that of the IDF was very proactive. I knew they went to just the spots where there could be trouble. Further, although the Palestinians were massively outgunned, their methods had grown increasingly sophisticated. They were the masters of the roadside bomb and other ambushes, which frequently destroyed tanks and other armoured vehicles.

I drove to the nearby South Brigade HQ, an agglomeration of tents and other temporary buildings surrounded by barbed wire, earthwork banks and sandbags. The entrance was heavily fortified. I had to get out of my car to shout up to the soldier on the bank above. They were expecting me, though.

The double wire gates swung open and I drove in. Major Huli Moshe was a surprise. I don't know what I expected, but the reputation of the IDF was so hard and uncompromising that this laidback, reasonable-sounding guy seemed quite out of place.

However, he was professional enough, and committed. As we sat in the command tent, he explained what his role was. He briefly ran through a catalogue of recent incidents that brought home to me just how dangerous the settlements were. His talk was all of 'the terrorists' and never of 'the Palestinians', as if the two terms were synonymous.

I put to him Mayor Avner Shimoni's proposal that the IDF should be sent into the Palestinian towns of Gaza to root the terrorists out. He smiled resignedly. 'Unfortunately, it isn't as simple as that,' he said. 'The smallest refugee camp in Gaza is many times bigger than Jenin, and look at the bloodshed there. The city of Khan Younis has 230,000 residents. There are Fatah, Hamas and Islamic Jihad there, but they expect us now and will be very hard to find. Then there will be the civilians caught in the crossfire.'

He remarked that, in some instances, the IDF were caught in the middle of disputes between the government and the settlers, and this made his job particularly onerous. In what sounded remarkably like a complaint, he said that many of his men were young conscripts who were itching to get their national service over so that they could return to their normal lives. Almost as an afterthought, he warned me that the patrol I was about to go on could be dangerous.

I was reassured to see that he was coming with us. As I climbed into the armoured jeep, I noticed that the driver, the radio man and another guy with a heavy machine gun across his lap were barely out of their teens. All looked tense. Further, although the jeep looked quite formidable from the outside, inside I could see that the 'armouring' wasn't that thick. 'What will this stop?' I asked, pointing to the metal jeep side I was leaning against.

'Small-arms fire and that's about it,' said the major. 'Nothing armour-piercing.'

Once again I was brought to the realisation that, for most of the violence, there wasn't much precaution you could take. Injury or death really depended on being in the wrong place at the wrong time. If a determined attack could take out a tank, what chance would we stand in this little jeep?

Each of the forts we visited was surrounded by earthwork embankments and had heavily sandbagged gate lodges. Termit, Girit, Aluf – their names had become part of the local geography. Even though our jeep was clearly marked, at every stop there was a laborious security procedure before we were allowed in. In the main, the heavily armed troops inside ignored our arrival, scanning the surrounding countryside intensely for signs of attack.

We drove down to the Egyptian border and along the fence. I guessed that this section was closely monitored by both the Israelis and the Egyptians. Then I saw a most strange sight. Coming towards us, but as if floating on a cushion of air, was a tank. It threw out sand on either side and looked as if it were floating on a cloud. I asked the major about it, but he would say only that it was specially designed to avoid mines and roadside bombs. I guessed it to be some kind of hovercraft, but it was as big and as heavily armoured as any tank.

If my brief tour with the IDF had been an ordeal, it was as nothing compared with the one that faced me the following evening. Debbie had arranged a dinner engagement for me with a family, but first I would attend synagogue with them. I had never been in a proper synagogue in my life. The ones in prison had all been converted cells. I knew something of the procedure, but should I be asked something or, worse, asked to do something, my ignorance of Jewish custom would soon be revealed. As it was, I felt something of an interloper, what with my perceived lack of 'Jewishness'.

Neve Dekalim's synagogue was the most substantial building in the settlement, next to the community centre. It was brick-built, with stained-glass windows and ornate balconies, yet here the ostentation ended. It was intended to be functional rather than decorative. Inside was quite beautiful, airy and spacious, with acres of polished woodwork.

Almost timidly, I walked beside Moshe, my host for the evening. On my head was my faded pink koppel and, around my neck, a tattered prayer shawl. In my hand I tightly clutched my battered copy of the Torah, which I had been given on reception into prison. A close examination would have revealed the stamp declaring it to be the property of Wandsworth Prison. I had had it throughout the 24 years of my sentence. It had travelled with me through some of the worst punishment blocks in the British penal system.

Everyone greeted me warmly, if not effusively. Quite clearly, this wasn't a social occasion and the serious business of prayers would soon begin. To my great relief I was largely an observer of the proceedings. I was probably saved by the fact that it was all in Hebrew, anyway. I wasn't asked to read any of the prayers.

Afterwards, I strolled with Moshe and some of his children through the surrounding streets. This was my first opportunity to examine him carefully. He was a big man, probably in his early fifties, and had the substantial waistline of so many of his fellow settlers. If they had a vice here, then it was probably that they liked their food. Similar to his fellows, he also wore a big bushy, black beard, black wide-brimmed hat, white shirt and black trousers. He too was religious, without being extremely orthodox. I found him to be both tolerant and non-judgemental. Clearly, I wasn't a religious Jew, yet there were no probing questions as to my particular religious orientation.

Dinner was an elaborate affair. The massive dining table was set with 11 places. I sat down to eat with Moshe, his wife and their eight children. These ranged in age from about two to eighteen. All were open and friendly and seemed to be individuals in their own right. None seemed cowed by some overweening authority.

Their manners and their behaviour were impeccable, even the young ones. In England, in a similar setting, there would inevitably have been at least one Kevin, that dysfunctional idiot of the TV series, who would have attempted to assert his own individuality with conduct that outraged others. There was none of that here. I could only reflect on what a healthy well-balanced family they were.

By now, I was getting an in-depth picture of what life for the settlers was like, but to give that any relevance I would also have to see what life for the average Palestinian was like too. For three days, I had been asking for permission to go into Khan Younis and for three days the military authorities had stalled. They had told me that it was too dangerous and that they couldn't be held responsible for my safety. Even Debbie and Dror said that it was madness. Once inside, no one could do anything to save me if things went wrong.

However, while in Jerusalem I had visited the Knesset, the Israeli Parliament. There I had spoken with an Arab Member of Parliament. He had given me the telephone number of Dr Jowed Tibi, a Member of the Palestinian Parliament, who lived in Khan Younis. I had recently spoken to Dr Tibi on the phone and he had told me that the Israelis had no right to stop me from entering. So I had continued to press my case.

It was about eleven in the morning when I drove to the Toffah checkpoint close to Neve Dekalim. This was the main point of entry to and exit from Khan Younis. It looked a serious place. Not one Israeli was to be seen. All were hidden behind concrete barriers and sandbagged emplacements, barbed wire stretched between them like some overgrowth of unruly vine. I had been warned that sniping and suicide-bomb attacks were a frequent occurrence here and that the IDF manning the checkpoint were always edgy.

There was a definite feeling of tension in the air, as Arabs in their flowing robes shuffled forward to thrust their papers through a small slit to an almost unseen Israeli, who would decide whether they could enter or not. I had parked my car in a rubbish-strewn bay at the side of the road, reasoning that it would be even more difficult to get in with it. When my turn came I had prepared myself for the inevitable row.

As we progressed upwards through the ranks of the checkpoint staff, all were agreed that my entering was out of the question. I stood my ground, saying that Major Moshe himself had finally okayed my entry. Several more phone calls later, I was grudgingly allowed through, but with the caution that I should be back by 2 p.m.

The steep hill leading up from the checkpoint was littered with rocks, broken bricks and shards of glass. I guessed that this had been the scene of many anti-Israeli protests. It was completely devoid of people, save for those making their way in or out of Khan Younis. I concluded that, in view of the many attacks on the checkpoint, this was a very dangerous area to linger in. I headed towards a crowd of people at the top of the hill.

As I neared the brow, the outskirts of the city came into view. It was a scene of unimaginable devastation. Whole buildings had been reduced to bare bullet-scarred frameworks, evidence of the Israelis' awesome firepower in response to sniping. They stood in fields of rubble, through which cats ran skittishly.

I had been told that taxis wait a few hundred yards beyond the top of the hill. As I made my way through the crowd of shabbily dressed Arabs, I was immediately surrounded by hordes of children begging for money. I had known that there was no way that I could enter the city unobtrusively, but I didn't want to attract any more attention than necessary. As it was, everyone was looking at me. To have given the children money would have provoked a scrum. I pushed through brusquely.

Just beyond the ruined outskirts, the city itself looked only marginally better. Tumbledown tenements jostled for space alongside jerry-built shops and warehouses. Piles of rotting rubbish lined rough, earthen, deeply potholed roads. The overwhelming impression was one of decay, squalor and grinding poverty.

In the main, although the shabbily dressed people looked at me curiously, they largely ignored me, apart from the children, that is. They followed me as if I were the Pied Piper and, when I paused to photograph some particularly distinctive poster or revolutionary slogan painted on a wall, they ran in and posed with victory signs.

I saw very few women on the street. Further, there were no signs of preparations to ward off an Israeli attack. At one intersection, there was a sandbagged wall alongside which four fatigue-wearing men sat holding rifles, and that was about it. They waved away my request for a photo. If Fatah, Hamas and Islamic Jihad were here, they were keeping a very low profile.

Just as the streets cleared of fallen masonry and rubble, I came upon a small crowd of drivers standing around their battered taxis. Galvanised, the baying mob surrounded me, all striving for my custom. I had already made up my mind before entering the city that I would try to stay in control of the situation. Any display of weakness would only have invited trouble. I pushed through them and pointed at the least battered of the taxis. As the driver approached, I told him, in a loud voice so everybody could hear, to take me to the house of Dr Jowed Tibi, Member of the Palestinian Parliament.

Dr Tibi must have been well known in the city, because the driver knew exactly where to go. A 20-minute drive brought me to a neighbourhood that, while still being dilapidated, was a definite improvement on the slums, chaos and decay of the outskirts of the city.

We pulled up outside a substantial apartment block and I rang a bell with the name of Dr Tibi beside it.

His apartment was on the second floor. The door was opened by a woman completely hidden in a black chador. She waved me in and indicated that I should go into a spacious well-furnished room. Then she disappeared. Not one word had been spoken.

Either I was early for the appointment or the good doctor had had a late night. He came to me straight from his bed. Dr Tibi was not a young man. The wispy, straggly beard, the long angular face and the premature balding spoke of a man in his late forties who looked a decade older. He seemed tired but, more than that, weary. There was an air of resignation about him, defeat even. I had been told that the recent military setbacks had seriously damaged Palestinian morale.

He was pleasant enough, though, and, whatever had kept him from his bed the previous night, he made a determined effort to pull himself together and give a good account of himself. His English, although somewhat fractured, came courtesy of a 13-month stay in Scotland while he was studying for his surgery qualifications. The fact that he was a surgeon made everything else fall into place. No wonder he looked tired and prematurely aged. In the course of his work, he must have seen terrible things.

He did his best to put me at my ease. He offered me refreshments and asked what my journey had been like. I told him of the tension at the checkpoint and my shock at the damage to the buildings on the outskirts.

There was no fiery rhetoric, but, with the massed might of the Israelis outside the gates, perhaps it was time for conciliatory words. However, his condemnation was implicit when he explained that this was how his people had to live, by asking permission to pass through checkpoints to go about their daily lives.

He was more condemnatory when he spoke of the damage inflicted by the Israelis firing into the city. 'But isn't that in reply to sniping at the settlers?' I asked. I told him of my experience in Neve Dekalim, the protective blast walls and mortars dropping almost every night.

'Where is the equivalence in replying to rifle fire with tanks and missiles?' he replied. 'And do the Israelis think that they ever hit the sniper with a shell or missile? No. It goes right through wherever he was and kills innocent civilians, so creating more martyrs and more hatred.'

I was about to reply that surely it was the same when someone planted a roadside bomb or burst into a classroom and slaughtered innocent Israeli children, but thought better of it. I was here to listen to Dr Tibi's opinions, not to engage him in a political debate. However, I did comment that many of the Palestinian attacks on innocents similarly created hatred among the Israelis. 'Wasn't it an infernal circle,' I asked, 'with no beginning or end?'

Dr Tibi looked thoughtful for a moment. No doubt he was trying to appear reasonable and it was difficult to maintain that appearance when defending violence in any form. Shrugging his shoulders in resignation, he continued on a slightly different track. 'All the time they are overestimating the strength of the Palestinian fighters. We have no tanks, no Apache helicopters, no F-16s. There are just a few men with rifles and a belief in a Palestinian state. Yet we believe that, the next time the Israelis suffer a big attack, they will use that as an excuse to invade us.'

I briefly considered mentioning, then rejected, the mayor of Neve Dekalim's suggestion that the IDF be sent into the Palestinian towns and cities to root out the terrorists. It would only have inflamed the argument. As it was, the interview was proceeding in a very reasonable tone.

But he was particularly scathing about America's role in the conflict. For the first time, I saw him become angry and it was reflected in his rhetoric. 'America is playing games with us. They say that Hamas, Islamic Jihad and the Popular Front are terrorists, yet these groups do not attack America. They only attack within the borders of their land, so they are freedom fighters. Now America wants us to put them in prison. This will lead to civil war with Palestinian killing Palestinian. Then the world will say, "Look at them fighting among themselves like animals. They don't deserve a state."'

I asked him if he thought there was a solution. Again, he looked thoughtful before replying, 'We say the land is ours. The Israelis say the land is theirs. So there should be two states. Arafat said that he would accept 20 per cent and we backed him on that, but the Israelis refused.'

I thought of Michael Goldschmidt's words when he said that the Palestinian Authority wanted every Jew out of first Gaza, then the whole of Israel. 'And would all the Palestinians accept that?' I asked.

Dr Tibi replied that the majority would accept it and make the minority fall into line. In view of the current high level of strife between the various Palestinian factions I couldn't help but conclude that even Dr Tibi didn't seem convinced by this argument. I was sure that the average Israeli wouldn't be.

I asked if he thought there was any hope for the future. 'At the moment there is little cause for hope,' he replied. 'The Israelis don't want to give us a state and no one is putting any pressure on them to do so. But the will of the Palestinian people is strong. For myself, they can only kill me. I would rather that than live in humiliation.'

Dr Tibi's tone had changed as his rhetoric had grown more fiery. Formerly slumped in the sofa, he was now sitting erect, his shoulders back and his head up. I detected a movement at the periphery of my vision and I looked up. Two of Dr Tibi's children had entered the room. There was a boy of about seven and a girl perhaps a year younger. He called them to him.

Sitting with his arms protectively around them, he said, 'I owe a duty to my children. I don't want them to grow up having to go through checkpoints.'

It almost seemed like a cue to signal the end of the interview. I looked at my watch and, to my surprise, saw that we had been talking for over three hours. I was already too late to get back to the checkpoint by 2 p.m. I would need a photo to go with the interview, though. He posed with his arms around his children.

Dr Tibi had phoned for a taxi. The same car was waiting for me down in the street. Dr Tibi said something to the driver in Arabic, then advised me to head straight to the checkpoint. He cautioned that certain areas of the city were dangerous for foreigners.

Once again, we raced through the narrow streets. Suddenly, I could hear a lot of noise up ahead. It sounded like many people shouting and the banging of drums. There was a big intersection up ahead. Moving across it was a flatbed lorry carrying several coffins bedecked with garlands of flows. Banners bearing slogans in Arabic draped the sides. Behind came a surging mass of people shouting and waving their arms in the air. There were occasional explosions that sounded like gunshots.

You didn't have to be an expert in Arab customs to work out that this was some kind of funeral procession. From the several coffins I concluded that they must all have died in some recent confrontation with the Israelis. The passion of the crowd was obviously inflamed. Almost by reflex, I sat forward in my seat to get a better view.

Waving me back with one hand, the driver pulled sharply into the side of the road behind a parked car. 'Better you're not seen,' he said, sounding afraid.

We waited for several minutes before setting off again. He looked relieved when we got back to where he had originally picked me up.

It seemed situation normal back at the checkpoint. A crowd still stood at the top of the hill, the downward slope deserted. Once again, I was immediately surrounded by children begging. This time I took out some money and tried to share it among them. It was a big mistake. They swarmed all around me, pawing at my shoulder bag and at my clothes. I had to break into a run to get free. They dropped back as soon as I started to descend the hill.

Suddenly, a loud, distorted, disembodied voice called out from a hidden loudspeaker. By the tone, it was clearly a warning of some kind, but it was in Arabic. However, I did have the presence of mind to stop. I realised that, from down in the checkpoint, all they could see was an unknown man with a bag on his shoulder, hurrying towards them. I must have looked very much like your average suicide bomber.

I stood stock still, placed my bag on the ground and held my passport out at arm's length above my head. Several seconds passed, during which I considered the certainty that there were several machine guns trained on me at that very moment. I mused on the irony of my surviving the dangers of a trip inside Khan Younis, only to be shot by mistake by the Israelis on the way out.

Suddenly, the hidden voice roared out again, still in Arabic. Clearly, they thought me to be an Arab. Equally clearly, I felt that I was running out of time. There wasn't even the option of going back up the hill. That would surely have caused them to open fire.

No doubt frustration fired my anger. This was becoming ridiculous. I guessed that the reason I had been told to get back to the checkpoint by 2 p.m. was that this was when the shifts changed over. This new shift knew nothing about the Englishman who went into Khan Younis earlier.

'English journalist,' I roared out, narrowly avoiding adding expletives to the ending.

'Who are you?' came a voice in heavily accented English from somewhere closer by.

'I'm the English journalist you let in at eleven this morning,' I shouted. 'Check your records. Phone Major Moshe.'

Several long minutes passed. I felt very exposed, stopped halfway down the hill. I was conscious of both the Israelis below and the Arabs above me. Should the latter cause some kind of disturbance, throw something or, worse, fire a shot, I could see the Israelis opening up on me. It was a situation that very much wasn't under my control.

Eventually, the English-speaking voice called out for me to come on down and I approached the checkpoint. A young soldier examined my passport while telling me that they were a new shift, just come on duty, as I had already guessed. I collected my passport and passed through. I felt elated as I got in the hire car. The feeling didn't last. As I put my bag on the passenger seat, I noticed that one of the pockets was undone. It was the one where I kept my English mobile. It was missing. I cursed myself for giving the kids the money. During the mêlée, one of them must have stolen my phone.

Back at Neve Dekalim, both Debbie and Dror were waiting for me. As I pulled up outside the Hof Aza building they rushed to meet me, concern clearly showing on their faces. They welcomed me back, but from their manner it was obvious that something else was on the agenda besides just relief at my safe return. Debbie asked me if I would come with them for a few minutes.

The three of us got into her car and a short drive took us to the heart of the settlement. We stopped outside a small neat chalet in a row of similar chalets. With Debbie leading the way, the three of us went inside. It was clean, if sparsely furnished, and didn't look as if it was currently occupied. I was wondering what this was all about, because Debbie and Dror were behaving like estate agents.

'Norman,' began Debbie, 'we have been thinking. And by "we" I mean the council and some of the community here. You have told us that you are not settled at the moment back in England. We are wondering if you would come and live here and be our journalist. We desperately need a good journalist to tell our side of the story and Dror is the first to admit that, although he does his best and we are grateful, his English isn't very good. We would give you this house to live in'

For a moment, I was completely at a loss for words. Whatever I had been expecting, it wasn't this. I tried to think clearly about the practical possibilities of the offer, but raw emotion surged through the thought process. I had come to Neve Dekalim fearing that they wouldn't even accept me as a Jew and here they were asking me to play a major role in their community. I don't do 'humble' very well, but I felt humble at that moment. And grateful.

I was conscious that any delay could seem like rudeness, but this was something I would have to think carefully about. It was a very serious decision to make. First, there was all the faith and trust that was being put in me and I didn't want to let anyone down. Second, I would be committing several years of my life. I managed to mumble that I was honoured by their offer, but that I would have to give it careful consideration. They told me to take all the time I needed.

That night, I stayed in Neve Dekalim, in a rented room in an unoccupied house. As I lay there, I pondered the statistical likelihood of my being the target of a mortar. Somewhere in the settlements, several fell every night. But you couldn't agonise about it – that way lay madness. You would just have to put it out of your mind, as everybody else did. Be that as it may, I was still conscious of the danger.

My thoughts drifted to the events of the day. I had seen something of the Palestinian side of the story, but nothing close to what I would have liked in order to achieve an even balance. Then I considered what Debbie and Dror had offered me. I still could hardly believe it.

It was true that I was unsettled back in England. More than that, with the end of my relationship with Marsha, there was nothing to go back for. Part of the problem, I guessed, was that I had spent most of my adult life in the long-term prisons. Away at 18, out at 23, away again at 25 and not out again until I was 50, I didn't really know what a 'life' was.

I had observed the way other men had put their lives together and had found that so much of it hadn't appealed to me. I would enjoy one part of their lives, but the rest, the majority, I couldn't bear. They had surrendered so much of their individuality, their freedom. They had settled for so much less than they had set out to achieve. Their lives had little meaning.

There was no meaning in going down the pub, watching TV and going to football matches. It was all just passing time, wasting time, and I had just spent 24 years sitting about, passing time. I had kingdoms to conquer, unscalable peaks to climb. For if I allowed my life to become like most men's lives then I would surely be in just another prison.

That was one of the reasons I had gone to so many dangerous places to do stories. At least there was some adventure in that. Another, more subliminal reason was that I had come to the conclusion that the mundane was an inevitable part of most men's lives and would surely become part of mine. Was I just to sit about, waiting to get old and die? There was no nobility in that. Perhaps it was better to search out an honourable death in pursuit of adventure.

I considered what options were available to me. Danny had suggested that I go to Colombia and set up a girlie bar with him in

Cartagena, a resort island away from the war. But I would tire of that very quickly and it smacked of running away from the world.

I was still mightily impressed by the work that ZAKA did. It stood out as a challenge to me. I was sure I could make myself strong enough to do it and it was worthwhile work, admired by both Arab and Jew. Also, in some ways, it would be penance for me. However, although I was old enough, I wasn't married. Would they forgo that stipulation just for me?

The more I thought about life in Neve Dekalim, the more it appealed to me. As the mayor had said, life was idyllic here apart from the terrorism. Other than that, I too had seen an almost perfect community, one where everyone pulled together and made sacrifices for others. Compared with the rat race of other societies, it seemed like Nirvana. What an irony it was that such a perfect society had been brought about by the ongoing Arab–Jew conflict.

I could also see a way to do my journalistic work with honour, too. I would set out right from the start to report on attacks both against the settlers and on the innocent Arab victims of Israeli firepower. Hopefully, I could still go into the Arab towns and cities.

For a while, I agonised about the rightness of the Israeli cause. I had come to Israel full of passion for Palestinian rights. But, as with most issues, when you looked closer there were complicating factors. All over the world, from Sri Lanka to Northern Ireland, different peoples were claiming the same bit of land, the rights to which were obscured by the mists of time.

Whatever the rights and wrongs of the contending causes in Israel, there was one inescapable fact. The Arabs and the Jews were both established communities here. Neither was going anywhere, so some accommodation would have to be reached eventually.

I remembered the words of Dr Tibi when he had said that Arafat would accept 20 per cent of the land and that the majority of the Palestinians would force the minority to accept it. I also recalled the words of Michael Goldschmidt, that, if he thought it would bring peace, he would give up his land willingly. But he knew that there were those among the Palestinians who wanted to drive every last Jew out of Israel/Palestine. So to give up anything at all would be weakness.

I was beginning to understand why so many Israelis seemed indifferent to the suffering of the Palestinians. They had become so traumatised by the suicide bombings that they now connived at even savage measures designed to stop them. However, I also felt that many of these measures were proving to be counterproductive in that they were alienating world opinion.

I was confident that I could make a principled defence of the above arguments, but there was always a ticking bomb underneath my accepting Debbie and Dror's offer. What of my criminal convictions? Would I be 'Norman the Writer' or 'Norman the Murderer' to the Jews of Neve Dekalim? In all conscience, I would have to tell them.

As I drifted off to sleep, I contemplated the particular point my life had reached. I didn't intend to join the IDF or otherwise fight against the Palestinians, but I would lay down my life to defend the children of Neve Dekalim. Who could deny the nobility of that? So, if Jew boy was searching for an honourable death, he could certainly find one in Gaza.